Photographic Memories

Photographic Memories
Jack Delano

Smithsonian Institution Press • Washington and London

© 1997 by Jack Delano
All rights reserved

Copy editor: Jan McInroy
Acquiring Editor: Amy Pastan
Production editor: Duke Johns
Designer: Linda McKnight

Library of Congress Cataloging-in-Publication Data
Delano, Jack.
    Photographic memories
    p. cm.
    Includes index.
    ISBN 1-56098-741-3 (alk. paper)
    1. Delano, Jack. 2. Photographers—Puerto Rico—Biography. 1. Title.
TR140.D43D43   1997
770'.92
[B]—dc20   96-44181

British Library Cataloguing-in-Publication Data is available

Manufactured in Canada
04 03 02 01 00 99 98 97   5 4 3 2 1

∞ The paper used in this publication meets the minimum requirements of the American National Standard for Information Sciences—Permanence of Paper for Printed Library Materials ANSI Z39.48-1984.

For permission to reproduce illustrations appearing in this book, please correspond directly with the owners of the works. All the photographs in this book either were taken by Jack Delano or are from his personal files. The original negatives of the images in the duotone section are either at the Library of Congress, at the Institute of Puerto Rican Culture, or in the author's personal collection. The drawings are either the work of the author or his personal property. The Smithsonian Institution Press does not retain reproduction rights for any of these these illustrations individually, or maintain a file of addresses for photo sources.

Contents

Acknowledgment   *viii*

In Pursuit of the Proximate: A Biographical Introduction
SALLY STEIN   *ix*

1 · From a Ukrainian Village to an American Metropolis   *1*

2 · Learning to Be an American   *6*

3 · Music in the City of Brotherly Love   *8*

4 · Movies, Pretzels, and Empty Pockets   *11*

5 · Becoming an Artist and Falling in Love   *15*

6 · Euphoria in Europe and Trouble at Home   *19*

7 · Going Underground—in a Pennsylvania Coal Mine   *23*

8 · New York: In Search of Fame, Fortune, and a Job   *27*

9 · Working with Stryker and Trying to Understand the South   *31*

10 · From Florida to Maine on the Trail of Migrant Farm Laborers   *35*

11 · On the Road   *49*

12 · Washington: Preparations for War   *52*

13 · The American Melting Pot   *55*

14 · Displaced Persons—and a Chance to Go to the Caribbean   *69*

15 • Puerto Rico: Welcome to the Tropics!   *71*

16 • The Virgin Islands: Blackouts and War Jitters   *75*

17 • Back in Puerto Rico: Poverty and Dignity   *81*

18 • The War Effort at Home   *84*

19 • Riding the Rails   *89*

20 • The Army Tries to Make a Soldier of Me   *95*

21 • A Secret Mission to Peru   *101*

22 • B-29 Bombers and Bloody Bodies in the South Pacific   *104*

23 • We Win the War but Lose a President   *108*

24 • Back Where Sugar Is King   *111*

25 • Producing and Directing Films   *116*

26 • Embarking on New Ventures   *125*

27 • Around the World in Ninety Days   *145*

28 • Managing a TV Station—and Political Turmoil   *162*

29 • Designing Museums and Books   *172*

30 • "Every Forty Years"   *180*

31 • New Avenues of Creativity   *195*

32 • The End of an Era   *207*

33 • Preserving an Instant of Time   *212*

    Index   *217*

This book is dedicated to the memory of Sonia and William, my parents.

◆

Art is a human activity having for its purpose the transmission to others of the highest and best feelings to which men have risen.

Leo Tolstoy

Acknowledgment

I probably could not have written this book without the help of Mary McHale Wood. She not only scanned every page with an eagle eye as I wrote, correcting my grammar and punctuation, but made innumerable suggestions to help me find the best way to express what I wanted to say. I can never repay her for all the Sunday afternoons she spent poring over my manuscript, questioning discrepancies, looking up the spelling of difficult words, not letting any detail escape her. She did this all in the name of good friendship—and I owe her an eternal debt of gratitude.

In Pursuit of the Proximate

A Biographical Introduction
SALLY STEIN

Jack Delano has titled his autobiography *Photographic Memories.* Reader beware: Though Delano is justly celebrated as a photographer, his work in photography plays a relatively minor role in this chronicle of his life. Yet I do not consider the title to be a misnomer. Ultimately, the anecdotal narrative may be the most direct route to comprehending the basis for his craft, and love, of photography.

As Delano here elaborates, photography was an abiding interest for much of his life, but it was just one of a number of compelling modes of communication and expression, including music and the traditional fine arts, along with film-, print-, and book-making. And of all these media in which he displayed quite remarkable gifts, photography in his view was the most contingent, involving the greatest collaboration with, and even indebtedness to, the world in front of the camera.

One can take this idea too far. And if you read Delano's words literally, you risk being misled. You might actually believe that he did very little in making his photographs, and that there is slight difference, as he insists at numerous points, between the world he encountered and the photographs he produced. What you should keep in mind is that such a belief was very important, probably crucial, to this photographer as he constructed many carefully composed, even staged, intricately balanced images of the world.

I mentioned earlier the issue of debt and photography's indebtedness to the world. Maybe Delano is such a good photographer because he is so acutely conscious of the various debts he has accumulated over a lifetime. Indeed, one thread of his story is an account of debts incurred, supplanted by other debts, and repaid most often only over time, with some still outstanding. The debts vary in size and character. Though only a few involve money, they all are recounted with distinct gravity . . . as if, so to speak, money had changed hands.

Photographic Memories

There is the 1946 Guggenheim Fellowship enabling Delano's return to Puerto Rico, which he had first visited five years earlier while working for the Farm Security Administration (FSA). This second visit became a permanent move. His initial plan of making a book-length study of the island was shelved as he became an active participant in emerging forms of Puerto Rican culture, adding to his photographic work first film and then TV production, at the same time that his wife, Irene, organized for the government a community-oriented graphic arts studio and subsequently a wide range of book and poster projects. But when he describes assembling his older and more recent Puerto Rican pictures in the 1980s for exhibition and subsequent publication, he sounds distinctly relieved by this act of summation. As a personal record of one island's historical changes and continuities over a period of four decades, the photographic book that appeared in 1990 fulfilled the original plan of a descriptive document and exceeded it, by adding to the documentary impulse the sense of duration that comes with deep attachment.[1]

Another form of trust he records here was that expressed by one World War II–era train engineer in his willingness to move not a mountain but its near equivalent, a mile length of freight cars—and only because the photographer envisioned a slightly better picture as part of his government assignment to cover the wartime transportation story. If that act of trust forged a bond across very different lines of work, Delano just as scrupulously notes the support extended by his mentors in the arts: particularly, the apprenticeship in documentary photography provided by FSA photography chief Roy Stryker; the generous loan of a movie camera by filmmaker Robert Flaherty that figured as both symbolic and material form of encouragement to expand his documentary practice; and the patience with which so august a figure as Pablo Casals treated Delano as he struggled to translate the art of music into a suitable filmic form.

Indeed, the second part of the autobiography, devoted to the life Jack and Irene Delano made in Puerto Rico, is filled with recollections of acts of confidence and generosity that made these newcomers feel profoundly welcome. Nowadays the art market has mostly supplanted the older forms of artistic patronage. But for a period of two decades, Luis Muñoz Marín, the first elected governor of Puerto Rico, employed Jack and Irene Delano in various professional capacities to help develop modern forms of public education and communication as part of his broad program for social reform.

Delano continues to speak with reverence of this man whom he considers friend and host, as well as historic political leader who governed the island with a broad base of support from 1948 to 1964. His photographic series of the public mourning at the 1980 funeral of Muñoz Marín, subsequently published in book form, has qualities of both private and public tribute.[2] In keeping with the memorial tradition, the images express the mourners' relation to the statesman and the sense of community that is deepened in the public act of paying tribute. Like most rituals, this one contains many echoes: most immediately, of the public mourning occasioned by the death of John Kennedy, with whom Muñoz had been frequently compared. Likewise, both Kennedy and Muñoz recalled for many the hopeful vision of FDR. This New Deal lineage was especially resonant for Delano, who had first developed his own documentary vision in that political context. Moreover, it was the New Deal that had first sent him to Puerto Rico, and it was the belief that New Deal progressive policy might be further developed to improve social conditions on the island that led Delano to return and then stay there. Just as Muñoz Marín readily acknowledged the influence of FDR's New Deal on his own vision of social reform coupled with modernization, so this series recalled and extended the way Delano had previously summarized the New Deal legacy by photographing the stunned expressions of ordinary New Yorkers on hearing the news of FDR's death on April 12, 1945. In both cases, the photographer sought to capture a multitude of reaction shots as a way of commemorating the public trust and sense of reciprocity that only rarely is achieved in political relationships.

But of all these records of trust that instilled a sense of profound obligation, arguably the most moving is the account of the *jíbaro* (variously translated as rural countryman, mountain folk, as well as peasant) family who in the late 1940s offered Jack and Irene shelter during a sudden downpour in the Puerto Rican countryside. Even after confessing that they themselves were without work and dependent on the kindness of neighbors, the rural hosts insisted that the strangers take with them a pair of eggs freshly laid by their one remaining hen. The pair-of-eggs conferred upon a pair-of-strangers is almost too good to be true. That Jack and Irene would later have two children, a boy and a girl, only makes the story seem more fabulous. But the way Jack recounts it, the *jíbaro* gift stands less as omen of a future family to be raised in Puerto Rico than as a quintessential blessing of cultural fertility.

What better way to repay a loan that compares with the proverbial shirt-off-one's-back than with another shirt, or else something closely comparable? If there is any way to match such precious gifts, this retrospective accounting suggests that the committed document might serve better than most forms of trade as fitting repayment, with interest.[3] Already in the first decades of photography Oliver Wendell Holmes had compared the photographic image to a layer of skin or membrane peeled directly from reality. Holmes in this instance was writing specifically about the stereograph, which in the mid-nineteenth century offered the most astonishing 3-D illusions, but his comments more generally addressed the way photography warranted the epithet "the mirror with a memory," thus promising to be the most reliable of witnesses, and even reality's surrogate. Certainly Holmes, who envisioned a "comprehensive system of exchanges" based on a "universal currency" of photography, would have appreciated the way this artist's sense of indebtedness has brought him back time and again to the intensive use of photography.[4] To record the world with a sense of passionate immediacy became the artist's familiar method of repaying debts, or at least of acknowledging their weight and significance.

And there is another thing, nearly paradoxical, in Delano's photographic memories: If photographs became a kind of currency, they also served as anchor. As with most photographers of his generation, Jack Delano had no formal course of training in the medium or, for that matter, any other systematic plan of becoming a photographer. But the autobiography indicates the way that photographs from an early period in his life were freighted with memory, or sometimes *as* memory. His life is punctuated by two major migrations, first in 1923 from the Ukraine to Philadelphia, and a quarter century later from postwar New York to Puerto Rico. Of his early childhood in a Ukrainian village, he recalls only a little. More surprising, he recalls almost nothing from the passage he made at the age of eight. After leaving his village and making a first stop in Kiev, he can recite only the names from the stages of his journey—Moscow, Riga, Hamburg, Southampton—before arrival in Pennsylvania by way of New York. That so momentous a voyage figures as a blank says a great deal about the trauma of uncertainty, of the disorienting quality of the present when the immediate future remains unimaginable. Characteristically, he does not dwell on that uncertainty in his own life, noting pointedly that his family in the Ukraine, though fearful of persecution as Jews, was relatively fortunate. But this fundamental experience of uneasy dislocations may explain the painstaking portraits of migrants that he made on the eve of World War II. These were not your most desperate of westward migrants or historic victims of war. Indeed, most of the rural Americans he portrayed as they faced the loss of their homes to make way for dams or army camps were slated to receive some compensation to assist their relocation. However minor it was in the larger scheme of things, Delano documented for all time the kind of terror that these lesser upheavals can produce, particularly for minorities, who had added reason to worry whether they could overcome discrimination and recover any semblance of security in their lives.

He cannot even recall how his family was so fortunate as to obtain passports in 1923. But it was these official exit papers with ID photographs that provided safe passage out of the Soviet Union. In retrospect, these same photographs provide the most permanent documentary record of his family before their arrival in this country to begin a new, typically immigrant, struggle to become that hybrid modern type we call "American." If America offered a relatively safe haven, the same travel documents also stand as evidence that identity was not formed in this country but rather recast here.

In Pursuit of the Proximate

That interwar American culture encouraged the recasting of identity, and the recasting of it again and again, is indicated by two photographs Jack made and kept from his early manhood. One from just around the time he graduated from the Pennsylvania Academy of the Fine Arts is doubtless the most dashing image we have of him. It incidentally demonstrates that he has already figured out the rudiments of photographic lighting technique, for it is the shadows, and the low brim of the fashionable fedora casting the largest shadow, that lend drama to the picture. If one strains, one can imagine Rembrandt as an influence for this young artist's self-presentation, but the pose appears most indebted to Bogart, particularly the side of Bogart that played cocky gangsters and gumshoes rather than truck drivers.

The fedora, trench coat, and theatrical shadows seem utterly alien to the next self-portrait, made in 1939 (see frontispiece). Young Delano is no longer crowding the camera and filling the frame with the same sense of self-importance. Rather, for this photograph he backed off to leave room in the frame for the modestly outfitted studio. He looks tired, and his rumpled clothes have a corresponding lived-in look, as if he's been up all night working. Most important, in his rather inconspicuous position seated on the low cot, he deflects attention from his own self to the portrait of a miner that occupies a larger and more central position on the wall behind him, a portrait that would hang prominently in his first public exhibition of documentary photographs he had made of a desperately poor mining community in central Pennsylvania. Thus, at the time he was preparing that exhibition for installation in the gallery of Pennsylvania Station in Philadelphia's railroad terminal, he made another self-portrait to seal his newfound identity, a portrait of artist-of-workers *and* artist-as-worker. If Delano had briefly identified with Hollywood glamour, he at this point declared quite different allegiance—to proletarian valor. Thereafter, as he attests repeatedly, he would make it his business to eschew all things Hollywood.

Other pictures and recollections are equally revealing of his formation as a young adult and an aspiring artist. Of his art school training, Delano mentions the Cresson fellowship—another debt—that enabled him to spend months traveling in Europe to immerse himself in the art of the past. The time spent educating himself in major museum collections left him impatient with his academic training and eager to experiment when he returned to school in Philadelphia. Indeed, he had gained such confidence from his travels in Europe that when he had the opportunity the next year to compete for a second fellowship, he defied the school's competition rules, which strictly prohibited the hanging of any work that was framed and any portrait that was larger than life size. On the contrary, he somewhat sheepishly recalls: "I did not frame anything, but a painted frame was an integral part of one of my illustrations, one portrait of a woman was much greater than life-size, and one illustration showed a group of people sticking their tongues out at the onlooker." These efforts were not applauded. Even Delano sounds somewhat self-critical as he now reports the outcome: "The jury did not seem to appreciate my infantile humor. I was not offered another trip to Europe."

Notwithstanding Delano's efforts to distance himself from these youthful acts of self-indulgence, they seem to be quite telling acts that will become integral to his way of working as a visual artist. Indeed, numerous aspects of this rule-flouting performance constitute what might be considered the emergence of his visual signature, which will change over time but will remain in some form as constantly as any feature of his work. First, there's the play with carnivalesque role reversal as a way of shaking things up, the very basis for the comedic interlude in his 1952 film *Los Peloteros*. Then there's the desire to go larger-than-life size. The already noted self-portrait from the late 1930s in which he's upstaged by the picture of a miner records the way he continued to employ shifts in scale to give prominence to ordinary working people. Though he would not make a habit of enlarging pictures to huge proportions, his subsequent work with film offered another avenue by which he could create dramatic enlargements of everyday issues. And even in his more modest-sized photographs, there is the abiding desire to emphasize the human subject—a very typical motive of progressive art of the 1930s but an idea to which Delano remained faithful long after the Great Depression had passed and many of the artistic and social principles of the New Deal had been deemed old-fashioned.

We should take special heed of Delano's admission of defying the school's prohibition against the use of picture frames by making a frame part of his rendering. If we take this act seriously—and the recurrence of frames in the rest of his work demands that we do so— this incorporation of a frame may seem at first quite at odds with his other typically 1930s gestures of larger-than-life heads and blatant mugging at the viewer. In some respects, framing constitutes the most conservative aspect of art, that which seals arts as finished, literally and metaphorically. But after studying Delano's stories along with his imagery, one might conclude that his art in various media involves the impulse to frame—and alternately to break the frame, or at least question its sanctity.

The frame or edge is an especially crucial aspect of photography. To the extent that photography is an art, its greatest work involves the act of framing, of defining what's significant and worthy of inclusion and how best to make a space for it in relation to all other included elements. To continue the economic metaphor, the frame might be considered the photograph's ledger, effectively delineating all significant entries. The infinite care that Delano took while composing within the frame of the camera is evident in the earliest FSA photographs. These are quite different from the photographs he made previously in the Pennsylvania mining region, which were composed rather simply of a single figure or couple of figures, or else of the dark spaces of the primitive mine conditions or the equally impoverished landscape of the community. Once he joined the FSA, he began to explore the possibility of putting such elements together. There are numerous reasons for this change. At the FSA, he was using more precise photographic equipment than he previously had access to (including the 8 × 10 view camera formerly used by Walker Evans to achieve results that combined remarkable detail with utter simplicity). Moreover, once at work for the FSA, Delano took quite seriously the sociological instructions he was receiving from Stryker and his circle of progressive social scientists, who were beginning to see in photography a way of comprehending patterns of culture and social organization. In 1941, Stryker authorized him to make an extended stay in Georgia at the request of Arthur Raper, who was conducting a sociological study of the Greene County area. Though Delano at times worried that much of his work for Raper would serve too literally as mere illustration of the main topics in the social scientist's forthcoming study, *Tenants of the Almighty*, it was during this extended period of work in Georgia that the photographer grew quite articulate about the value of including in his documentation of a region more than just a mix of portraits and landscapes. At this point Delano began to systematically enumerate the various kinds of pictures that might situate people in their environment, thereby establishing further linkages between the way the organization of work and community would vary according to economic resources and social relationships.[5]

In addition, Delano's new autobiographical account suggests that perhaps there is a more intimate connection for this framing impulse than the extracurricular training he absorbed from FSA managers, academic affiliates, and stellar photographic predecessors. His immigrant father earned a modest living making furniture. And there is something akin to the literal work of carpentry in many of young Delano's compositions. He seems fascinated with the process of enclosing a scene to indicate the basic elements that make up a life, a family, or a community. And far more than the mandarin Evans, but rather with the earnestness of any journeyman builder, he was careful to leave openings: windows, mirrors, halls, and doorways often connect the scene with another view, adding depth, which in turn demanded more attention from the viewer, and provided more possibility for interplay between what was inside and what was beyond the frame.

The desire for interplay between what's inside the frame and what's beyond its borders is enunciated most emphatically when Delano recollects with tremendous pride the open-air screening of one of his early films made in Puerto Rico. The film, he states clearly, was made with the people, and for the people. But the effect he conveys is not so much one of a blurred boundary between art and life as a productive relationship of reciprocity. In this account, life mirrors art that mirrors life:

Photographic Memories

> I remember once attending the preview of a short documentary about the sugarcane industry. The showing was to be held at a crossroads in front of a country store in a sugarcane field. We used no professional actors in our films, finding plenty of acting talent among the country people. *The cane-cutters in our film were just like the men coming to see the movie.* . . . On this occasion, just at dusk, miles before we arrived at the country store, we found posters produced by Irene's workshop all along the roadside, announcing the film showing. They were everywhere—on trees, walls of houses, doors of country stores, telephone poles—everywhere. Each poster carried the word "gratis" (free) in big letters, and a line that read, "Film produced in Puerto Rico." The air was filled with music coming from a loudspeaker on the Jeep of the local group leader and his voice announcing that the film was about to start.
>
> In the fading light, we could make out streams of people coming along the mountain trails toward the projector in front of the store. There were children, old people, women with babies in their arms, almost everyone barefoot, to stand in a crowd of about two hundred and socialize with neighbors, exchanging news and gossip while waiting for the film to begin. *When it was quite dark, the projector was turned on. A sudden hush fell on the gathering. The people stood openmouthed, transfixed by the images flickering on the screen. Sometimes they would point at the screen and laugh in delight at the familiar faces and scenes they recognized.* This was no Hollywood movie with gorgeous, otherworldly ladies and gentlemen. *They were looking at people just like themselves.* (Emphasis mine.)

To prove his point that this was "no Hollywood movie," Delano at this juncture in the telling adds to the scene another figure, this time with the dramatic force of industrial machinery:

> No sooner had the film started than a little steam locomotive hauling cars of sugarcane appeared on the nearby narrow-gauge tracks. The bright beam of the headlight fell on the screen and obliterated the image. Immediately an angry chorus of shouts rose up from the audience: "Turn off the headlight! Turn off the headlight!" The engineer not only turned off the headlight but kept the train standing there so he could watch the movie too.

Just as a film might do, Delano closes this scene by pulling back. In this retelling, his documentary—doubtless *Caña*, made in 1947—recedes into the background. By broadening the scene, he shifts attention from the film being screened to the rural audience, which now includes a train and its director (the engineer), as well as the film's director, who has nearly merged with the crowd of witnesses. Thus, half a century later, Delano has made a new version of the story of field workers uniting, in which the image of the people—distinctly framed and illuminated but still very accessible—stops all in their tracks. In effect, he has outdone photographer O. Winston Link, who made a memorable photograph from the same era of a train speeding by at night as a movie is projected on the screen of a rural drive-in.[6] In Delano's scenario, even the iron horse is tamed and brought into the charmed circle of performing viewers and viewing performers.

The incredulous will note that with this recollection there's a doubling of an earlier, wartime anecdote of the stateside train conductor who agrees to back up the train a few feet. We never learn whether that very obliging person ever saw the picture he helped make possible. Probably not; it was wartime, after all, and both engineer and photographer were on tight schedules. As if by magic, the first accomplice is repaid in the form of a fraternal emissary who at last gets an unexpected break in the midst of his own laboring journey.

Delano's chronicle contains many such loops. *Photographic Memories* might be subtitled a metachronicle, a summary chronicle of not only diverse episodes in his life but various chronicles he has made. And in keeping with his passion for musical composition, many stories replay as variants and refrains. The issue of money saved and then used improperly comprises a key Depression memory that later resonates as powerfully in the 1952 film he directed, *Los Peloteros*, albeit with notable differences.

In the first version of this tale, Jack is class treasurer of his high school. Already worried about whether the collected dues are safe in the bank, he grows even more worried when his father, who is struggling to keep his business afloat, persuades Jack to lend him the money. The father repays the loan before the breach of trust is discovered, but not before the son has felt compromised. Two decades later, he may have drawn upon that memory of conflicted allegiance while directing the feature-length film, based on a script by his colleague Edwin Rosskam. In that film, young boys in a poor country town pursue their dreams of playing in the junior baseball league with proper uniforms by collecting cans, shining shoes, selling snacks, and finally staging a neighborhood circus. But hard work and collective resourcefulness are not immediately rewarded. With a gender twist that mixes biblical echoes of Eve's original temptation with 1950s lures of consumer culture, the ambitious wife of the unofficial coach embezzles the funds to fulfill her acquisitive dreams of nicer clothes and furniture. In the end, both the team and the town are vindicated. Even after the coach has sold his pig to make up the funds, he is so disgraced that he can view the league at play only from a position of exile behind a fence. Following this denouement, the film closes as it opened, with town elders conversing at night on the porch of a rural store, concluding from this recollected episode that they need not wait for outside help to achieve some progress in their community. With the ballplayers as their model, they should be able to build a school through their own efforts. "But," one member of the group counsels, "we must be very careful about choosing our leader."

Just as the overall film proceeds by the allegorical mode of a story-within-a-story, so, too, many of the individual scenes are staged to incorporate distinct visual representations—whether silhouette, mirror, family photograph, or clothes mannequin—that serve diverse functions in relation to the narrative. As with stories (or, for that matter, leaders), the right kind of image may inspire positive action, while the wrong kind may just as readily mislead. But even if the image thus figures as a kind of moral compass, the multiplication of so many compasses has at the very least a distracting effect, and at most a disorienting one.

Why would Delano persistently experiment with such destabilizing devices? There is an immediate explanation that may suffice. In this way, the socially committed modern artist tacitly acknowledges his own sense of an ethical charge while making new representations designed for circulation among a class for whom any picture, particularly a new kind of picture, may be especially potent. But if at one level Delano's deployment of representations incorporated within another representation works in a quite traditional emblematic fashion, at another level the same device has a less specifically moralizing effect. Contemporary literary theory has much to say about the representation that contains another representation. The most radical version proposes that the effect is like an infinite regression into an abyss—the *mise en abyme* rather than the traditional illusionistic staging of the *mise en scene*—whereby the categories of representation and reality become virtually interchangeable.[7] Regarding Delano's frequent play with the picture that encloses other pictures, I am inclined to borrow from this model while still veering away from the abyss or the underlying idea of virtual interchangeability of reality and representation. Far from producing easy closure, Delano's picture-within-the-picture insinuates the principle of complexity into the scene as well as into the act of looking. By containing a representation, the picture alerts the viewer to the charged nature of all imagery—including, of course, the one most immediately on view. Moreover, such signs of complexity arguably serve an even more important function in the representations of supposedly simple lives, which—however reduced—should not be perceived as lacking the means to imagine the world and one's place in it.

Quite literally, Jack Delano might be considered the ultimate FSA photographer. Though he was one of the last to join the New Deal operation, it made a profound impression on him, and he absorbed its style, working methods, and values deeply. Moreover, of all the FSA photographers, he arguably continued the longest to work in comparable contexts of making publicity to support the work of progressive governmental agencies committed to social improvement. But in at least one key respect, Delano departed from the FSA style of photography: He rarely included the increasingly pervasive advertisement that figured so prominently in the imagery of other 1930s photographers. To take just two examples, consider FSA photographer Dorothea Lange's ironic inclusion of the ad "Next Time Try the Train" so that it appears to be addressing two migrants traveling by foot down an empty stretch of California highway, or for another example outside the FSA circle, think of Margaret Bourke-White's scene of the victims of the Louisville Flood waiting in line for relief assistance, mocked by the coincident billboard overhead that proclaims: "There's No Way Like the American Way."[8]

Such blatant contrasts were reigning devices of the reform school of 1930s American documentary. Yet even though Delano displayed a penchant for playing with pictures inside pictures, he never made part of his repertoire this particular use of advertising-as-reality's-foil. Indeed, on one occasion in a letter to FSA photography chief Roy Stryker, Delano proposed a new category of exterior signage and decoration that might warrant documentation in color, and he proceeded to name all manner of vernacular signage while conspicuously omitting any mention of billboards and other standard forms of corporate advertising.[9] In keeping with his aversion to Hollywood, Delano must have doubted whether advertising once admitted to the scene could ever be kept in its place. From the visual evidence, he must have thought it preferable to exclude the advertisement from his field of view rather than risk having it swamp the everyday, turning the tables so that ordinary reality became the foil of ads, the insignificant "before" of the commodity-blessed "after."

Similarly, though Puerto Rico between the 1940s and the 1980s became a prime market for consumer goods that mainly were imported from the mainland, Delano's vision of the island strictly limited such crass signs of modernization. He was enough of a realist to avoid censoring all forms of advertising. But with regard to ads, he was exceedingly selective, admitting some small signs, usually in Spanish, and permitting also the more playfully theatrical figures of mannequins, but excluding most oversize advertisements and billboards from his view. There seems only one way to explain this wholesale avoidance. He found the increasingly large, pervasive, uniform and uniforming advertisements so repellent that he could not bear to contribute to their dissemination, nor could he bear to have them overwhelm his vision of society as an organism capable of drawing on its own resources for sustenance and transformation, no matter how limited those resources were. In their place, he consistently sought to incorporate in the scenes he composed other, more traditional, sorts of pictures, just as he sought to envision the function of culture as providing a different sort of guide to, and measure of, development.

In his autobiography, it is equally characteristic that a fleeting reference to increasing crime in Puerto Rico—one common sign of the triumph of acquisitive values—is immediately counterbalanced by a recollection from the recent past of having his car break down in a dangerous neighborhood. Instead of becoming easy prey, he is once again the beneficiary of the kindness of strangers, even more surprising for their youthfulness. The handful of young street kids, who ordinarily seek every opportunity to make a bit of money, end up marshaling additional kids to push his car out of traffic. This specific recollection immediately reminds me of so many visual images Delano has made of the arduous daily tasks that require communal orchestration. Once they accomplish this feat, the children surprise him a second time by refusing his offer to pay for their assistance. Just as Jack figures for these boys as a "grandpa" and thus is accorded special respect, their unexpected generosity to an elder reminds him of the residual values that first attracted him to the island: "These boys—tough street kids—had been brought up to believe that when you do some work for someone, you expect to be paid, but helping an old man in trouble, that you don't do for money. You do it *por amor al prójimo* (for love of thy neighbor)."

While encountering the Spanish phrase and its conventional translation, I ponder for the first time that "neighbor" means literally "that which is proximate or nearby." In some respects, photography is sui generis the art of the proximate, capable of rendering only that which is close at hand or in the immediate vicinity. But the proximate quality of the photographic image is frequently offset by its indiscriminate use as a medium of mass reproduction and dissemination. Delano's practice with photography offers one model of use that not only conforms to the principle of *por amor al prójimo* but helps preserve it. Just as Delano has made few concessions to the mass appeal of advertising, so too since he moved to Puerto Rico his prime considerations for making pictures have been how the immediate community of Puerto Ricans might regard such images and how such images might intensify the act of regarding into the act of respecting.

Familiarity, the saying goes, breeds contempt. Many modern theorists of photography have argued that the pervasive use of the medium contributes to the devaluation of all things through a process of overfamiliarization.[10] And indeed, when Oliver Wendell Holmes first spoke of photography as a kind of second skin, he paired this analogy with the irreverent proposition that once we possess an exact copy of the Parthenon, we need not think twice about the fate of the original; even more, his language implies, we might actually take pleasure in its destruction.

Jack Delano is not that sort of modernist (maybe this is where his origins in a small Russian village inform the rest of his biography). He displays little irony and no contempt. Likewise, his photographs have had the effect of refuting Holmes's thesis that photography produces a perverse relation to the original.[11] On the contrary, his photographs have helped fuel an impassioned political debate by serving as a measure of what has been lost or is at perilous risk of extinction.

Delano's photographs of Puerto Rico systematically attest to a different cultural heritage in terms of architecture, spatial organization, modes of work, and modes of nonverbal communication through clothing and gesture. Such visual demonstrations of difference have impelled me as an outsider to study more of the history of this anomalous U.S. territory—my typical ignorance constituting yet more evidence of the culture of imperialism. In the course of preliminary study, what has astounded me is the regularity with which Delano's photographs appear in all manner of discourses on Puerto Rico, ranging from those advocating independence at all costs, to those promoting statehood as the most efficient means of accelerating the engine of progress, to those still committed to the "midway" philosophy of Muñoz Marín, the post–World War II architect of commonwealth status.[12]

I am struck particularly by the central role of Delano's imagery in two of the more radical critiques. I recently viewed a new documentary film on Puerto Rico that drew heavily on Delano's photographs and films to challenge anew the reformist path of Muñoz Marín, with whom Delano worked so closely, while simultaneously reconsidering the legacy of revolutionary Nationalist Pedro Albizu Campos. This film made the case that the decision of Muñoz Marín and the Popular Democratic Party to moderate the road to independence may have put too much weight on short-term material gains that the commonwealth route seemed to offer. In the process of further integration of Puerto Rican and U.S. economies and societies, the possibility of independence may have been radically reduced, foreclosing not only political but cultural autonomy. Yet the vision of what may have been lost in terms of a distinctive culture is conveyed in large measure by use of Delano's films and photography made for the reformist government.[13]

A recent critical essay on the imagery of DIVEDCO, the Division of Community Education, to which Delano made such a signal contribution with his films, is inclined to brand the imagery as utopic, more specifically as ignoring the contradictions of increasing industrialization and dependence on foreign capital. And yet, the very penetrating critique concludes, even if utopic, these works must not be ignored: "The qualities of these films endure, not the least being the belief in the possibility of Puerto Rican fulfillment, and the images of the vitality of a people who are capable of taking hold of their conditions and transforming themselves."[14]

Delano's imagery offers no decisive answers, nor does it seek such finality, except in the sense that the social coherence he treasured may have been more fragile than his renderings of it. I have always marveled that in his extensive efforts to document changes in Puerto Rico, he only rarely depicted the arrival of tourists in a period when tourism was a key element of the burgeoning service economy and doubtless had considerable impact on local culture as well. At least as noteworthy, Delano never depicted the departure of native residents, when the massive outmigration in the postwar era was both a sign of the limited success of industrialization and a key element in the process of further social integration with the mainland.

Like the proverbial half-full glass, his renderings seek to shore up such major social ruptures, by emphasizing those aspects of tradition that remain vital and self-sustaining and by emphasizing the many crucial links in the necessarily social process of cultural communication and preservation. On one occasion while studying changes in Puerto Rican locales photographed decades earlier, Delano was heartened to discover muralists in the town of Juncos carrying on the tradition of cultural preservation by decorating the underpass of a modern highway with a view of the town as it appears above. They not only shared his interest in local history but had selected virtually the same view of the town that Delano's colleague, Edwin Rosskam, had recorded a half century ago. Such coincidence of purpose inspired new documentation, not of the town of Juncos but of an emerging generation of local guardians of the town's current image.

Delano's recent photograph includes the older photograph held by muralists in front of their independently conceived handiwork. As such, it is a typically Delano picture in at least two ways. He has always enjoyed slightly tricky pictures, in which the viewer must puzzle through the relations between one image found inside another. But this formal game, though it offers its own genealogical challenges, also connects to his deepest cultural concerns.

In his various endeavors in photography, film, books, and even music, Jack Delano has always considered how art might fit into everyday society and make a difference by helping people see their lives, environments, and heritages more clearly. In this way, the picture-in-the-picture might be said to symbolize Delano's fervent belief that art should strive to find a place in all of our lives . . . thus generating more meaningful lives and more meaningful art . . . in an endless process that links present to past.

Notes

In writing this essay, I am especially indebted to the cooperation, insights, patience, and art of Jack Delano. Thanks also to Pablo Delano, who carries on traditions as son and photographer, and to Evelyn Figueroa, lively guide and prod in Puerto Rico and Washington, D.C. Finally, thanks to Professor Ronald E. Ostman, Department of Communication, Cornell University, for generously sharing his biographic research, which greatly facilitated my sense of chronology and artistic diversity in Delano's awesomely multifaceted career.

1. Jack Delano, *Puerto Rico Mío* (Washington, D.C.: Smithsonian Institution Press, 1990).

2. Jack Delano, *El Día que el Pueblo se despidió de Muñoz Marín* (Carolina, P.R.: Borinquen Lithographers Corporation for Fundación Luis Muñoz Marín, 1987).

3. Some may object to my conflation of the ethic of reciprocity with the more market-based contract of repayment, which appears even more burdensome when interest is compounded. The conflation is deliberate for two reasons. In the recent debate about the nature of the gift and its relation to the economic, I am persuaded by Mary Douglas's argument that there are no free gifts, nor have gifts ever been "free." She considers this point central to Marcel Mauss's classic anthropological essay *The Gift*, first published in 1924, newly translated by W. D. Halls, and published with Douglas's foreword (New York: Norton, 1990), pp. vii–xviii. For an eloquent counterargument that seeks to recast the gift outside of market relations (precapitalist or capitalist), see Lewis Hyde, *The Gift: Imagination and the Erotic Life of Property* (New York: Vintage, 1979). In his introduction, Hyde acknowledges the "optimistic" cast of his work that avoids addressing the relations between gifts and obligation (p. xvi). Yet the principle of obligation is the issue that Mauss considered to be the basis for "the bond of alliance and commonality" (Mauss, p. 13). Hyde's metaphysics of the gift seems an insufficient surrogate for that bond. Likewise, I contend that in Delano's chronicle two marked strains are the sense of obligation and indebtedness, as well as the quest for just such a sense of alliance and commonality that Mauss considers the informing reason for all gifts.

4. Oliver Wendell Holmes, "The Stereoscope and the Stereograph," *Atlantic Monthly* 3 (June 1859): 738–48.

5. See Delano's correspondence with Roy Stryker from April and May of 1941, and particularly the detailed description of work in progress contained in his letter of May 7 (Roy E. Stryker Papers at the Photographic Archives, University of Louisville).

6. See O. Winston Link's "Hot Shot East Bound at Iaeger, West Virginia, August 2, 1956," reproduced in Rupert Martin, ed., *Night Trick by O. Winston Link: Photographs of the Norfolk and Western Railway* (London: Photographers' Gallery, 1983), p. 11.

7. For a theoretical summary of this critical discourse, see Lucien Dallenbach, *The Mirror in the Text* (Jeremy Whiteley with Emma Hughes, trans.) (Chicago, 1989); see also Daniel Arasse's deftly modulated use of this theory in his recent monograph, *Vermeer: Faith in Painting* (Princeton: Princeton University Press, 1994), particularly chapter 3, "The Picture-within-the-Picture," pp. 22–39.

8. The photograph by Lange was first featured in the portfolio of FSA photography assembled by Edward Steichen in *U.S. Camera Annual* (New York: William Morrow, 1939), p. 47. The photograph by Bourke-White first appeared in *Life*, February 15, 1937, p. 9.

9. Delano to Stryker, September 23, 1941, Stryker Collection.

10. For two versions of this argument, see Walter Benjamin, "The Work of Art in the Age of Mechanical Reproduction," in the collection of his essays edited by Hannah Arendt, *Illuminations* (Harry Zohn, trans.) (London: Fontana/Collins, 1973), pp. 219–54; also, Susan Sontag, *On Photography* (New York: Farrar, Strauss, 1977).

11. Holmes, "Stereoscope," pp. 747–48.

12. The term "midway" philosophy is enunciated by the historian closely associated with Muñoz Marín; see Arturo Morales Carrión, *Puerto Rico: A Political and Cultural History* (New York: Norton, 1983), p. 291.

13. See the film by Raquel Ortiz and Sharon Simon, *Mi Puerto Rico* (Somerville, Mass.: Ortiz/Simon Productions, Inc., 1996). Notwithstanding the considerable use of historic film and photography by Delano, and the film's title that is quite similar to Delano's 1990 book, *Puerto Rico Mío*, this recent film is an independent production made without Delano's participation.

14. Antonio Lauria-Perricelli, "Images and Contradictions: DIVEDCO's Portrayal of Puerto Rican Life," *Centro* 3, no. 1 (Winter 1990–91): 92–96.

1 ·

From a Ukrainian Village to an American Metropolis

If you were to look for the town of Voroshilovka on the map of the present-day Ukraine, you wouldn't find it—the Nazis destroyed it completely during World War II, and it was never rebuilt. But in 1914 it was a thriving little village of three or four thousand souls about 120 miles southwest of Kiev on the River Bug. That's where I, Jacob Ovcharov (nicknamed Jasha), was born on the first of August. During my early years, I always thought that my birth had something to do with the outbreak of World War I. Not until later did I discover that the war was precipitated by the assassination of Archduke Ferdinand in Sarajevo on June 28, more than a month before I was born. Although the two events were obviously not related, the war and the revolution that followed did have a profound effect on what was to happen to me in the years to come.

Looking back after eighty years, I cannot remember much about life in Voroshilovka. It was a typical Russian village of those days: It had no electricity, no running water, no telephone. Its most characteristic feature was a long, dusty main street that ran to the marketplace, where we children could buy a pickled apple for a kopek. Merchants and tradesmen made up most of the population, and on market days the town would be filled with peasants from the countryside bringing in their produce. Men and women bathed in the nude on alternate days in the river while we children splashed about with water wings made of cow or pig bladders filled with air. The town boasted a modest little church and also a synagogue for the Jewish community. Jews and Christians of the Greek Orthodox Church lived side by side, and although there was always fear of "pogroms" (raids) against the Jews by the Cossacks (I had heard rumors of frightful atrocities), I remember no such occurrences disturbing my childhood days.

Perhaps that was because of the rather privileged position of my parents. My mother, Sonia, was the town dentist—a graduate of St. Vladimir University in Kiev. (I still have her graduation certificate.) This was no mean accomplishment for a woman in those days, and a Jewish woman at that. Her patients were people from all walks of life in the town who knew and respected her work and peasants who came in from the nearby farms complaining of a toothache. During the revolution, money was worthless, and when she pulled a tooth for a peasant, she was usually paid in produce—eggs, chickens, geese, or perhaps a baby goat, so we never really lacked for food. Besides, when the revolution came to town, she was commissioned as an officer, with the rank of captain, in the Red Army medical corps. That meant not only a guaranteed supply of food, commandeered from the peasants by the soldiers, but also protection from any possible vandalism or persecution.

In contrast to my mother, who was a very realistic and strong-willed person, my father was rather impractical and easygoing. His name was Vladimir, but everyone knew him as Vova. He was a teacher of Russian and mathematics in the local school. In such a small town he was considered part of the intelligentsia. After all, he had graduated from the normal school, he was well-read, and he was interested in all sorts of cultural affairs. An amateur violinist and guitarist, he gave me my first violin lessons when I was about six years old. I also remember him setting up a still life with cups and saucers and teaching me to draw. He was acquainted with world literature and could recite the soliloquy from *Gamlet* (there is no *h* in the Russian alphabet). He knew of Mark Twain and Jack London and introduced me to an extraordinary literary character he called Donkishoht (Don Quixote). His only sibling, my uncle Shlomo, was an accomplished violinist who played professionally at weddings and parties, and it was he who made me study the violin seriously.

We lived in a one-story stone house on the main street of Voroshilovka. My mother had her office in part of the house, and there was a kitchen with a huge oven where all the cooking was done and the bread was baked, just as in a bakery. The wall between the kitchen and the main dining room was hollow, with an opening at one end covered by an iron door. In winter, we used this as the heating system of the house by keeping a fire going in the hollow wall. I remember people standing with their backs and the palms of their hands up against the wall to keep warm on freezing winter days. I remember this particularly because of an incident my parents and friends used to tease me about. It seems that one evening when I was quite small I came up to warm my hands on the wall and it was so hot when I touched it that I was shocked and wanted to shout *"chepyot!"* (it's hot!). But what came out of my mouth was *"pechyot!"*—the correct word but with the first syllable reversed.

Not far from our house stood the mansion of one of the rich landowners. It had been a target of the revolutionary army when the artillery came through town, and the structure showed the scars of heavy bombardment. As children, we would crawl through the gaping holes in the walls to play games inside.

But I really have no memory of any serious fighting in the town. We lived a rather tranquil life and, except for what happened to the landowner's house, we were hardly aware of the war. We got along well with our neighbors, we had many friends, and we were never molested. My mother (the captain) felt quite secure in her position, but my father (the worrier) was quite concerned about what would happen to us after the revolution. His concern was shared by my mother's relatives in the United States, who kept writing, urging us to leave the country, for fear of the chaos that was sure to follow the revolution. They offered to pay for our passage, and they painted a glorious picture of what we would find in the States.

I, of course, had no part in making the decision, but one day I learned that we—my mother, my father, my little brother, Sol (five years my junior), and I—were leaving Voroshilovka.

My family and I in Vinnitza in 1923, just before we left for the United States.

Many people were fleeing Russia, and it wasn't easy to get out. As children, we couldn't help hearing horror stories of men, women, and children being arrested or shot trying to sneak across the border illegally into Romania. But we didn't have that problem. I don't know how my parents managed it, but we all had perfectly legal passports (which I still preserve). My father's passport was issued December 15, 1922, in the name of Vova Ovcharov "and two children, Jacob, eight years old and Solomon, aged three." My mother had a separate passport in her own name, Sonia. With our documents in order, off we went to the "promised land."

There was no railroad station in Voroshilovka, so our first destination was the town of Vinnitza. There we stayed just long enough to put on our best clothes and pose for a family picture taken by the town photographer. Then off we went to the great city of Kiev to spend a few days with relatives. I had never been in a big city before and was overwhelmed by everything I saw. Just imagine! Our relatives lived in an apartment! They had electric lights and a telephone! To reach them you had to take an elevator! (It's just like an animal cage, I thought.) A prank I learned from the boys in the building was to run down the halls ringing all the doorbells and then dash out into the street to avoid being caught. But the most memorable experience in Kiev was my visit to the theater.

My parents took me to a children's theater production of a musical play called *Ivan Durachok*. Today I realize that Ivan Durachok is the same character we know in Puerto Rico as Juan Bobo (Juan the Fool). The play was about the pranks and mischief of Ivan, but what stuck in my mind was the scenery, the costumes, and, above all, the final, wondrous scene when Ivan rides off into the sky on the back of a beautiful white horse! It must have been in Kiev also that I witnessed what seemed to me to be a magical scene—a park with an ice-skating rink that had a gazebo in the center. In the gazebo a band played waltzes while young skaters whirled around in a great circle, sometimes pushing elderly people in chairs equipped with runners.

After a brief stay in Kiev, we continued our odyssey by train to Moscow, then to Riga in Latvia, to Bremen in Germany, and from there by steamer to Southampton, England, where we landed on June 17, 1923. Strange that I don't remember anything of this long journey, nor of the ten days we spent in England before embarking for the United States. The inspection card issued to us by the American consul in Southampton shows the date of departure as June 27, to "Immigrants and Steerage Passengers." We left for New York on the S.S. *Homeric* of the White Star Line in berth number T-141. All I remember about the ship is that it had four huge smokestacks.

We traveled third class. Crossing the Atlantic took eight days, and to me the only significant thing about the voyage itself was that I made my debut as a violin soloist, picking up a few pennies by playing ditties for the amusement of our fellow passengers.

Then one starry night everyone rushed up to the crowded decks to behold a magnificent sight—the lights of the skyscrapers of New York. As we passed the Statue of Liberty and entered the harbor, the sky suddenly lit up with a brilliant display of fireworks. The flares were of all colors—red, green, white—shooting up from platforms or tugboats in the harbor. Never in my short life had I seen such a thrilling sight. It was even more exciting than the theater in Kiev. In my childish innocence, I assumed that this was the Americans' way of welcoming us immigrants to their country. Not until the following day did I learn that we had arrived on Independence Day, the Fourth of July, and what that day meant to the American people.

We were herded through Ellis Island, with its health inspectors and immigration officers, and onto the ferry for the mainland. A long wrought-iron fence held back a noisy crowd of people who had gathered to get a glimpse of their newly arrived relatives. It seemed like pandemonium to me, but suddenly, out in the crowd, my mother spotted her cousin, our Uncle Louie, who had made all the arrangements for our journey. He had come, with his wife and two sons, to take us to his house in Bristol, Pennsylvania. And he had a car. A real car! I think it was a Buick. Now I knew we were in America.

2 ·

*Learning to Be
an American*

Bristol was a small town about twenty miles north of Philadelphia. My uncle had settled there many years earlier and started a furniture store. He was now a successful businessman, a member of the board of directors of the local bank, and a highly respected member of the community.

He was determined that we should learn English and become "Americanized" as soon as possible. Though I knew not a word of English, I was immediately enrolled in the local elementary school. To find out in which grade I should be placed, the teachers gave me several examinations; I passed the only one I understood—mathematics. In Uncle Louie's house, speaking Russian was frowned upon, and his family did not understand the language.

But children learn languages easily, and I had no trouble picking up English from my playmates. Soon I became fluent in the language. (Unfortunately, because of all the pressure to become thoroughly American, I gradually forgot all my Russian.)

Curiously enough, it was while I was learning English that I ran into my first example of racism in the United States. I had many playmates in town and was soon participating in the games they knew. We played cowboys and Indians, we went trick-or-treating on Halloween, I learned about baseball and football, and I played peg-ball in the street. One day while I was out playing with the gang, we saw a tall black woman on the corner waiting for a bus. In Russia I had never seen a black person. I didn't know they existed. The black woman on the corner seemed exotic to me, like someone out of the Arabian Nights stories my father used to read to me. Then one of the boys said to me, "Go up to her and say ————." I didn't understand what that meant, but he assured me that it was very complimentary. So I went up to the woman, smiled, and said, "————." The next thing I knew, I was stretched out on a bed in my uncle's house with a swollen black eye and everybody around me asking, "What happened? What happened?"

It was in Bristol also that I had an unhappy introduction to another aspect of American culture—Chinese food. One evening we sat down to dinner and were served some strange food that my uncle had ordered especially from a nearby Chinese restaurant. I had been brought up on beet soup and other staples of a Russian diet, and the idea of eating all those noodles that looked like worms to me was repugnant. "Worms, worms," I kept repeating. "I won't eat worms." I was so adamant in my refusal and raised such a ruckus, to the embarrassment of my parents, that I was sent to my room with no dinner at all. (Paradoxically, I have since then become very fond of Chinese cuisine.)

We were welcome to stay in my uncle's house as long as necessary, but after a few months it became apparent that we were imposing too much and that my parents should find work and move our family to a home of our own. In a town as small as Bristol, there was no urgent need for the services of a teacher of Russian or a dentist unlicensed to practice in the United States. With the advice and encouragement of Uncle Louie, we decided to move to Philadelphia, where he had arranged for my mother to be accepted in a two-year graduate course at the dental school of Temple University that would qualify her for a license to practice in the United States. As for my father, he could find no position anywhere as a teacher of Russian and had to be content with a job in an upholstered-furniture factory.

3.

*Music in the
City of
Brotherly Love*

We lived in a small apartment on Franklin Street, near Girard Avenue, in central Philadelphia, in one of those row houses that have three steps leading to the front door. Money was very scarce. My father's earnings were not enough to support the family. So my mother, through the many friends she had made at the dental school, managed to acquire some of the tools of her profession, including a foot-powered dental drill and some medicines, and she set up a little office in her bedroom. Little by little, word spread through the neighborhood that the Russian lady dentist was treating patients in her house and that she was an expert. Of course, she first worked on members of the family and friends. (I still have a few fillings she put in for me.) For a long time no one seemed to question whether this was legal or not.

It was difficult for her to continue with her studies at the university. She had to look after the household, take care of her two children, and study textbooks in a language she did not understand. Besides, it must have been frustrating to have to go over material she felt she already knew perfectly well. The climax came the day of final examinations. She herself knew the answers to all the questions, but she noticed that some of the other students were having difficulty and saw no reason not to help them. She didn't understand why she was expelled. "After all, the idea is for them to learn, isn't it?" she insisted. "What difference does it make if they learn from me or from the professor?"

My father, in the meantime, was having his own problems at the furniture factory. He had never done any physical work, and having to deal with hammer and nails as he learned a trade was not easy. The other workers in the shop, most of them unskilled immigrants who had been working there for a long time, soon became aware that this was a strange character, an "intellectual," and they sometimes made fun of his clumsy attempts to stuff a sofa. But he managed to gain their respect in a rather unusual way.

They all knew that my father spoke Russian. One day a worker approached him and said, "So you speak Russian, eh? Well, that's nothing. Mike, here, he speaks FRENCH, don't you, Mike?" *"Oui,"* said Mike. Then to my father, "Can you speak

French too?" Now, my father couldn't speak French at all, but he had learned a few words of the language while studying to be a teacher, so he said, *"Oui. Oui."* "Well, let me hear you say something in French to Mike," said his tormentor. My father suspected that Mike was bluffing, so he boldly blurted out a stream of French-sounding gobbledygook that meant nothing but sounded great. Poor Mike stood openmouthed. His bluff called, he could only slink away in defeat while my father rejoiced in his victory. From then on, my father was treated with more respect. "He speaks not only Russian *but also French!"* his coworkers would exclaim.

As for my brother, Sol, and me, we were immediately enrolled in school—I in the sixth grade and he in kindergarten. My father also took me to the Settlement Music School on Queen Street in South Philadelphia, where, after an audition on my violin, I was accepted and given a partial scholarship. I had to pay only three dollars a month for classes in violin, theory, harmony, chamber music, counterpoint, orchestration, and related subjects. Settlement was a special school for underprivileged children in a poor neighborhood in the city. But the teachers were excellent, many of them faculty from the Curtis Institute of Music who taught at Settlement on a pro bono basis. Several times a week after public school, I would take streetcar no. 7 down to the music school for my classes. On Saturdays I would be there all day. There were tennis courts on the roof of the building, and between classes the budding "virtuosi" used to practice to be tennis stars also. Two years after I started at the school, Sol was also admitted to study the violin.

The director of the school was Johann Grolle, a tall, impressive, kindly white-haired man from Holland. He conducted the chamber music classes—string quartets, trios, sonatas—and took a personal interest in every student. Once when I didn't have a formal suit to wear at a student recital, he lent me one of his own suits and a pair of shoes, all of which were two or three sizes too big for me. The discomfort did not deter me, however, from announcing nervously to an audience consisting mostly of proud parents, "I will now play 'The Swan,' by Saynt Sayns [Saint-Saëns]." Mr. Grolle also conducted the school orchestra, and he introduced us not only to the great works of classical literature but to some contemporary music as well. It was here that I first played works by Hindemith, Bartók, and Prokofiev.

Mr. Grolle was assisted in his administrative duties by Miss Evans, a sweet lady who looked after all the records and bookkeeping, and by Miss Finnegan, a strict disciplinarian whom I shall never forget. She didn't know anything about music (I think she was tone-deaf), but she knew how to run a tight ship. It was Miss Finnegan who escorted a selected group of us students on Saturdays to the Academy of Music on Broad Street, where the school had a reserved box, to sit through the concerts of the Philadelphia Orchestra conducted by Leopold Stokowski. At the time I did not appreciate the wonderful opportunity I was being given to become acquainted with magnificent performances of great orchestral music. Sometimes during a Bruckner or Mahler symphony, my mind would wander off to the tennis courts at school or I might even begin to doze. It was especially difficult for me to take the Wagnerian operas. Sitting through the entire four operas of *Der Ring des Nibelungen* at the age of ten, I frequently fell asleep, only to be stirred awake by Miss Finnegan poking me in the ribs.

My violin teacher, Emmanuel Zeitlin, was a gentle, wise man and a very good violinist. One day when I came in for my lesson, he asked me about my other interests in addition to music. What book had I recently read? (*Scaramouche*, by Rafael Sabatini.) What did I do in my spare time? What were my hobbies? (Making model ships and airplanes.) Finally he said to me, "You have a good ear and a lot of talent, but unless you give up some of these other things and spend more time practicing the violin, you are never going to be a virtuoso." He was right, of course. I gave up the idea of becoming a concert violinist but did not give up my interest in music, concentrating on playing chamber music and studying composition.

For solfège lessons, I turned to a teacher from the Curtis Institute of Music. She had a house in the suburbs and I would pay for my lessons by mowing her lawn. From her I learned sight-reading in different clefs, transposition, and something of Gregorian chant and medieval music.

Composition, counterpoint, and harmony were taught by Professor Jacob Weinberg, a specialist in Hebrew music, which he did not teach. I say "professor" because he was the first person I ever saw who wore pince-nez. For him we had to harmonize Bach chorales, learn about the figured-bass system of harmonic shorthand, and compose original pieces.

The school auditorium, where monthly student concerts were held, boasted a small but extremely good organ. I would sometimes spend hours at the instrument, improvising and composing, until one day Miss Finnegan told me I could no longer use it—all my practice time was consuming too much electricity.

I spent twelve years at the school, first as a student, then as a teaching assistant, and finally as a teacher. After the first few years, I took up the viola and began playing it professionally. My brother, Sol, in the meantime, was accepted at the Curtis Institute of Music, where he studied with the internationally acclaimed violinist Efrem Zimbalist. Soon, with Sol as first violinist and me as violist, we organized a string quartet and managed to get a half-hour weekly program on a local radio station.

4.
Movies, Pretzels, and Empty Pockets

I was ten years old when we moved to Philadelphia, and I had never seen a movie. Now, around the corner from our house on Girard Avenue there was a theater, and there I saw my first film. It was Milton Sills in *The Sea Hawk*, a swashbuckling pirate adventure story. I sat enthralled in the dark theater, my heart pounding with excitement, without understanding where all those images were coming from. When the film was over, I went around to the back of the screen to see if the pirates were still there.

There was a pretzel factory not far from the theater. If you brought your own little paper bag, for three cents you could have it filled with pretzels that had been broken in the manufacturing process. It was a small luxury that we could sometimes afford.

The combined earnings of my parents were barely enough to support the family. We never actually went hungry, but neither was there ever any money for luxuries. For example, one Christmas, my parents gave my brother and me a pair of roller skates, one skate for him and one for me, while many children in the neighborhood received gifts such as bicycles and electric trains.

Not far from Philadelphia, there was a summer camp for underprivileged children run by the Catholic charitable organization called Big Brothers. It cost only ten dollars a week, so that's where my parents sent me, for a week. I was a strong, husky boy, and everybody in camp wanted me on their baseball team. That's how I learned about the great American pastime. But I had never played real baseball before, and every time I came up to bat I struck out. This happened so often that a kindly counselor, seeing my distress, came up to me, put his arm around my shoulder, and said, "Look, kid, you gotta keep your eye on the ball, see? Don't look at me, or the pitcher or anybody. Just keep your eye on the ball. Okay?" I took his advice. The next time I came up to bat, I hit a home run. Simple, I thought. Why didn't somebody tell me that before?

One luxury we did enjoy was the radio. When Uncle Louie bought himself a fancy new radio, we inherited his old battery-powered one. It came with a bell-shaped speaker and several batteries that had to be constantly recharged. We would often stay up late at night, gathered around the speaker listening to symphony concerts or comedy programs. I shall never forget the excitement when we heard the broadcast of Lindbergh's arrival in France after he had crossed the Atlantic. And when Jack Dempsey and Gene Tunney fought for the world heavyweight boxing championship, we remained glued to the radio for the entire fifteen rounds.

In 1928, I graduated from the James G. Blaine Elementary School and entered Central High School for Boys, located on Broad Street in the center of town. Just a few blocks away was the William Penn School for Girls. Central High was supposed to be the oldest high school in the country, founded by Benjamin Franklin, people said. Of course, in Philadelphia, everything was said to have been founded by Benjamin Franklin, but it really must have been an old school—my graduating class was the 158th! It was the only high school that still granted a bachelor of arts degree.

Central High was racially integrated. There were many black students, and some of them were my friends. In our graduating class, a young black man was vice president, and I was treasurer.

The school curriculum was based on the liberal arts and the classics. Students were required to take Latin or Greek and a modern European language—French, German, Italian, or Spanish. I remember taking a course in philology and having to write a paper about Sanskrit. Our Latin teacher was an old man we called Ducky Hawes because of his propensity for flunking students with a D. He was somewhat careless in his dress and often sat at his desk with his fly open. One day while he was out of the room, one of my classmates, a top student, wrote on the blackboard, in perfect Latin, "The joys of men lie between the legs of women." He got into deep trouble for what we students thought was a show of brilliant wit.

In addition to languages, the school offered excellent science classes, good laboratories, an art department, and a ten-inch refracting telescope for students interested in astronomy. I belonged to the art club and the astronomy club and would often spend evenings at the telescope. As an astronomer I knew nothing of mathematics, but I was fascinated by the mysteries of the universe, a fascination that has never left me. At the music school, I had become enamored of a pretty young blond violinist who shared my interest in astronomy, and sometimes after a late rehearsal we would go for long walks, holding hands, looking up at the star-filled sky, and babbling, not about the romantic moon but about light-years and galaxies and satellites and the curvature of space.

By this time, my family had moved to a different house, on Twenty-ninth Street, in the Strawberry Mansion section of town near Fairmount Park. It was far from our house to the high school. During the week, I had to go by streetcar no. 9 to Central High and often, after that, continue on to the music school for an orchestra rehearsal. But Sundays were different. On Sundays I could go to Fairmount Park to fly kites, go running around the reservoir, or watch the rowing crews from the University of Pennsylvania practicing on the Schuylkill River.

Our new house was a two-story building. The first floor was occupied by my father's furniture business (yes, he had decided to go into business for himself), and the second floor held our living quarters and my mother's little dental office. The staff and employees of the Victor Furniture Company, as my father called his store, consisted entirely of my father himself. He built the furniture, he put it on display in the store window, he was the salesman, bookkeeper, delivery man—everything. I am sure he was a very good teacher of Russian, but I know he was not a very good businessman. He was always in debt to the building and loan association and always worried about how to pay his bills. After all, this was 1929 and the early 1930s. The country was in the depths of the Great Depression. Banks were failing and everyone was having financial troubles.

As treasurer of my graduating class, I was nervous about the $150 in class money I had in the Bankers Trust. What if the bank closed? I kept watching the newspapers for bank failures and kept taking the money out of one bank, putting it into another, then withdrawing it from that one to deposit it in yet another, hoping to stay ahead of the failures. It was during this period that my father came pleading for me to lend him $100 of that money I had in the bank. "If I don't pay off those building and loan people tomorrow, I'll lose the business," he said. "I'll pay it back in two days." How could I do such a thing? It wasn't my money. Suppose the class needed the money right away? But how could I let my father go broke while the money that would save him lay idle in a bank? I lent him the money, feeling like a criminal, convinced that I would be put in jail. But he paid it back in two days, as he had said he would. I was saved and no one was the wiser.

Our neighborhood consisted mainly of lower-middle-class people of about the same economic level as my family. Many of them, including my mother and father, belonged to a group they called the Workmen's Circle, a secular Jewish fraternal organization of liberal leanings that met every now and then at alternate houses. Though the purpose of the meetings seemed to be mainly social, the gatherings also served as a place to discuss serious issues of the day. When the group met at our house, I would be in the adjoining room trying to understand the heated discussions of the case of Sacco and Vanzetti, the two anarchists arrested in Massachusetts and accused of murder, and of the *Scottsboro* case, in which nine young black men in Alabama were accused of raping a white woman and sentenced to death. Both cases made headline news day after day. I was especially impressed by the passion of a young woman who would come to the meetings to urge people to write to their congressman or to sign petitions for the release of the prisoners. I suppose that it was at these meetings that I began to develop a concern for the oppressed and persecuted that was to last me for the rest of my life.

5.

*Becoming an
Artist and
Falling in Love*

I graduated from high school in 1932 and applied for scholarships to the University of Pennsylvania (in science) and to the Pennsylvania Academy of the Fine Arts (in art). The university turned me down because of my abysmal grades in mathematics, but the academy offered me a partial scholarship on the basis of some drawings I had done in the art club, so my choice was clear.

My brother, Sol, meanwhile, embarked on a career as a musician. In the years to come, as we followed our separate careers, he as a concert violinist and I as a graphic artist and photographer, we seemed to drift further apart and to have less and less in common. The one thing that held us together was our love and concern for our parents. Even as students we hardly ever saw each other. He was always at the Curtis Institute studying or playing somewhere to earn a little money, while I was at the art academy trying to become a successful illustrator.

The art school was on Broad Street at the corner of Cherry, in the center of town, just two or three blocks from the city hall. The long streetcar ride from my home every day got to be too much for me, and I persuaded my parents to let me rent a room somewhere near the school. "Fine," they said. "Our friends the Kormans run a little store in their house just four blocks from the school. We're sure they have a spare room they can rent you." What I didn't know was that they also had an attractive daughter and my parents hoped we would make a good match. I now felt that I was a true bohemian artist, with my own room near Chinatown, and my artist friends, who would gather to carouse and argue about everything from the influence of African sculpture on modern art to the poetry of Baudelaire.

Most of the students at the school were as poor as I was, and we all depended on federal financial aid—the NYA, the National Youth Administration created by the Roosevelt government. I was a member of the advisory committee that had been created at the school to help administer the program. Funds were limited, and one had to learn to live cheaply. I usually ate lunch at a nearby Automat restaurant, where for twenty-five cents I could get a sandwich, coffee, and a piece of apple or cherry pie. And dinner at Linton's or in Chinatown usually came to about thirty-five cents.

The school was proud of its tradition as the place where Thomas Eakins and other great American painters had taught and worked. It was pointed out to us that the very room where we were given a weekly criticism of our work was where Eakins had taught anatomy and dissected cadavers. The school also boasted of being the first art academy established in the country, having been founded in 1805.

Courses were offered in drawing, painting, composition, perspective, sculpture, illustration, mural painting, and the history of art. I decided to major in illustration. The richest and most successful artist that we students knew of was Norman Rockwell, who did the illustrations for the *Saturday Evening Post*, which was published in Philadelphia. All of the illustration students dreamed of being as successful as he was so they could work for the many magazines of those days that used illustrations by famous artists—N. C. Wyeth, Joseph Pennell, and others. Courses in drawing, composition, and related subjects were required of everyone. The drawing class conducted by Professor Laesley, a sculptor, was especially memorable, partly because it was the first time I had seen a nude female model and partly because the teacher had the habit of smudging his fingers on the dirty floor and unabashedly using the dirt to put dots all over the model's body to explain the "movement" or "the axis" or the interplay of muscles.

In general, all the teaching was strictly academic. Only one teacher, Henry McCarter, almost surreptitiously opened our eyes to contemporary art. A short, chubby old man with white hair and a red nose, he liked to have a little drink once in a while. On Fridays in the former anatomy room, enveloped in a slight aroma of cognac and surrounded by a group of admiring students, he would look at the work that we brought in for criticism, and on Mondays he would give an illustrated talk in the school auditorium about the work of the impressionists and Picasso, Miró, Braque, and other modern painters.

One day around lunchtime, in the same auditorium, I heard someone playing the piano. I recognized the piece as Beethoven's "Appassionata" Sonata. Quietly I opened the door and tiptoed in to listen. There on the platform I saw a young woman furiously pounding away at the piano. She had a mop of black, disheveled hair and wore a leather jacket and jeans—quite a daring outfit in those days. I don't know if it was the music of Beethoven or the hair that did it, but I fell in love on the spot. I learned that her name was Irene, that she was sixteen years old, and that she had come from Toronto to study painting at the academy on the recommendation of her distant cousin, the painter Ben Shahn, while her father, Dr. David Esser, was pursuing postgraduate studies in ophthalmology at the University of Pennsylvania in Philadelphia.

In the weeks that followed, I did my best to get Irene to pay some attention to me, but to no avail. I was as bald then as I am today, and she thought I was one of the teachers trying to make a pass at her. (My parents had been concerned about my losing my hair when I was in high school. They took me to the Skin and Cancer Hospital in Philadelphia, where I was thoroughly examined by a group of bald doctors and sent home with my tonsils removed.) I finally managed to make an impression on Irene when she had trouble with her perspective classes. I was good at perspective drawing and offered to help her do her assignments. I usually charged other students a quarter for such coaching, but for Irene it was free.

Irene's father provided her with a generous monthly allowance, which she often shared with her less affluent friends. She shared a room with her friend Maggie and sometimes made small loans to students with no expectation of being repaid. I became one of the most frequent borrowers. She smoked cigarettes constantly, and I picked up the habit too, partly to impress her and partly because it was the thing to do for an artist.

By the time I was in my third year at the academy, I had moved out of my room in the Kormans' house and forgotten about their daughter. One of my fellow students, Joe Tonner, had rented a big house on Cherry Street with many rooms, which he offered to rent to art students on a cooperative basis. Irene moved in and I soon followed. Before long, the house was filled with eight students from the academy and Irene's cousin Olga, each with his or her room and studio space. The house became a lively artistic center. All of us were involved in our own work, but there was also a great deal of collaboration and interchange of ideas. Naturally, in a group of young artists living together, it was inevitable that there should also be drinking parties, consumption of endless packs of cigarettes, and other attributes of bohemian life.

One day we decided to invite our favorite teacher, Henry McCarter, for dinner. Joe was an excellent cook and prepared a great feast. As for the wine, when we asked Mr. McCarter what he would prefer, he immediately said, "Chablis." Stimulated by the Chablis, Mr. McCarter kept us entertained the whole evening with stories about his experiences in Paris when he studied with Puvis du Chavanne and hobnobbed with such artists as Cézanne, Degas, Renoir, and Seurat.

We were fascinated by his stories of the turbulent life in the art world of Paris at that time—artists' organizations issuing proclamations, manifestos, declarations of principles, and new ideas in the world of art. Exhibits and controversies kept alive the concept that art *mattered*. Although we were living in a different time, we were stimulated and inspired by his tales.

Those were exhilarating times for an aspiring young artist. Every season, operas and ballets were performed at the Academy of Music, and when extras were needed there were always plenty of volunteers at the art school. I sometimes appeared as an Egyptian soldier, a French grenadier, or a German villager. In my fifth year at the academy, I took part in the Ballets Russes de Monte Carlo, cast as a Polovtsian warrior, trying to look ferocious in an ornate costume, spear in hand, with a little camera poking out of the folds in my shirt, taking pictures of a Japanese ballerina, Sono Asato, who seemed to me to be the most beautiful creature on earth.

The late 1930s was a time of deep economic depression but also a time of experimentation. And it was a time for social awareness and political involvement. The New Deal government had raised the consciousness of people toward the complex problems facing the country, and newspaper headlines made us aware of the threat of war. In Spain, General Franco, with help from Hitler and Mussolini, was trying to overthrow the democratically elected government, and in China, the Japanese armies were already swarming over Manchuria.

Japanese ballerina Sono Asato during a performance by Ballets Russes de Monte Carlo.

Some young men we knew had volunteered to go to Spain to defend the Republic, and a national campaign had been started to boycott Japanese goods. Irene and I were among a group of students at the school who sympathized with liberal causes. Horrified by the atrocities committed by the Japanese army in China, we prepared an audiovisual show urging people not to buy Japanese products, especially silk stockings. The show consisted of slides made from photographs in newspapers and magazines, collages and original drawings. It was accompanied by live narration, and background music and sound effects from discs (there were no tape recorders in those days). The show was grippingly dramatic, and we were invited to present it at social clubs, religious groups, fraternal organizations, and trade unions. Also around that time, the National Negro Congress was about to celebrate its annual meeting at Convention Hall in Philadelphia. To decorate the hall, Irene and I organized a group of students to paint huge, mural-size portraits of Frederick Douglass, Abraham Lincoln, Sojourner Truth, Nat Turner, and other important figures in the struggle against slavery. We also helped paint picket signs for the stevedores' union when the threat of a strike surged on the Philadelphia waterfront. The union had been very active in supporting the boycott of Japanese goods.

None of these extracurricular activities interfered with our creative work at school. Every student was passionately involved in his or her particular project and worked at all hours of the day and night. The quality of the work was most evident at the end of each year, when we all competed for the coveted traveling fellowships to study abroad.

6 ·

*Euphoria in
Europe and
Trouble at Home*

The school had been endowed by the Cresson family with a fund that enabled talented students to spend several months overseas for travel and study. Each student who competed for the award was assigned a wall in the school gallery to display his or her work—painting, illustration, mural design, and sculpture. A jury of faculty members then selected the eight or ten students who would receive the awards. In 1935 I was granted a Cresson Traveling Scholarship. It provided me with $2,300 for travel to Europe, with no strings attached. I could go where I wished, stay where I wished, and do whatever I wanted. There would be no questions asked and no report required. I was thrilled at the opportunity to travel, to seek out the work of the great artists I had studied in school who showed a concern for ordinary people, for people like my parents. I had always admired and respected the fortitude of such people in the face of the trying circumstances that often troubled their lives. They worked hard, never complaining, never earning much money, always willing to make any sacrifice for the welfare of their children. I suppose that it was from them that I learned to respect the dignity of ordinary, hardworking people, a respect that was to last me the rest of my life. As an artist, I often thought that if members of the nobility could have their portraits painted to hang in galleries and museums, my parents, and people like them, deserved no less. I most admired the artists who recognized this nobility in ordinary people.

In those days, $2,300 was a lot of money. I had never seen so much money before. After getting my passport, visas, and other documents in shape, I said good-bye to my parents and to Irene and my friends at school, then went off to New York to book passage for Europe. This was to be my first trip outside the United States. (To tell the truth, except for my short stay in Bristol, I had not been outside Philadelphia since our trip from the Ukraine!) I left New York aboard the brand-new luxury liner *Normandie* (third class), headed for Le Havre. The *Normandie* had just crossed the Atlantic on her maiden voyage and on the return journey was attempting to break the world's speed record. Though I was in no hurry, I had to put up with the constant violent trembling that shook the ship from stem to stern as the engines were pushed to the limit. Every time I set myself up comfortably in a lounge chair in the middle of the deck, the ship's vibrations soon had the chair bouncing along and pushing up against the railing. Back I would go with my chair to the middle of the deck, only to end up at the railing again. But we did beat the world record, and I suppose that's what counted—four and a half days from New York to Le Havre.

Paris! I was really in Paris! I could hardly believe it. And Paris was only the beginning of my journey. Before going home, I would visit England, Italy, Austria, Holland, and Spain—but not Nazi Germany. In every country I went looking for the art I had seen only in books and in the slides that Mr. McCarter showed us. Museums, cathedrals, libraries—I spent hours spellbound by the frescoes of the Italian Renaissance, fascinated by the Persian and Indian miniatures and illustrations in the medieval books at the British Museum, and awed by the paintings of Goya at the Prado in Madrid. I made a special trip to Amsterdam to see an exhibit of Van Gogh's drawings and paintings. I was especially attracted by the work of artists such as Van Gogh, of course, and Brueghel, Daumier, Toulouse-Lautrec, Giotto (just look at the sympathetic way he rendered ordinary people in his religious paintings), and the extraordinary Japanese woodcuts Hokusai did of the boisterous life in Tokyo.

    I was overwhelmed by all this great art and felt that it was far beyond anything I could hope to achieve. It certainly made my humble aspirations to be a magazine illustrator seem cheap and tawdry. I had bought a small camera in Europe just to take some tourist pictures, and now I began to think that perhaps in photographs I could show the same concern and understanding of ordinary people that I found so compelling in the work of the artists I admired so much.

    Life did not consist only of visits to museums and galleries, however. There was plenty of time for sight-seeing too. How could one be in Paris and not visit the Eiffel Tower or go for walks on the Champs Elysees? How could one be in Rome and not see the Coliseum? How could one be in London and not go to Madame Toussaud's? In Paris, I ran into a violinist friend who had studied with me at the Settlement school. He had been living in Paris for several years and gave me a tour of the city. The climax of the tour came when he took me to his favorite brothel, but I was too embarrassed and scared to do anything but stare at all those naked girls. I later learned that my friend had died of syphilis.

    After four months in Europe, I came back to Philadelphia a changed man, changed in a way perhaps not intended by the scholarship committee. The exposure to contemporary art—cubism, abstract expressionism, surrealism—had changed my attitude toward the academy. I began to rebel at what seemed to me the stodginess and old-fashioned concepts that prevailed in all the classes. The following year, when I was again eligible to compete for a traveling scholarship, I decided to break all the rules in displaying my work on the wall assigned to me. Several strict regulations had to be followed in the entries; for example, no work was to be framed, no portrait could be more than life-size, and so on. I did not frame anything, but a painted frame was an integral part of one of my illustrations, one portrait of a woman was much greater than life-size, and one illustration showed a group of people sticking their tongues out at the onlooker. The jury did not seem to appreciate my infantile humor—I was not offered another trip to Europe.

During the summer Irene had gone back to Canada to work as a counselor at a girls' camp. I missed her very much, but that did not stop me from falling for the charms of a petite and vivacious blond girl at school who seemed to enjoy my company. She visited me often at the cooperative house and sometimes spent the night. At other times we would go out in the evening to find a dark corner at the nearby Pennsylvania railroad station where we would sit and talk or just caress each other. When Olga, Irene's cousin, learned of my philandering, she sounded the alarm to both me and Irene. For fear that I would lose Irene, I cut off my affair with the little blond charmer, and when Irene returned, we resumed our friendship, which continued to grow into a much closer relationship.

During my last year at the academy, I was under constant pressure from my friends and fellow students to change my name. In high school and during my first years at the academy, my friends used to call me Ovchy. But now most of them felt I would have a hard time professionally with a name that everyone found impossible to pronounce and difficult to spell. During one rowdy party at the cooperative house, the subject of my name came up. A group of students, stimulated by an ample supply of beer, began chanting, "Change your name, change your name, change your name." "All right," I said. "You pick a name for me." They put several names on little pieces of paper into a hat and out came the common names in the phone book—Smith, Brown, Thompson, Jackson, and so on. "No, no, no," I replied. "At least my present name is different, it's original. Come up with something else." At that point a young woman, a mural painter, spoke up and said, "Look, Jack, if you like, I'll write to my family in Maine and see if they will adopt you as a member of the Delano [pronounced Del-ay-no] clan." And that's the way it happened. She wrote, and the family replied that they would be delighted. From then on, with my parents' blessing, I began using the name Jack Delano. In March 1940 I went to a lawyer and had the change legalized by the Eastern District Court of Pennsylvania. (I had become "Jack" some time before, when my parents learned that the most famous man in America was Jack Dempsey, the boxing champion of the world.)

Now, after five years at the academy, I was out on my own—and out of work. I still lived in the cooperative house, where I could see Irene every day, but I needed to earn a living somehow. I found myself thinking of my little camera; perhaps I could use it to make some money. I remembered the idea that had occurred to me while I was abroad: If I could not be a great artist, perhaps I could learn to be a good photographer. So I set up a darkroom in the house and tried to drum up some business.

A friend who worked for an advertising agency offered me my first freelance job. "It's for a soap ad," he said. "Just a girl's hand with a bar of soap. Very simple. You can do it. It pays a hundred dollars." I could think of no hand more beautiful than Irene's. She willingly posed for me and I took the picture. The result was a handsome glossy print, well lighted and technically excellent. What I didn't realize was that Irene had the strong, muscular hands of a stonemason or a carpenter, not the delicate, dainty, smooth hands the agency was looking for. When I didn't get the job, I became convinced that I was not really suited for commercial work.

Though I was not living with my parents, I visited them frequently. One day I learned that my mother had received a summons to appear in court. Her dental practice had expanded considerably, and it seemed that one of her patients had been a police undercover agent. We were all afraid she would be sent to jail for practicing without a license. The judge questioned my mother patiently. Did she know that what she was doing was illegal? Yes, she did. Would she promise to quit the practice if he let her go? No, she would not. "As long as I have to provide food and clothing for my children, I must continue working," she told him. The judge shook his head as if to say, "What can you do with a woman like that?" and suspended her sentence. But the experience must have scared her, because she began turning down patients and eventually closed her office. With my father's business constantly on the verge of bankruptcy, the additional income my mother brought in had helped to keep the family afloat. It soon became evident that I would have to help out. I must find a job. But where? How?

7 ·

*Going
Underground—
in a Pennsylvania
Coal Mine*

In an effort to ameliorate the grave problem of unemployment in the country, the Roosevelt administration initiated various work-relief programs for the unemployed, all under the name of the Works Progress Administration. The WPA provided jobs not only for skilled and unskilled workers but also for artists, writers, musicians, dancers, and other workers in the creative arts. Some of the accomplishments of these groups were outstanding. The Federal Theater Project produced innovative shows that were successful on Broadway and throughout the country. The Writers Project had writers doing research on state history to produce a guidebook for every state. Painters were doing murals in post offices and other public buildings. And in Philadelphia, the Federal Arts Project was employing artists to do, among other things, renderings of folk art objects that would culminate in the book *An Index of American Design.* As an unemployed artist, I qualified for a job at the agency and was put to work photographing Pennsylvania Dutch furniture and other expressions of folk art at a salary of ninety dollars a month.

That was not precisely the kind of work I had hoped to do with my camera. I was interested in social conditions, and I thought the camera could be a means of communicating how I felt about problems facing the country and that therefore I could perhaps influence the course of events. I thought I could portray ordinary working people in photographs with the same compassion and understanding that Van Gogh had shown for the peasants of Holland with pencil and paintbrush.

At the time, the daily newspapers had been publishing articles about problems in the anthracite coal–mining region of Pennsylvania, where the mines had been shut down during the Depression. The miners, left with no other source of income, were going into the mines illegally and extracting coal to sell wherever they could. This practice was called bootleg mining.

At the Federal Arts Project in Philadelphia, most of us were members of the Artists Union. Our sympathies were with the unemployed miners. I presented a proposal to the head of the Arts Project (whose name I do not remember) to go into the mining area with my camera, live with a mining family for a month, and do a documentary study in photographs of the conditions in the community. There was no precedent for that kind of photography in the Federal Arts Project, and the administration was loath to approve my proposal. Their hesitation came partly from the fact that the federal arts programs in general had been under attack in Congress as a waste of money and as "boondoggling." After much pleading and persuasion, and with the support of the Artists Union, however, the proposal was finally approved.

The miners union was interested in helping me and arranged for me to live with a miner's family in the town of Pottsville, Schuylkill County, the center of the bootlegging activity. (There was no hotel or motel in town.) During my month's stay, I photographed activities not only around Pottsville but in Minersville, Shenandoah, and Mahanoy City as well.

Pottsville was a dirty, dreary town with an open sewer running along the main street and houses that tilted this way and that because of the coal-mining tunnels under the streets. On the surrounding hills lay piles of slag, and one could often see women and children picking through the rubble in search of any salvageable bits of coal. Here and there a makeshift derrick, powered by an old automobile motor, was silhouetted against the sky. From a rusty cable dangled the elevator cage that took the men down the mining shaft. The bleakness of the countryside was emphasized by the seemingly permanent brooding black clouds that hung in the sky.

In contrast, the people were warm and friendly. Most of them were of Polish origin. The family I stayed with fed me well (mostly fried potatoes) and made sure I was comfortable. The men enjoyed trying to teach me some words of their language, mostly curse words. They took me down into the mines with them, helped carry my equipment, held extension lights for me, changed flashbulbs, kept me from bumping my head in the low tunnels, and, in general, made sure I was safe and sound. Luckily for me, I was too ignorant to understand how risky all this was because no safety measures were being observed.

Many of the miners showed the effects of various lung diseases, but there was no health insurance in those days. In spite of the hard times, Saturday night would find a lively group of people at the corner bar enjoying a couple of drinks, dancing a mazurka or polka, and singing Polish and American songs. The Delaware and Lackawana Railroad went through the area, and a song I often heard went like this:

Where do ya worka John?

On de Delaware Lackawan

Whadaya do a John?

Oh, I push an push an push . . .

Whadaya push a John?

On de Delaware Lackawan,

Oh, I pusha push de truck,

Where do ya push de truck?

On the Delaware Lackawan, two, three, four

The Delaware Lackawan.

Another song was this:

My sweetheart's the mule in the mines

I drive her without any lines

On the tailboard I sit

And I chew and I spit

All over my sweetheart's behind.

After a month in Pottsville and the surrounding area, I returned to Philadelphia with several hundred negatives of life in the coalfields, feeling triumphant after my first big photographic assignment. An art gallery in the old Pennsylvania Railroad Station on Fifteenth Street near City Hall offered to put on an exhibit of my pictures.

Working in the darkroom I had set up in our cooperative house, I developed all the negatives and, with Irene's help, made a selection of the images for the exhibit. (In later years, I was to rely heavily on Irene for this sort of help. She had a wonderful sense of how photographs would affect one another when placed side by side.) All my friends helped with making the large prints, many of which were 42 x 60 inches (no frames). For lack of better facilities, we had to wash the prints in the only bathtub in the house. Mounting was another problem, but on a large table of plywood, with wallpaper paste and many helping hands, we got the prints ready in time for the show.

The exhibit was a resounding success. Newspaper reviews were favorable, but best of all, one of the people who came to the opening was the great photographer Paul Strand. He had been living in Philadelphia and had come to the show because of his interest in the work of the Federal Arts Project. I had read somewhere that way back in 1917, he had stated that to produce an honest photograph, the photographer had to have "a real respect for the thing in front of him." The word "respect" became the guiding principle of everything I was to do in the future. And "the thing in front of me" became the basic reason for taking a photograph. I felt honored when Strand congratulated me on my work and promised to recommend me wherever I might apply for a

Photographic Memories

Some of the enlargements for the exhibit of Pennsylvania coal miners in 1938.

job. For my portfolio, I prepared a selection of 8 x 10 prints, mounted them back to back, and had them spiral-bound in the form of two books.

All this recognition and success seemed to go to my head. I felt that all I had to do was go to New York, and fame and fortune would come to me easily. But I had another powerful reason for going to New York: Irene had moved there. She was working on murals at the New York World's Fair as assistant to a well-known painter—Anton Refregier.

8.

New York

In Search of Fame, Fortune, and a Job

Although fame and fortune kept eluding me, I had no trouble finding Irene. She was living with a young couple in a small apartment on West Twenty-eighth Street, but she had no studio space to do work of her own. Later she rented space in a large loft shared by several artists of the "New York School," on Union Square at Fourteenth Street. I, in the meantime, had found a cold-water flat on West Eighteenth Street that served as my living quarters and studio. In an enclosed back porch, I set up a darkroom in the expectation of getting a lot of freelance work as a photographer.

The heating system in my apartment consisted of one small potbellied stove in the living room. In the winter the place was bitterly cold because I sometimes didn't have a quarter to buy a little bag of charcoal at the grocery store across the street. One time when I went to work in the darkroom, wearing an overcoat, hat, and gloves, I found all the solutions frozen solid. The furniture in my apartment consisted of old crates and packing boxes. The only window in the place faced the brick wall of the adjacent building, so I made a large photograph of the New York skyline at sundown and pasted the print over the window.

Life in New York was not easy. The few freelance jobs I was able to get were barely enough to pay the rent. Irene kept lending me money, and my parents helped out when they could. I did some work for a ballet company and also a charitable institution, the United Fund, where I was told that my services were needed because their regular photographer was too old and sick to work anymore. Several years later I learned that his name was Lewis Hine; I was a great admirer of his work.

Irene and I saw each other almost every day. We became interested in films and went to all the film festivals. The work of the great directors fascinated us. We saw their films over and over again until we knew them by heart. We idolized such directors as John Ford, René Clair, Jean Renoir, Fellini, Rossellini, Eisenstein, Pudovkin, Fritz Lang, and Orson Welles. We sought out, and became acquainted with, the producers and directors of documentary films at a company called Frontier Films, which had just completed the film *Spanish Earth*, written by Ernest Hemingway. With Irene footing the bill, we bought many books on filmmaking and borrowed a little 16mm camera to make experimental films that lasted three minutes, the duration of a 100-foot roll of film. The subject matter usually had a surrealistic flavor. I remember one scene of goldfish swimming around Irene's foot in a fishbowl. One time, for a mystery thriller, we were up at dawn in front of the two statues of lions at the New York Public Library. The story called for the lions to follow an escaping fugitive with their eyes. We animated the eyes by sticking black plasticine pupils on their eyeballs and moving the pupils bit by bit while shooting frame by frame.

We did everything together, and sometimes when we worked very late Irene would spend the night with me. It became evident to both of us that a deep relationship was developing, which I hoped would eventually lead to marriage. We knew we would have to have Irene's father's permission to get married. He had never met me, and he wanted to come to New York for a visit. Dr. Esser was a meticulous man, and we were afraid that if he saw the hovel I was living in, he would never give his approval. So we decided to try a bit of deception.

Irene found a building near my street where furnished apartments were available for rent by the week. I moved in, and all our friends helped me furnish it with books for the bookshelves, food for the refrigerator, clothes for the closets, and a few old magazines scattered about. It really looked as if I had been living there for years. When Dr. Esser arrived (he could stay only a day), I welcomed him into "my apartment." He gave it a cursory inspection and seemed to be properly impressed. That evening we had dinner together and afterward he returned to Toronto. The next day I quickly moved back to my cold-water flat. I don't know if he was fooled or not, but he never voiced any disapproval of his future son-in-law.

It was about this time (1939) that I began seeing the work of the Farm Security Administration photographers in such magazines as LOOK, *Survey Graphic, Saturday Review*, and in books as well—for example, *U.S. Camera*, Walker Evans's *American Photographs*, and Dorothea Lange's *American Exodus*. In 1938 the Museum of Modern Art presented a Walker Evans exhibit called "American Photographs." When the show went on tour, I remember making a special trip to the Boston Museum of Fine Arts to see it. I spent almost the entire day at the exhibit, stunned by the simplicity, sureness, power, and grace of the images. But I must confess that I was also somewhat disappointed in some of them; they seemed to be too cool, precise, and emotionally aloof, like technically perfect, interesting specimens of humanity rather than human beings of flesh and blood and joys and sorrows.

The extraordinary images by Dorothea Lange, Walker Evans, Arthur Rothstein, and Ben Shahn had a profound impact on me. The country was in the heart of the Great Depression, and here was art seriously concerned with the plight of the dispossessed, the needy, and the landless. I was deeply moved by the pictures, and I thought that surely people everywhere and legislators in Congress would be equally affected and therefore impelled to do something to alleviate the misery of so many of our people.

It seemed to me that that was the kind of photography I had tried to do in the Pennsylvania coal mines. I could think of no place I would rather work than at the FSA. With high hopes, I sent my two coal-mining books to Roy Stryker, head of the Historical Section of the Farm Security Administration in Washington, D.C., and applied for a job. A reply arrived in a few days, by telegram. It read: "Sorry. No openings available. Good work. Do not give up hope. Read the following books. Roy Stryker." There followed a long list of books on economics, geography, history, sociology, and even a Department of Agriculture pamphlet on canning vegetables.

During the next several months, I kept up a correspondence with Stryker while anxiously waiting for a favorable response. Then I received the following telegram: "Arthur Rothstein resigned. Will work for LOOK magazine. Position available for you. Salary $2300 a year plus per diem and mileage. Must have car, know how to drive and have license." It was followed by this letter:

> The main thing on which I would like you to spend a little time is economics and geography. I recommend that you get a copy of J. Russell Smith's *North America* from the library.
>   . . . When you first start to work, we are going to send you out on short trips of two, three, and four days; then back to Washington, to get your developing and printing done and we can have a chance to talk over your approach, and incidentally, have quite a little time to work out larger plans. There's a lot of work in the nearby vicinity that ought to be done—and it's always being postponed in favor of the jobs that are half-way across the continent.

I found out much later what influenced Roy Stryker to offer me the job. Edwin Rosskam, a fellow Philadelphian, was working at the FSA as a designer of publications and exhibits. He may have put in a word for me. I probably also had the support of the photographer Marion Post, who had worked for the *Philadelphia Evening Bulletin* and who was on Stryker's staff and knew of my work. But perhaps the most important influence was that of Paul Strand.

Many years later, when I was visiting a niece in New York, she said to me, "I think you should know that Paul Strand lives in the basement apartment of this building. He is very sick. Would you like to see him?" Would I indeed! I rushed downstairs and knocked on the door of the apartment. Strand's wife, a white-haired woman in her sixties, answered my knock, and when I introduced myself she said, "Oh, do come in. I'm sure he'll want to see you."

He lay wrapped in several blankets on a large bed. He looked wan and sickly, but when he caught sight of me he smiled and beckoned for me to come closer. Then he pointed a trembling finger at me and said, "I'm responsible for you, you know. I'm responsible for you, and don't ever forget it." That was the first and last time I saw him. He died shortly after.

But to get back to my departure for Washington, D.C.: I had no car, I had no license, and I didn't know how to drive, but I was so elated at the news that those seemed like minor problems. With a loan of $250 from Irene, I bought an old Dodge convertible, and a friend of Irene's gave me driving lessons in the area around Times Square. "If you can drive here, you can drive anywhere," she said. I passed my driver's test with no trouble, and off I went to Washington.

Getting out of Manhattan through the Holland Tunnel was a bit of a problem, though. I hadn't realized when I bought the old car that the steering wheel was quite loose. All through the tunnel, I kept weaving from lane to lane, sure that I would be stopped by the police and arrested. Then, when I got onto the New Jersey Turnpike, I felt the car bumping along rather badly and suddenly saw one of my front wheels rolling along up front, trying to get to Washington ahead of me. I retrieved the wheel, mounted it where it belonged, and somehow managed to arrive in Washington intact, which surely is proof that God takes care of fools and madmen.

9 ·

Working with
Stryker and Trying
to Understand
the South

Arriving in Washington on May 6, 1940, I found myself at the door of a new world, a world I had never experienced before. Except for my trip to Europe, I had done very little traveling up to that time and had never been below the Mason-Dixon Line. Now I would soon be in the South, the South of lynchings, of racial prejudice, of poverty and despair—according to the newspapers and books I had read. From my first assignment on, I was to learn what racism meant both to blacks and to whites in all the Southern states I visited.

I had heard that Stryker was a dictatorial and authoritarian person, so I looked forward with some trepidation to meeting him. After all, I was not a well-known photographer like Walker Evans or Dorothea Lange. I had very little professional experience. Compared to them, I was just a young upstart barely beginning a career. What if I failed on my first assignment? What if Stryker didn't like the way I worked? What if? What if?

But my fears were allayed when he welcomed me into his office with a bear hug and a broad smile that exuded only warmth and cordiality. He immediately introduced me to some of his staff—Russell Lee, John Vachon, Marion Post, and Edwin Rosskam. I assured him that I had indeed gotten J. Russell Smith's *North America* and was reading it. That seemed to clinch our friendship. Then, after a long and enlightening briefing session, he sent me out on short assignments to nearby areas in Maryland, Virginia, and North Carolina, accompanied by Rosskam, who would be my mentor and guide for the next several days. The pictures I brought back seemed to please Stryker, and soon he sent me out on my own to North Carolina to photograph social conditions in the rural areas of the state's tobacco country. It was good to have Roy's confidence and I knew I was doing a good job, but occasionally a few little problems did come up. Here is an example from a letter to Irene in New York, dated May 21, 1940:

> I am sending you some discarded negatives which will give you some idea of my ability to *overexpose* and *underexpose* and get stuff *out of focus.* (Sorry I can't send you any *blanks,* some of them were beauties!) But don't be disturbed, my quota of discarded negatives is no higher than that of the other photographers. . . .

Photographic Memories

My impressions of some of the other photographers at work.

Please I—there's one thing you must do for me. I know you don't have the money to get my laundry but if you don't tell him to hold on to it for a little while I'll lose it altogether. There are some good shirts in there.

Now in the South on my own, I was struck by signs of racial segregation everywhere: separate drinking fountains for blacks and whites, separate waiting rooms at bus and railroad stations, separate schools for children, separate sections on buses and trains and in movie houses, and separate churches—even in the nation's capital. I must have expressed my concern about these problems to Roy, because in one letter he wrote me: "The observations in your letter of the 9th were most interesting: I guess you will have to develop some callousness if you are going to stay in the South. At least, that is what everyone else seems to do. I am afraid I would have some difficulty doing it though."

I was having to learn strange new rules of behavior: Don't shake hands when in-

troduced to a black person, don't address a black man as "mister," don't be surprised if you're not allowed into a restaurant with a black friend of yours, don't this and don't that. But I was also learning something of Southern hospitality and getting used to being addressed as "honey" or "love" by waitresses in restaurants. I seem to have a pretty good ear for languages and didn't realize that I was beginning to talk like a Southerner until one day, when I was talking to Irene on the telephone, she snapped at me, "Oh, stop putting on that Southern accent!"

I had been brought up in a big city and had no appreciation for or understanding of rural life. As a child I knew only that food—eggs, butter, cheese, bread, and milk—all came from the corner grocery. It never occurred to me to think of the farmers and their wives and children who produced these things, working the land and casting anxious eyes at the sky to see what the weather would be the next day. Land and the soil were, to me, just "dirt," not something that had to be nourished, protected, and revered. A few scraggly pine trees that somehow managed to survive through holes in the pavement in front of our house were as close as I ever came to agriculture. But now, driving through the Southern states, past gangs of farmhands, their backs bent as they toiled under the broiling sun in fields of tobacco, cotton, corn, and vegetables, I began to understand how much human effort went into agricultural production and how much the land meant to the people whose lives depended on its care and cultivation. And when I saw so many abandoned, gutted fields scarred and bleeding from erosion, I understood the meaning of the old Mexican proverb

> God forgives always,
>
> Man sometimes,
>
> Nature never.

I got the impression that Stryker was very protective of his photographers and had great respect for their talents. One of his important accomplishments in their behalf, for example, was to have the personnel office create the position of Artist-Photographer for the Historical Section, to differentiate us from those who did the routine photographic work for the Department of Agriculture. The title carried with it not only recognition of special status but also a higher salary.

His instructions to us about what to photograph were often quite detailed. I did not resent his "shooting scripts," which were often lengthy and very specific, because as I got to know him better I realized that they were not *orders* and that I could take many liberties if I felt it advisable. After all, his was a historical vision, which I respected. To me it meant that although we were a Farm Security Administration program and part of the Department of Agriculture, anything I saw that reflected social conditions in America was fair game for my camera. (After all, the official title of our photographic unit was the Historical Section.) I also realized that Stryker was under constant pressure from the FSA supervisors to get the kind of "public relations" pictures they wanted. In one letter he wrote:

> You remember we agreed that you would contact the FSA man (whom Arthur knows very well), gather his ideas and take whatever seems feasible at this time? Be sure that these are marked for the file when they come in. I will have to depend on you to take care of this particular item. *This method will help keep the FSA man out of our hair.* (Emphasis mine.)

But often his ideas of what to cover were only general—"Photograph everything on Route No. 1 from Maine to Florida," he might say, or "Follow migratory agricultural workers up the eastern coast from Florida to the Canadian border." It was apparently in one of these inspired moments, after I had been on the staff for less than two months, that Stryker decided to send me on my first long trip—yes, to follow migratory agricultural laborers.

10 ·

From Florida to Maine on the Trail of Migrant Farm Laborers

I started in Florida and began working my way north—Georgia, South Carolina, North Carolina, and on up into Virginia and Maryland—following people working in the turpentine camps, tomato fields, and peach orchards. It was while I was driving through Virginia that my attention was caught by billboards and signs reading, "Marriage License $10. No Physical Exam Required. Get Married in 24 Hours." A brilliant thought occurred to me. After two months as an FSA photographer, I felt that now I had a steady job, I was making a fairly good salary, and I could support a wife and family—and incidentally, settle my debts with Irene. I called Irene in New York and asked her to come down and meet me in the town of Accomac, on the Eastern Shore of Virginia, and marry me.

    She arrived the next day with her mother and sister. Irene's father, Dr. Esser, was in Toronto and did not come. I really didn't know why he stayed away, though I thought perhaps it was because he would have felt uncomfortable being there with Irene's mother, since they had recently been through a bitter divorce. My mother and father came from Philadelphia, and we were all set to have a great celebration. But the marriage couldn't take place: it was the Fourth of July and the office of the justice of the peace at city hall was closed. I was still too uncertain of my relationship with Roy Stryker to take time off without his permission, so I sent him a telegram requesting authorization to take the next day off to get married.

    Then I got a taste of Stryker's sense of humor. He replied in one word: "No." So we all stayed over in a guest house, and of course, Irene and I ignored his orders and were married. Right after the ceremony we began our honeymoon by following farm laborers into Delaware and, later, on up to the Canadian border. The honeymoon would last for the next forty years.

    It was against regulations for spouses to travel with the photographers, but Roy looked the other way in our case. Having Irene along as wife, companion, assistant, and critic was extremely helpful. She had a great talent for developing rapport with people and getting the attention of women and children as I clicked away with my camera.

Photographic Memories

Besides, she was much prettier than I, and people tended to look at her rather than at my camera. In addition, she willingly took over such tasks as changing film in the cameras, taking notes, keeping a diary, writing captions, and—best of all—editing and criticizing my work.

Now together, we set out in a new car, a Dodge coupe that was a wedding present from Irene's father, with camera equipment and all our worldly possessions in the trunk. We traveled through all the states from Florida to Maine, photographing people on cotton plantations, on tobacco farms, and at agricultural fairs; recording aspects of the lives of farm families, sharecroppers, fishermen, teachers, and, of course, migratory farm laborers; documenting religious ceremonies, funerals, baptisms, and graduations. We soon realized that we were learning much more about our country from our work than we had from all the books that Roy had us read.

Irene and I in Aroostook County, Maine, in the 1940s, with our new car, a wedding gift from Irene's father.

Migratory farm laborers, mostly blacks, moved farther and farther north as the crops ripened, picking tomatoes, potatoes, other vegetables, and fruits. Watching them at their backbreaking work under the broiling sun, I couldn't help thinking how desperate they must be for a little money, to withstand such hard labor and such poor working conditions. Yet back they came, year after year. Some of them, often entire families, traveled in their own cars, following the crops. Others were transported by contractors from farm to farm in trucks. Still others were herded about in the boxcars of freight trains. Their living quarters in work camps varied from bad to horrendous, a situation that the FSA was trying to remedy. With the help of FSA supervisors, we were able to photograph conditions in some of these camps. But at one camp in Delaware, I was refused admission. Tough-looking guards barred the way, and no photographs were allowed. No pictures, period. So I made a drawing of the place from memory. It resembled a concentration camp—a cluster of barracks-like structures enclosed by a rectangular barbed-wire fence with watchtowers at each corner. Between two of the towers was a huge gate, which was opened for trucks to take the workers out to the fields at dawn and shut tight after they were delivered back at sundown.

My next assignment took me to Georgia. Arthur Raper, a noted sociologist, was working on a book about Greene County and would need photographs to illustrate his text. Since the FSA had an active program of aid to the farmers of the county, it would be advantageous to both the FSA and Raper to have a photographer document conditions not only in Greene County but in Heard County as well. I was delighted to go; the more counties, the better! I arrived with Irene in Greensboro, the county seat, eager to get to work, and registered at the Colonial Terrace, the only hotel in town.

Roy had given me a twelve-page document titled "Pictures for the Greene County Study" (probably prepared by Raper), which included a list of everything from "oak forest in color" to "washing dishes." I had become accustomed to receiving all sorts of materials from Roy as I prepared for my assignments—pamphlets, reports, so-called shooting scripts, and long letters of suggestions of what to look for—so this list was no surprise. I knew Roy well enough by then to realize that he did not expect me to follow the document slavishly but to use my own judgment and consult him when in doubt. Besides, it would have taken me at least fifty years to cover everything on the list! It became obvious that I would have to come back to Greene County, which I did several times during the following year. I returned not because I was obliged to follow the list but simply because I found it a fascinating project in which to be involved and because both Irene and I learned a great deal and found it exciting to work with Arthur Raper.

Arthur was himself a Southerner, from North Carolina. He lived on a farm in Greene County with his wife, Martha, and their four children. Because of his sympathy for the black community, he sometimes found himself at odds with many of the townspeople. In school, his children were sometimes taunted as "nigger-lovers," and I heard that he himself was once brought before a grand jury, accused of having addressed a Negro as "mister." Apparently it didn't help his standing in the community to be escorting a "Yankee" photographer around town.

Irene and I kept notebooks and diaries of some of our first impressions and experiences in Georgia. Here are a few extracts:

> Arthur's story of driving home from a lynching and giving a lift to a guy who had a [severed] thumb in his pocket.
>
> Miss Lucille Welch, on seeing picture of kids in costume on May day said they reminded her of Klansmen. Told story of a train that passed their neighborhood. It was loaded with Klansmen and scared the neighborhood to death. Arthur said: they didn't get off, did they? No, but we were afraid they might.
>
> Arthur's story—"Raper should be electrocuted *under* the electric chair. He's not good enough to sit in it." Quoted from a man in Siloam who had killed a Negro last year. Nothing happened to him, of course, but he talks and talks about Raper. Arthur's fears of his office burning up, and his family. Story of being run out of town, grand jury investigation. Ignorance of what Arthur is doing.
>
> In Columbus, Georgia I saw a horrible fight between a Negro and a white man. The Negro had accidentally broken a window in the door of a Greek restaurant. The owner immediately ran out and started to beat up the Negro. A crowd gathered. The Negro tried to protect himself from the blows. Soon he was bleeding and pleading, "Don't hit me! Don't hit me!"—not daring to strike back. One person was wonderful: a young girl—redhead, pert, pretty, about twenty years old, in a white uniform (probably a waitress or beautician). Only she spoke up to the crowd, in a loud voice and with tears in her eyes, "Don't hit that nigger! He can't hit back! It isn't fair! Don't hit him!"
>
> When we were last here one nite [*sic*] at dinner [at the Colonial Terrace], Alma Jackson [home demonstration gal FSA] told about a "good nigra" who had turned "bad": "Why, they just had to shoot him right there on the street."

Arthur spoke with a gentle Southern accent, and for all intents and purposes he seemed like most of the men of his generation and education in the country. Although he disagreed with most of the community on the question of race, he was not an activist and was never strident. He was a scholar, a sociologist. A good Lutheran, he attended the local church every Sunday and taught Sunday school. Arthur was a gentle person, and except for the most rabid racists among the poor whites, the community seemed to consider him a "good man." By his easy manner and nonconfrontational attitude, he managed to maintain good relations with the influential intellectuals who were in power—the lawyers, bankers, judges, and news media.

It was only because of Arthur's influence that I was able to get access to the county jail, for example. As for arranging for me to meet poor farmers, tenant farmers and sharecroppers, both he and the FSA county supervisor were very helpful. Although people everywhere, both black and white, were cooperative and respectful, I always felt a kind of reserve on their part, especially among the black people, when I was accompanied by a white person in authority, which made me a little uneasy about saying or doing the "wrong" thing. During this first visit, as well as my subsequent visits to Greene County in 1941, Arthur Raper's help was invaluable. I was able to get not only all the material he needed for his book *Tenants of the Almighty* but also many, many more photographs that I felt would make a valuable contribution to the FSA file.

I don't know how Arthur arranged it, but the guard at the county jail permitted me to go inside and take all the photographs I wanted. He ordered the prisoners to "dance for the photographer," and I began snapping pictures as fast as I could, fearful that the guard might change his mind. When I needed someone to hold an extension light for me, I handed it to the guard, saying, "Hold this, please." He was so startled that he did what I asked without thinking.

I was so nervous and excited by the opportunity to get these pictures that I blocked out all my personal feelings. I had only one thought in my mind: I must not fail to get these pictures! I must not fail to get these pictures! I'll never have an opportunity like this again! It was only afterward, relaxing back in my hotel room, that the realization of what I had witnessed came upon me. The bitter irony of striped prison attire combined with song and dance seemed almost surrealistic. How humiliating it must have been for those men to be obliged to perform for me, as if they were trained animals! The idea that they had been ordered to put on a show for the photographer was abhorrent. Yet they did have a guitar, and I am sure they sometimes entertained themselves. After all, I reasoned, this is the sort of thing that produced the soulful music of the blues.

At other times, however, I was on my own, without Arthur to help out. This happened, for example, when Irene and I were back in Greene County to continue our work with Raper. Early one Sunday morning, we passed a little church where a group of well-dressed black people were preparing to go inside for the service. I spoke to the minister, a tall, dignified man, and explained what we were doing. When I asked for permission to take pictures in the church, I could see by the cold expression on his face that he wished we would disappear and leave him alone, but after a long, awkward pause he nodded and said we could go ahead.

With Irene holding the extension light, I began taking pictures of the congregation. Flash! Flash! Flash! as people tried to concentrate on their prayers. Then I asked Irene to stand up front next to the altar, facing the people. She refused, saying in a loud whisper, "I'm not going to stand up and embarrass those people by flashing the light in their faces." I insisted, pleaded, but she remained adamant. "We've bothered these people enough. Why can't you leave them alone now?" We were indeed embarrassing everyone by having our fight in public. Finally, with a venomous look in my direction, she did as I asked, and I got my pictures. As the congregation burst into song, we gathered our equipment, thanked the minister, and tiptoed out of the church.

We drove off in silence, and for the next three days Irene would not speak to me. Not long after, when Viking Press published Richard Wright's book *12 Million Black Voices*, with some of the pictures I'd taken that day, we finally felt somewhat vindicated for our brazen behavior. By that time Irene and I were back on good speaking terms.

12 Million Black Voices: A Folk History of the Negro in the United States was published in 1941. Written in the first person—"We millions of black folk"—Richard Wright's evocative and passionate text was illustrated by Edwin Rosskam with photographs from the work of FSA photographers, including sixteen of mine. Author and photo editor worked together to produce one of the most important books to come out of the FSA. This publication proved to be an example of the power that could be achieved in a creative combination of text and photographs.

Stryker and everyone else seemed quite happy with the Greene County photographs. I was particularly pleased and flattered when one reviewer of Raper's *Tenants of the Almighty* wrote: "No other photographer, not even Dorothea Lange, can show shining through a body of land, or buildings, or hands and backs and faces, the living spirit of the people more clearly than Jack Delano."

At the bus station in Durham, North Carolina. May 1940.

Planting cotton in
Heard County,
Georgia. May 1941.

A view of the old sea town of Stonington, Connecticut. November 1940.

A preacher and his wife, who lived in a converted schoolhouse with their two grandchildren. Heard County, Georgia. April 1941.

In the home of an
FSA borrower.
Greene County,
Georgia. June 1941.

Mr. and Mrs. Andrew Lyman, Polish tobacco farmers and FSA clients. Windsor Locks (vicinity), Connecticut. September 1940.

Pumpkin pies and Thanksgiving dinner at the house of Mr. Timothy Levy Crouch, a Rogerine Quaker. Ledyard, Connecticut. November 1940.

Convicts in the county jail. Greene County, Georgia. June 1941.

11 •

On the Road

For weeks and sometimes months, we would be away from Washington, keeping in touch with Roy by mail or telegram. We had no fixed address, staying at motels or hotels wherever my assignment took us. Mail could reach me only at the General Delivery window of the post office in the next town on my itinerary. There I would eagerly go, hoping to receive contact prints of the film I had sent to be developed, some correspondence from Roy, perhaps even a paycheck. Because I sent my film to Washington for processing every few days, there was always a period of waiting anxiously to see the results and to know if the cameras were functioning properly. What a relief it was to get a telegram reading, "All film O.K."

For emergencies, I always carried with me a little kit so I could develop some film just to find out if the 35mm cameras were behaving well. One evening at a hotel I tried developing a roll of film in the bathroom. With Irene's help, I made the room as lightproof as possible and processed the film in a little developing tank. The negative looked beautiful when I took it out and put it in the bathroom sink to wash for a while. In the meantime, we went down to the cafe to have some coffee. When we returned, imagine my dismay when I looked at the film and found it completely transparent—all the emulsion had come off and gone down the drain. I had inadvertently left the film to wash in *hot water!* (I never made *that* mistake again, but there would be others.)

Except for my personal CONTAX 35mm camera and a Rolleiflex, all the rest of my equipment came from the FSA. This included a Leica, a 3¼ × 4¼ Speed Graphic with cut film magazines, each holding twelve films, a view camera, and, for a brief period, an 8 × 10 view camera with a three-way convertible lens. (It was the same camera Walker Evans had used, I was pointedly told.) The most exciting thing about going to the post office was being handed a parcel that we knew to be prints of my last couple of weeks' work. The laboratory made contact prints of all the larger negatives, and 5 × 7 enlargements of all the 35mm work. (There was a special Leitz auto-focus enlarger for this purpose.) With prints in hand, Irene and I would first edit the pictures, marking "kill" on the surface of any of the contact prints we felt were not worth keeping and indicating the same instructions on the 5 x 7 enlargements by making a tear halfway through the ones we wanted to be discarded.

I had heard that Roy sometimes punched holes in the negatives he thought should be killed, but he never did that to any of mine. He did sometimes want to keep some that *I* was not particularly fond of, but he never insisted on killing any that I preferred to keep. With Irene, however, I often had serious disagreements. She was always concerned with maintaining high aesthetic standards at all costs, whereas I was sometimes inclined to keep a photograph for its documentary value alone. Therefore we often got into serious arguments about which pictures were worth preserving. I don't know how Irene developed such discriminating tastes in dealing with visual images and their effects on each other, but she was always instantly aware of any fault in composition, balance, contrast, or lighting. Perhaps when she was a child, her artistic tastes were influenced by her mother, who was an exceptional designer of batik and other decorative textiles. Perhaps her musical training (she was an excellent pianist) made her aware of the importance of form and structure in a work of art. She was never satisfied with her own painting at the art school, and many canvases remained unfinished because they didn't meet her impossible standards of perfection. Her criticism of my work was always uncompromising, but I learned to rely greatly on her good taste and we usually managed to resolve our differences in the interests of marital harmony.

Once the contact prints arrived, we spent many long hours, far into the night, writing captions for them. Each negative had been numbered in the laboratory (by hand) and identified according to its size by an initial letter. For instance, the letter *A* after a number meant an 8 x 10 negative, the letter *D* stood for 4 x 5 or $3\frac{1}{4}$ x $4\frac{1}{4}$ negatives, *E* was $2\frac{1}{4}$, and *M* (for "miniature") was for 35mm negatives. These numbers appeared on the edge of each negative (44536-D, 22756-E, etc.). We then proceeded to identify each image by its negative number, often simply marking it with the word "kill," indicating that we did not think the negative worth keeping.

The captions were usually quite short, containing some basic information to be included with the photographs in the picture file. In addition, we often wrote what we called a general caption of several pages, providing much more detailed material, which we had accumulated in our notes. The general captions were stored in a separate file from the pictures but were made available for researchers, writers, and historians.

In addition to cameras, the trunk of our car was filled with flashbulbs of all sizes, some of them blue for color work. I always preferred to work in natural light, but that was sometimes impossible, and in those cases I tried to simulate natural light as closely as possible with flash. I could have kept the flash on the camera and taken a photograph that produced a fairly accurate document of what was before me. But that would not have been the *truth* of the scene—only its outward appearance. There would have been something fundamental missing: the special, individual *light* that enveloped everything. It would often be the light that attracted me in the first place. After all, it is sometimes the quality of the light that makes the difference between a simple documentary fact and a powerful statement about reality. I suppose this preoccupation with light came from my early fascination, during my student trip to Europe, with the paintings of such artists as Vermeer and Rembrandt. Flash on extensions also made it possible to reveal foreground and background with equal clarity and produce an effect of deep space. My interest in such effects probably resulted from my time in Europe and the exposure to paintings of the Renaissance, when Western art discovered perspective.

Speaking of flash, I was once told that Ben Shahn never used flash because of a sad experience he had had. He had been accustomed to using an angle-finder on his Leica 35mm camera, to catch people who were unaware that they were being photographed. (An angle-finder permits the photographer to look straight ahead while the camera is actually pointing to the side at a right angle.) One of the photographers (I think it was Arthur Rothstein) convinced Ben to try using a flashgun. They mounted the apparatus on his little camera and put in the flashbulb. Ben held the camera up to his eye, with the angle-finder positioned as usual, and when he pressed the shutter button, the flashbulb went off right in front of his eyes. That was the last flash picture that Ben ever took.

But I was interested in all sorts of lighting. I sometimes would replace a regular bulb in a lamp socket with a flashbulb and then turn on the light switch on the wall. I once even tried using old-fashioned magnesium powder to photograph a farm family in Connecticut. The lightning-like flash and billowing smoke that filled the room scared everybody to death, including me.

12 •

Washington

Preparations for War

After every protracted stay in the field, we returned for a brief period to Washington. Irene and I had rented a little apartment in Bethesda, Maryland, which served as our headquarters and where we left many of our belongings when we were away traveling. During our stay, we would meet with Roy to discuss our work and plan the next trip. Sometimes he would send me off on some special assignment. Once it was to do a story on the trucking industry around Washington. Another time the subject was National Airport, where I spent several days. And once I was told to rush out to the White House, where a press conference was being held, and get a portrait in color of Franklin D. Roosevelt, the president. In a panic, I gathered up my camera, stuffed a bag full of blue flashbulbs, and dashed off to the White House.

When I arrived at the gate, I met several press photographers coming out and saying, "Too late. Too late. It's all over." But I kept going, and when I reached the pressroom, there was the president, alone except for the security guards, who refused to let me in, saying, "It's all over. You're too late."

But the president, seeing my distress, quietly said, "Oh, let him in. For just a moment, no more." With trembling hands, I put one blue flashbulb on the camera and one on the extension light. "Hold this, please," I said to one of the Secret Service men. I focused the camera, pressed the shutter button, and POW! one of the bulbs exploded! I thought with all those Secret Service men present I would surely be shot on the spot. But the president remained calm. In a gentle but firm voice, he said, "All right, young man. You get one more chance and that's all. Now hurry up." I needed no further urging. I repeated the shot with no problems and left as quickly as I could. Fortunately, it came out well.

Roy was pleased with the work I had done in the South and now began preparing me for a different sort of assignment. The war was raging furiously in Europe and the Far East. Adolf Hitler's armies had already subjugated most of Europe and were blasting their way into Russia; German submarines were prowling the Atlantic; Japanese troops were pouring across China like a tidal wave. And the industrial might of the United States was dedicated to turning out tanks, guns, and ammunition for the beleaguered French, British, and Chinese. The United States was still officially neutral, but it seemed only a question of time before we, too, would be involved in the war. The whole country was rallying for such an eventuality.

From coast to coast, in almost every state, a furious building program had been launched: army camps, training centers, aircraft and munitions factories. To make room for all these installations, the government needed land, and thousands of people had to be evacuated from the land that was appropriated for this purpose. That was part of our new assignment: "Get the story of the displaced families and the problem of their relocation: also, get the story of the thousands of workers settling in trailer camps and shanty towns to work on the construction projects." Not only industrial workers were being rallied in the war effort but farmers as well. Food production had to be increased, and farmers were being urged to produce more and more. Many industrial workers took up part-time farming.

I had started with the FSA in May 1940. Now, on my next assignment, I would spend from August 1940 to February 1941 in the northeastern states, with only a two-day return to Washington, in January. I left Washington with a nine-page brief titled "Information on New England," which included detailed descriptions of the agricultural resources of the region and also industrial installations such as shipyards, steel mills, aircraft factories, and a submarine base. Another book on Stryker's required reading list was *The Flowering of New England,* by Van Wycks Brooks. My first destination was eastern Pennsylvania, with which I was already familiar because of my mining pictures. In the town of Mauch Chunk (now named Jim Thorpe) in the coal-mining area, I began doing some work with the 8 x 10 camera.

When I was given the camera in Washington, the laboratory technician in charge asked me if I knew how to use it. I assured him that I was thoroughly familiar with the camera, but that was untrue—I had never used an 8 x 10 before. I thought I could figure it out for myself, though. The first thing I learned was that on a windy day, I needed someone to hold on to the tripod legs to keep the camera from blowing away. Thank goodness I had Irene along. She volunteered and performed the task beautifully. Then, after producing several double exposures, I discovered how to insert the slide into the film holders in such a way as to indicate which film had been exposed and which hadn't. (This, after receiving the following telegram from Roy: "No need to economize film. You have taken 16 pictures on eight pieces of film." I thought surely I would be fired.) Then I noticed a nick on the front of the lens and wrote to Roy about it. He replied that Walker Evans had dropped the lens, but it didn't seem to affect its sharpness. "Go right ahead and use it," he said, implying that if it was good enough for Walker it was good enough for me. He was right. In the town of Mauch Chunk, and later in Connecticut and Massachusetts, the camera worked wonderfully on landscapes and architectural elements of the New England towns.

13 ·

*The American
Melting Pot*

From my time in the northeastern states, several memorable situations come to mind, some of them relative to the nature and morality of documentary photography. In the Connecticut River Valley, for example, I did some work among tobacco farmers, some of whom I got to know fairly well. The diversity of ethnic groups in this region was fascinating—Poles, Italians, Portuguese, Irish, Armenians, French-Canadians, Jews, and Native Americans. Mr. and Mrs. Andrew Lyman were of Polish origin. The Lymans were working in their tobacco barn when I came upon them. After chatting for a while about the problems of growing tobacco, I asked them to let me take a photograph of them. At first, Mrs. Lyman demurred. With a giggle, she said, "Not in this dress. Let me change my clothes." But after a bit of flattery, she agreed to pose with her husband, just as she was. There they stood, posing stiffly for the photographer, staring morosely at the camera, not at all like the jolly people they really were. So I said, "Mr. Lyman, I think your pants are falling down." The peals of laughter that followed were just what I wanted, because *that* was what they were really like.

Was that cheating? Should I have photographed them just as they stood, posing so seriously for their portrait? Was it right for me to interject myself into the situation? Perhaps some purists, with their exaggerated notion of "reality," would think my intervention improper. But to me, a photograph is not reality. It is only an *interpretation* of reality. I do not believe that photographs do not lie. They lie all the time—though not intentionally, of course. In my view a photograph should not pretend to represent reality. The best it can do is *interpret* reality. It cannot tell the complete truth, but it can try to get at the *essence* of the truth. For me, the Lymans enjoying a good laugh was much closer to what they were really like than the Lymans standing stone-faced before the camera.

A situation of a different sort presented itself in the area around Watertown, New York, where huge tracts of land were being taken over by the U.S. Army for building military installations. The FSA was trying to deal with the relocation of the farmers. Among those being moved was a family named Sampson. I photographed the Sampsons in their home before they moved out. They were a large family, and I confess that to get them all in the photo, with decent composition, I posed some of them. In doing so, I believed, and still do believe, that I was not violating any of the sacred tenets of documentary photography. The photograph did not falsify any of the "reality" of the Sampson family. It simply showed them as they were, or might have been, on any day I may have visited them.

As I was driving away from their farm, I passed a lone little wooden structure standing in the middle of a vacant field. Curiosity led me to stop and take a look inside. It was an abandoned one-room schoolhouse with windows and doors wide open. On the blackboard, written in a childish hand, was this message:

> I have swept and put things the way they used to be. I hope the government does not destroy the old building. It has been a good school to everyone around here I know of, and everyone seems to like it here. They took the seats, drawers and other articles away, but it is still the same old schoolhouse we went to. We are all moving away now and I will miss some of our neighbors. Maybe it will do the government more good than it did us. Well, I am going now and shall never be around this part [sic] again. I live in South Rothen. My name is Mabel Sampson, Watertown, N.Y. RFD 1.

I photographed the blackboard, and I am glad the print is in the FSA file, although I know that it is by no means a work of art. But, of course, I was not trying to create a work of art. To capture and preserve those eloquent words was far more important than producing an aesthetically pleasing photograph.

I know that any artist in the visual arts is always fascinated by light, color, texture, and the interrelationship of forms. But for me, the most important thing—to use the term as Paul Strand used it: "the thing in front of the camera"—is the *subject*. To do justice to the subject has always been my main concern. Light, color, texture, and so on are, to me, important only as they contribute to the honest portrayal of what is in front of the camera, not as ends in themselves. If the photographer is talented enough or fortunate enough to assimilate these factors into his passionate interest in the subject, the result might be a work of art. My favorite subjects happen to be people, and the world they have created. The more I have studied people and shown concern for them, the more I have learned about myself. I suppose that is one of the main rewards of being a documentary photographer.

Thanksgiving Day 1940 found us in Ledyard, Connecticut, at the home of the Crouch family. Mr. Timothy Crouch was a Quaker, by profession a stonemason. The family had always lived in Ledyard and celebrated Thanksgiving together. Mrs. Crouch and all the children had worked for days preparing the feast, and there were twenty people for dinner, to share a twenty-pound turkey with all the trimmings. The meal had to be served in two shifts.

Instead of trying to photograph the entire family at the dinner table, I took advantage of a large mirror in the dining room. Spread out on a shelf in front of the mirror were the pumpkin pies—traditional symbols of Thanksgiving—and in the background, reflected in the mirror (in reality, behind my back), sat the family enjoying their meal. I often used mirrors in this way to give the illusion of an additional spatial dimension and sometimes to reveal things outside the view of the camera.

In Tunbridge, Vermont, at the county fair, we ran into an unusual situation. Wherever I went with my camera, people would shy away from me. I didn't understand why until finally, with Irene's help, we met a woman who confided in us. She said that a team of LIFE magazine photographers had been there the previous week and had antagonized everyone in town with their domineering manner. "They acted as if they owned the place, ordering people about, asking for this and asking for that." Apparently the experience created some ill will toward all photographers. It took us several days of going about without any cameras to establish good enough relationships with the people to get their support. The resulting pictures, in black and white and color, proved that those days devoted to "public relations" were well worthwhile.

Much of our time was spent in the state of Maine. Up near the Canadian border, in French-Canadian country, almost all of Aroostook County was devoted to growing potatoes, providing one-fifth of the country's supply. The FSA was involved in aiding farmers who were participating in a seed-production program. I had been given specific suggestions about what to look for in potato country, but I was also interested, on my own, in the special character of this area, where one heard more French spoken than English, and where families bore such names as Labbé, Duprey, Gendreau, Coté, Lévesque. Irene and I set up our headquarters in the town of Caribou, at the Vaughn Hotel, and from there traveled throughout the St. Johns Valley. I had been advised to brush up on my French or be reduced to talking with my hands, which is what truly happened when the advice was ignored.

It was here in Aroostook County that I made a most unusual request to the Washington office: I needed authorization to hire an airplane to take some shots of potato farms from the air. I could imagine the stir that my request caused in the FSA bureaucracy. What? An FSA photographer taking aerial shots? Unheard of! Finally, after many phone calls to Roy, I received the following telegram:

> This authorization to hire airplane for the purpose of obtaining photographs showing isolation feed [sic] potato farms. Estimated expenses twenty dollars to be paid by

you and claimed on travel voucher supported by receipt and assurance that lowest possible rate was obtained re paragraphs 11 and 80 travel regulations

Roy Stryker

I took the pictures with the Speed Graphic camera I had. The result was usable but not very good. Shortly afterward, I received a letter from the technical department with specific instructions on how to use the Speed Graphic for aerial work.

Tobacco farmers in Connecticut, potato farmers in Maine, poultry farmers in New Jersey—we were fulfilling the agricultural aspect of our assignment. (After being engulfed in a sea of thousands of white chickens at a poultry farm, I wrote to Roy that I didn't ever want to see another live chicken the rest of my life.) But at the same time, we were not neglecting the industrial part of the assignment. In Hartford, Connecticut, I spent several days photographing the Pratt and Whitney aircraft engine plant and then the Hamilton-Standard Propeller Company. In Bath, Maine, I did a photo story on the shipyard and the itinerant construction workers. Here, thirty-three vessels were under contract at Bath Iron Works, twenty-two of them destroyers. The steel industry kept me occupied in the Pittsburgh area—in the towns of Midland and Aliquippa and at the Jones and Laughlin Steel Company, in the vicinity of Pittsburgh. Most of the workers were of Slavic origin—Russians, Ukrainians, Serbs, Poles. One evening, while I was photographing steel mills from a highway overlooking Aliquippa, a police car drove up and two burly officers stepped out to question me. Who was I? Why was I taking the picture? Why take a picture at night? My explanations did not satisfy them, and I was escorted to the police station under suspicion of being a German spy. They couldn't understand why an employee, supposedly, of the Department of Agriculture in Washington (FSA) was photographing steel mills in Pennsylvania. Fortunately, I had a sufficient number of credentials from the FBI and the Department of Defense, as well as press cards, to calm their fears. After making several telephone calls—to their superiors, I suppose—they finally let me go.

While in Ithaca, in the Finger Lakes region of New York, I received a letter from Roy containing a paragraph that has been quoted countless times, often misinterpreted and therefore the subject of much controversy. Here it is:

Please watch for "Autumn" pictures, as calls are beginning to come in for them, and we are short.

These should be rather the symbol of Autumn, particularly in the Northeast—cornfields, pumpkins, raking leaves, roadside stands with fruits of the land.

Emphasize the ideas of abundance—the "horn of plenty" and pour maple syrup over it—you know—mix well with white clouds, and put on a sky blue platter. I know your damned photographer's soul writhes, but to hell with it. Do you think I give a damn about a photographer's soul with Hitler at our doorstep? You are nothing but camera fodder to me (except that you are on the other end of the camera).

Knowing Roy as I did, I could not take this seriously and only smiled at his awkward attempt at cynical humor. He was obviously writing this with tongue in cheek because he was under some sort of pressure. Many of his letters had hints of his worries about the budget and the survival of the FSA.

He was engaged in a constant struggle with congressmen and senators in his efforts to keep the agency afloat. He usually kept such problems to himself, to protect the photographers from worry, but occasionally he would share his concerns with us: "You have been hearing reports of the Byrd Committee's desire to completely annihilate the Farm Security Administration. There is plenty to be worried about in this situation. . . . There will be plenty of fighting to do."

And again, at another time: "Things look quite satisfactory, as far as the budget is concerned, but with the mood in which Congress finds itself, one should not be surprised at anything. If we all go out, it will be a common problem."

To make matters worse, there had been reports that some of the early FSA photographs had been used by the Nazi propaganda machine to show how deplorable things were in the United States. I was not surprised by Roy's request for some "positive" images. I did not feel that he was "selling out" to the "reactionaries."

Reading between the lines of that paragraph, I knew what he was saying to me (and the other photographers): "Listen, guys, we're in deep trouble here and it would help me a lot if you could get me some shots of 'bountiful America'—without in any way abandoning what you have been doing so well all along. After all, there are many beautiful and wonderful things in this country. You know that as well as I." I don't think it was asking too much of us, especially in view of all the freedom we enjoyed when we were in the field doing our work.

To tell the truth, I often took photographs of that sort without any urging from Roy, simply because that was part of the America I saw.

Before leaving the northeastern states, I spent a fascinating time with farm families of different ethnic groups. I shall never forget, near Colchester, Connecticut, meeting a tall, white-haired, long-bearded Jewish farmer wearing a skullcap and looking for all the world like a biblical prophet, tilling his field behind a horse-drawn plough. The town itself boasted a thriving Jewish community, with a Hebrew school and a synagogue where I was permitted to take photographs. In Rhode Island and Massachusetts, I found many families of Portuguese, Armenian, Italian, and Finnish origin working not only in agriculture (tobacco, dairy, poultry) but also in the mills and factories of industrial New England.

The family of Russell Tombs moving out of their home, which was in the area being taken over by the army. Caroline County, Virginia. June 1941.

James Edwards, a migratory agricultural laborer who had been following the seasons since 1928. Georgia. 1941.

A landowner who was moving some of his property out of the army camp area. Spartanburg, South Carolina. 1941.

Air service command. Enlisted man shaving in the wooded area occupied by the 25th service group. Greenville, South Carolina. July 1943.

A farm laborer's widow living on a Farm Security Administration project near Manatí, Puerto Rico. 1941.

In the huge slum area known as El Fanguito. San Juan, Puerto Rico. January 1942.

Boy in sugarcane fields bringing lunch to his father. Guánica, Puerto Rico. 1942.

Sugarcane cutter working in a field that had been burned, near Guánica, Puerto Rico. 1941.

14 ·

Displaced Persons—and a Chance to Go to the Caribbean

The relocation of displaced persons as a result of the construction of military facilities and public works continued to be a major concern of the FSA. Before long I was back in the South again—the Camp Croft area near Spartanburg, South Carolina; Camp Stewart near Hinesville, Georgia; a powder plant under construction near Childersburg, Alabama; maneuver grounds in Caroline County, Virginia. Everywhere clusters of sad people huddled, seemingly stunned by the prospect of having to leave their homes and land, to be moved to they didn't know where, all in the name of national defense. At the same time, sprawling trailer camps festered on the outskirts of towns, sheltering itinerant construction workers who hoped to find high-paying jobs building barracks, munitions plants, airfields, maneuver grounds, or powder plants. Life was not easy for them or for the people being relocated from their land to make room for all these new facilities.

I found a particularly poignant situation in the Santee-Cooper River Basin, near Charleston, where the government was building not an army installation but a dam. A tired old black woman said to me, "I worked half-naked and barefoot to get this land and I got old getting it." Now she had to move because her seventeen-acre farm would soon be covered by a huge lake. The entire community had to be relocated. People loaded their jalopies or mule-drawn wagons not only with all their worldly belongings but even with bones from the local graveyard where their ancestors had been buried. Everyone received some payment from the government for the property expropriated, but that did not compensate for the years of toil they had spent on their own land. The landscape presented a bleak, desolate vista of tree stumps stretching to the horizon and, occasionally, a short staircase leading nowhere—the remains of a church. I wrote to Roy:

> It's pathetic to see what's been happening to the people in these "areas." . . . In Spartanburg, in Hinesville . . . it's the same story. They have lived there so long, are attached to their neighbors and friends, have after many years, perhaps, reached the stage of owning their own little piece of land, and now comes the "guv'ment" and tells them they have got to move.

Some of the older Negroes especially, who were born and have always lived in the same shack, just can't conceive of having to move—and furthermore can't believe the gov't will ever pay them for their land.

Part of this southern tour included another visit to Greene County, in Georgia, to complete the work I had been doing with Arthur Raper. Again I was staying at the Colonial Terrace, when one afternoon I received a telephone call from Roy. He asked if I would be interested in going to the U.S. Virgin Islands. "And while you're there, you might stop by for a few days in Puerto Rico, where we have an FSA program," he added. I immediately said yes, of course, and went to the library to look for an atlas. I had no idea where those places were.

At that time, the Virgin Islands and Puerto Rico were both under the U.S. Department of the Interior, Division of Territories and Island Possessions. It seems that the governor of the Virgin Islands, Charles Harwood, had sent a communication to Secretary of the Interior Harold Ickes requesting the services of a photographer. He was preparing a report for Congress asking for financial aid and felt that photographs of the deplorable conditions on the islands would help. The FSA had the best-known photographic team in the government, so his letter eventually found its way to Roy Stryker. "I am sure that a pictorial record of present conditions in the Islands will be extremely helpful," the governor wrote, "not only in assisting us to convince Congress as to the need for improvement but also from other standpoints as well. . . . I shall expect to hear from you when your plans for the photographer have become definite."

Why Roy chose me for this assignment I don't know, except perhaps because I, in Georgia, was closer to the Caribbean than some of the other photographers, who were in the middle or far West, but I am ever grateful that he did.

I rushed back to Washington to make arrangements for my trip. Irene would not be allowed to accompany me this time—Roy made that quite clear—but she helped me pack my cameras, film, flashbulbs, clothes, credentials, a few little bags of silica gel (a drying agent to protect the film and lenses from excessive humidity), a little book of Spanish for beginners, and letters of introduction to the director of the FSA office in San Juan and to Rexford G. Tugwell, the governor of Puerto Rico. This was the last week of November 1941, and German submarines were reported to be prowling the Atlantic Ocean, but there was no alternative for travel to the Caribbean except by steamer. On a chilly November 27, I took my leave of Irene and sailed from New York aboard the SS *Coamo*, bound for San Juan, Puerto Rico. I expected to return to Washington in a couple of weeks.

15 ·

Puerto Rico

Welcome to the Tropics!

At 6:30 A.M. on December 1 we docked at pier no. 1 of the port of San Juan. Little boys were diving for coins thrown into the water by tourists. Street vendors were selling cones of crushed ice, calling out the different flavors. "¡Ajonjolí! ¡Parcha! ¡Frambuesa!" Passengers were jostling each other going down the gangplank. Everyone was shouting greetings in Spanish to arriving friends and relatives and receiving them with hugs and kisses. In the bustling crowd, I was looking for my baggage and sweating under the blazing sun—I couldn't believe it was December. At 8:00 A.M., when nearly all the passengers had disembarked, a young man in a white suit came running toward me, calling, "Mr. Delano, Mr. Delano!" He introduced himself as Ventura, the public relations officer of the FSA in San Juan. In slightly accented English he apologized for being so late and immediately escorted me to the Palace Hotel, only a few blocks from the waterfront.

    I had been in all sorts of hotels during my travels for the FSA, but never in one like this. A wheezing, cage-like elevator took us to the fifth floor and I entered a bright, spacious room, with a ceiling at least twelve feet high. A four-poster bed with a mosquito net stood along one wall. The three windows looking out on the street had no glass, only louvered shutters. Two huge louvered doors opened out onto a balcony ringed by an ornate wrought-iron railing. Before me, the morning sun sparkled in the Bay of San Juan while a little ferry chugged across to the town of Cataño on the other side. Beyond that, on the horizon, the central mountain range stood silhouetted against the cloudless, deep blue sky. And a gentle breeze rustled the curtains on the windows. I stood staring at the view and thinking, "Wow! So this is Puerto Rico!"

    In the afternoon, Ventura arrived to take me to the FSA office. When I commented on his good command of English, he explained that he was an agronomist and had studied in the States for several years. Now he was working for the FSA and was going to take me to meet the administrator, Mr. Ralph R. Will, and make arrangements for a car and a driver-interpreter to take me out on the island. As we walked along the street,

I noticed that most people, including pretty young girls, would smile at me in passing. At first I thought this must be due to my magnetic personality, but I soon realized that that was not so at all; nearly *everyone* smiled at everyone else! It just seemed like a simple, natural way for human beings to greet each other.

But on the street we also had encounters of a different sort: beggars. They were everywhere—on street corners, on doorsteps, in restaurant entrances, at the post office, and walking the streets. It was only later that I learned that in Puerto Rico there was no institution or program for care of the indigent.

As promised by Mr. Will, bright and early the next morning, my driver-guide-interpreter appeared at the hotel with a car and ration books for gasoline and tires. Our destination was to be the city of Ponce, by a route that would take me through several small towns across the central mountain range to the sugar fields on the plains of the south coast. I was eager to get to work and often asked the driver to stop so that I could take photographs. I was fascinated and disturbed by so much of what I saw: layers of lush blue-green mountains in the distance, barefoot children running along the roadside, vast sugarcane fields bustling with sweat-drenched men swinging machetes, humpbacked zebu oxen hauling cane to the sugar mills, thatch-roofed huts of poor farmers roasting under the blazing sun, and the horrendous slums festering in the towns and cities. I had seen plenty of poverty during my travels in the deep South, but never anything like this.

Yet people everywhere were cordial, hospitable, generous, kind, and full of dignity and a sparkling sense of humor. Wherever we went, no matter how dire the poverty, we were welcomed into people's homes and offered coffee. (I had never before in my life drunk so much coffee!) Coffee, Puerto Rico–grown, of course, was usually served by pouring hot milk into a cup and adding a few drops of *essence* of coffee (coffee concentrate) called *tinta* (ink). A little bottle of it was kept on the table at all times. (To me it looked just like the soy sauce served in Chinese restaurants, but it sure tasted like good coffee.)

In the city of Ponce I was taken to what was called the Land and Utility Project, where I took some shots in color. Here, on land belonging to the owner of a large sugar mill, people could rent a plot of ground—for eighty cents or a dollar a month—on which to build a house, with the aid of funds from a government housing program. Water privileges were available from a public faucet for twenty cents a month. The program was designed to provide housing for people who were living in a slum area called El Machuelito, where living conditions were infrahuman. Even here, the unquenchable sense of humor of the people was evident in the jokes they told about their own misery. This is one: A man comes home from work and sits down to dinner. He looks at the plate before him and says, "What's the matter, woman, no meat today?" And she replies, "Oh, yes, there is. It's under that little grain of rice on your plate."

The next day Ventura called to say that we were going to a Christmas party at the home of an FSA borrower. The man had just received a loan of five hundred dollars to get an oxcart and other equipment for his farm, and he was going to celebrate the birth of Jesus and the loan at the same time. (I didn't know at the time that in Puerto Rico, Christmas celebrations begin right after Thanksgiving.)

In the early evening, as we approached the eight-acre farm of Don Ezequiel, near the town of Corozal, we could hear from a distance that the party was already in full swing. The woods nearby seemed also to be celebrating. They were full of chirping sounds that I thought came from birds but later learned were tree frogs (*coquís*). The little wooden house was bursting with people—some making speeches, others reciting poetry, and everyone dancing, singing, drinking, and eating roast pork and all sorts of sweets I had never tasted before. In one corner, a group of country musicians kept things lively on native instruments. I was introduced to everyone and immediately made to feel as one of the family. They knew I didn't understand Spanish, but it didn't seem to matter. We communicated anyway. People kept serving me food and drinks and when the girls asked me to dance, they couldn't understand when I tried to explain that I didn't know how to dance. Impossible! In Puerto Rico, everybody can dance! The warmth, cordiality, and generosity of everyone made an indelible impression on me. I didn't yet know that I would find the same characteristics everywhere on the island.

For the next several days, I traveled throughout the island photographing children in school, sugarcane workers in the fields, hospital facilities, and the company villages called *colonias,* composed of barracks for landless agricultural workers and their families. Through the Department of Agriculture, I made arrangements to photograph the processing of sugar in the grinding mills. This was harvest time in the cane fields and forty-three sugarcane mills were grinding around the clock, steam engines puffing and hissing and chimneys spouting black smoke into the sky day and night. For the cane-cutters living in the *colonias,* it was the only time of the year when they earned any money, and most of it went to pay off their accumulated debts at the company store.

But I was afraid I was unduly prolonging my stay in Puerto Rico. After all, my main reason for coming was to document conditions in the Virgin Islands. On the morning of December 7, I came down from my hotel room to arrange for my flight to St. Thomas. In the lobby of the hotel, I noticed a group of people gathered around the radio listening to a voice I seemed to recognize. I came closer to the radio and heard President Roosevelt speak of the Japanese attack on Pearl Harbor. We were at war! But, war or no war, I had an assignment to complete, and I had to get to the Virgin Islands.

Photographic Memories

Air transportation consisted of a single-engine, cloth-covered biplane that carried three passengers. The fare, San Juan to St. Thomas, was ten dollars. I wired the office of the governor in St. Thomas of my coming and took off from the San Juan airport the very next day.

16 ·

The Virgin Islands

Blackouts and War Jitters

The flight to Charlotte Amalie, the capital of the Virgin Islands, took thirty-five minutes on the Powelson Company plane. I was met at the airport by a car and driver sent by Government Secretary Robert Morse Lovett and taken to the Grand Hotel in the center of town. Dr. Lovett had called a meeting of the townspeople that evening at the plaza in front of my hotel to calm their fears about the war and to pledge allegiance to the United States. The meeting ended with the singing of "God Bless America." I recognized the melody instantly but had a little trouble with the words. I was not yet accustomed to the singsong lilt of Virgin Islands English.

Alone in my hotel room, eager to get to work the next day, I couldn't help thinking about Irene in New York. When would I see her again? Travel to and from Puerto Rico was almost impossible. With war regulations in effect, only people with urgent military or government business were given priority for travel. And telephone communications were carefully controlled because of military needs. When would I be able to get back to the States? The waters of the Caribbean were swarming with German U-boats. Survivors from torpedoed ships were often brought into San Juan. (In 1942 the SS *Coamo*, on which I had arrived in Puerto Rico, was torpedoed and 187 lives were lost.) There was nothing I could do, except hope for the best.

I worked in Charlotte Amalie for a few days, shooting mostly street scenes, the marketplace, and general views of the town. Although the overwhelming majority of the people were black, there was an isolated part of the city called Frenchtown that was inhabited exclusively by families of white French-speaking fishermen, and there I was able to get many portraits and family groups. The island economy was dependent almost entirely on its port facilities and tourism, so I went over to the larger and more agricultural island of St. Croix. Here sugarcane, rum, and cattle were the basis of the economy. Here also an FSA agent was available to assist me.

I stayed in the principal town on the island, Christiansted, at the Penthany Hotel.

Posters and leaflets had been distributed all over town by the Office of the Coordinators for Civil Defense, announcing the precautionary measures to be taken in case of air raids:

> DEFENSE BULLETIN—WE ARE AT WAR.
>
> The enemy may strike here any time and probably without warning. Your own life and that of your neighbor may depend on your strict observance of all safety measures.

Then came a list of instructions to be followed in case of air raids or other disasters and the siren signals for blackout, air raid warning, all clear, and fire.

In a letter to Roy, I wrote: "Everyone here complains that they don't have enough money for food. . . . My main difficulty so far has been the antagonism of the people toward the cameras. It's really pretty serious when you try to get some decent portraits and everyone ducks and closes the door when they see you coming down the street."

My diary included the following notes:

> Writing this after having been here six days and wondering if I'll be getting my pay check within a reasonable time. Wondering also why I haven't heard from Irene and Roy. Is mail being held up? or does it really take that long for mail to reach here? Has Irene had an auto accident and what is she doing anyhow? and I wonder what the folks are thinking. Are they worried about me? What are they hearing in the States about these islands now? I wonder whether I'm going to be here long enough to finish what I set out to do? Wonder also if I'm going to have any trouble about citizenship. Mr. Penthany, the owner of this hotel, has just returned from a short trip to San Juan, with stories about hearing that St. Croix and St. Thomas were being bombed. St. Thomas seems to be a pretty tough place now. The navy has taken over the wharf which the government wanted me to photograph as part of their plan to have it enlarged and they've had several blackouts there too. Everyone is talking about the rumor that a fierce battle is going on in Martinique but no one knows if it's true or not. The planes connecting us with San Juan have had their windows blacked out so passengers cannot see out. Mr. Penthany says the ride from St. Thomas was terrible —several women getting sick on the plane because of the windows and also lack of ventilation. . . .
>
> Night. Have just returned from the movie (Boris Karloff). It's pretty hot tonight and across the road a radio is shrieking some Puerto Rican song over and over again. It's kind of a lilting tango sung by a hoarse-voiced contralto and male chorus. Other than that the only other sound in Christiansted is the noise of crickets and frogs.

Earlier tonight the streets were full of people, more than half of them black, gathered at street corners and at the bar down the street—girls wearing the wide-brimmed hats and the fellows in clean white shirts. All their bodies start swinging to a song from the Wurlitzer ("Kiss the girls good-bye.") They talk fast in their sing-song English—"Hey, Mon! What time it be?" "Look out de heel!" "You have been to de moooovie? How it was?" Now a pack of dogs have found something and there is a distant barking and yelping up the street that stops as suddenly as it started.

Every now and then I think—what if something happens and I can't get back to the States? When will I see Irene again? I wouldn't mind getting stuck somewhere if only she were with me. This war is no monkey business. It may be long and bloody and I wonder what part we'll play in it. What our job will be. And nobody knows anything except what comes over the morning and evening broadcast—and both are usually the same. The Christiansted newspaper carries about 20 lines of war news and not many people read that. The talk in the streets is not of the war but light chatter—gossip about the neighbors, the weather, what happened during the last blackout, how the fish are coming in, etc.

A small boat came in today (it was due yesterday) but I got to the post office too late to see if there was anything for me. It's just an old sailing vessel and takes a day to get here from San Juan. (Less than an hour by plane.) I had to mail my film on it—the plane company won't take packages.

Everyone has gone to bed now—Mr. Parker, the new chief of police (a Harwood appointee), the WPA man, who's the most pessimistic person in the house, has it all figured out how the Nazis could attack the islands. Feels a little better now that he's discovered that 12 army planes have come here to stay and are conducting a 24 hour watch. Also the quiet little Puerto Rican girl who never says anything—just smiles at the table talk, and the moustached little Puerto Rican who always sits at the end of the table, and bombastic Mr. Brady, who has been coming here for 27 years to stay 4 or 5 days and sell the people dresses and dry goods. And I think I'll go to bed too. I hear a mosquito buzzing around—can't help thinking of the word "malaria." . . .

In spite of feeling so sorry for myself, I spent the next couple of days traveling around with the FSA agent, photographing people working in the sugarcane fields, and visiting some of the old sugar mills still standing since the islands were colonies of Denmark. We also drove over to the other main town of St. Croix, Frederiksted. Here I photographed the unspeakable conditions in the local insane asylum, where people were kept in dungeons reminiscent of a medieval horror tale.

Returning to the Penthany Hotel in Christiansted, I was handed a cable that had just arrived. It read: "Am at Palace Hotel in San Juan. What shall I do? Irene."

Imagine my joy! How did she manage it? What would Roy think? Who cares what Roy would think?! I rushed to the telegraph office and wired her to come to Christiansted right away. The FSA agent took me to the airport (we drive on the *left* in the Virgin Islands), and there we met Irene. On the way to the hotel, she told us that she had booked passage on a freighter out of Baltimore and had come zigzagging through the Atlantic for ten days to get to San Juan. She carried a Rolleicord camera with her all the time. When I asked what she needed the camera for, she replied, "Well, if we were torpedoed, *somebody* should be able to get some pictures."

Here are some excerpts from her diary:

On the BARBARA—Bull Line freight and passenger ship to P.R. (Dec. 11th.) Boat seemed to almost "steal" out of harbor at about 9 p.m. Everyone on ship inside for it was furiously cold in Baltimore that day. In the afternoon I heard blaring on the radio. Germany & Italy had declared war on us—which was what I (and I guess everyone) expected. We slid along the bay watching all the lights of working shipyards glide by. The ship is small and you get real close to the water. Many flat cars are ominously piled on the front of the ship. I have a room on the captain's deck with a young woman and her 8 year old child. She rattles on about how frightened her family is—for her husband works for the Atrundel Corp.—a civil engineer.

This young woman, coming from a poor family, puts on "the dog" to the point she sneers at the Negro people in Baltimore until I feel hollow inside. She looks down on everyone she conceivably can. Tells me her husband was a strike-breaker (almost happily—but I think I detected just a speck of humiliation).

Her child is going to grow up to be a bastard—she does all the things anyone ever read not to do. Doesn't realize the child has just as good a head as she.

A few people begin to sit in the movie room. A large P.R. family—a beautiful little girl with pigtails—the father is slight—always with a worried look. During the whole voyage, except when he was sick, he kept turning the dial on the radio (a forlorn expression on his face) and all that would come back was loud screeches of static.

At dinner that nite, three men at the next table, who had had a little extra to drink, kept singing *constantly*, "Jim doesn't bring me any flowers" and kept asking one guy, whose name was Jim, "Why don't you bring me any flowers?" But even they looked worried and forlorn.

The captain's table was full of "ladies"—a couple of young girls and a couple not so young.

The third day aboard we started to *roll*. It developed into a real storm and the little wench in my room took sick immediately. And so I was left with the brat—to take him to the bathroom, put him to bed, etc. Most people disappeared from the dining room. My little wench, on our first nite out, had come down to dinner and said, "It's just terrible (real horrified). Those men came to dinner without *coats* on!"

"Those men" were a few husky guys—(one 6 ft 4″ tall, like a ruler, and the other 6 ft 4″ *round*) who were coming down to P.R. to drive Caterpillar tractors and build the new naval base.

Then the kid got sick and I had my hands full cleaning up his vomit when I was pretty near to vomiting myself. But they were both safely in bed—looking green and not talking much. The boat continued to rock and with it came a notice on the board that there would be blackouts every nite while we were at sea. You could feel everyone getting tense. The big, husky workman would pace the deck every nite, his face usually quite red, and carry on conversations outside our porthole—about how he couldn't sleep, how he wished to see land again.

The next night the bulletin board notice said everyone was to sleep with their clothes on. More frightening.

One huge woman, who was going to P.R. to meet her husband in the army with her children, got a little hysterical. "Why didn't I stay in the good old USA? Why did I have to get on this rotten old boat at all?" Shrieking.

Now that Irene was with me I didn't care how long we would stay in these islands. I was enjoying the work, learning constantly, and with Irene to help, we were getting a lot of good work done.

Blackout regulations were in effect on St. Croix, so every night we would draw the blinds on all the windows. As a further precaution, when we had to change film in the cameras or film holders, we would get under the blankets in bed to make sure no light would escape from the tiny flashlight we turned on momentarily when it was safe.

Everyone in town was nervous about the presence of German submarines in Caribbean waters. Rumors were flying thick and fast, sometimes the result of a vivid imagination or wild exaggeration. One night some fishermen came in with a story about being out fishing when suddenly "a big black thing" popped out of the water in front of them. An officer in uniform stepped out and said in perfect English, "Which way to Puerto Rico, please?" They pointed "that way" and the "thing" vanished back into the water, without so much as a thank-you.

So it was not surprising when one evening there was a knock on our door—the police! Someone had reported a light flashing from our room, surely signaling to a German submarine. Much as we tried to explain that we had been changing film in our cameras and that the light leak must have been accidental and that I was a federal government employee, nothing would satisfy the polite but insistent officers until we agreed to accompany them to the police station. There they telephoned the governor's office to inform him of their capture of two German spies. After a long telephone conversation with someone, they turned to us, apologized, and escorted us, much relieved, back to our hotel.

17 •

*Back in
Puerto Rico*

Poverty and Dignity

After ten days in the Virgin Islands, we returned to San Juan to continue our work in Puerto Rico. We stayed at the Palace Hotel, on the fourth floor looking out toward the bay, only a few blocks from the waterfront. As in most seaports of the world, the waterfront was also the red-light district. Irene had been brought up in a rather cloistered environment where the word "sex" was used only in referring to gender (the female sex, the male sex). Late one evening we were sitting on our balcony, enjoying the evening breeze, when she noticed two young women standing under a street lamp on the corner of the deserted street. To me, they were obviously prostitutes hoping to meet some clients. But Irene, in her innocence, said to me, "Jack, don't you think it's awfully late for those girls to be out alone at this hour?" What could I say? I just gave her an affectionate hug.

With Irene along, I traveled through every one of the seventy-seven municipalities (today there are seventy-eight) of the island, photographing schoolchildren, sugarcane workers, tobacco farmers, coffee pickers, workers in the glass factory and the cement works, longshoremen on the waterfront, women in the little garment factories, people in their homes and in church. Irene was fond of the folk art we found in many houses, especially the little carvings of saints, but she soon learned not to admire them too much, for when she did, they would always be presented to her as gifts.

Roy began to be concerned about our long absence and kept urging us to return to Washington. But we were enjoying our work too much and kept inventing excuses for prolonging our stay. We just mailed our film back to Washington regularly and tried to explain how much work still needed to be done in Puerto Rico.

One of the places we visited in San Juan, for example, was the infamous slum area called El Fanguito (the Little Muddy Place). Here, more than 20,000 people had built flimsy homes of scrap lumber on an enormous stretch of swampland. The houses were connected by shaky footbridges over the stagnant water. There was no electricity or sewage system. When we arrived at the edge of the area in our government Oldsmobile, our guide, well dressed in a white suit, refused to go in with us, so Irene and I went in on our own. The people were just as warm and friendly as everywhere else, and we had no difficulty taking all the photographs we wanted.

When we came back early one morning, the sight that most impressed us was of people, young and old, coming out of their shacks to go to work, the girls in pretty dresses, the men in white suits or shirts. Most people smelled of rubbing alcohol and carried their shoes in their hands, as they stepped gingerly along the flimsy bridges to the dry area. We could not but admire the spirit of such people, who would not allow their poverty to affect their self-esteem.

One day in the mountains, late in the afternoon, we set up the camera before a breathtaking view of a cane-filled valley. I was about to press the shutter when a thunderclap announced one of those sudden tropical showers. Hurriedly we gathered up our equipment and ran toward our car, far down the road. As it began to pour, we heard a woman's voice cry out, "Por acá, Señora. ¡No se moje!" (Over here, Señora. Don't get yourself wet!) The voice came from a wooden shack on the roadside, and there we ran for cover.

The darkness inside made it hard to distinguish our hosts, but as our eyes adjusted to the gloom we could make out some of the details of the house. It was made from a haphazard collection of old planks and scrap lumber. Rain poured through holes in the rusty tin roof. The furniture consisted of a small table covered with oilcloth and one rustic bench, on which we sat at the insistence of a pale, barefoot, smiling little woman. A tall, gaunt man stood in a corner with arms folded. From behind his legs, two small children peeked at us timidly. Another child, bundled in rags and obviously ill, lay on the floor.

Through the doorway in the back, we could make out several glistening eyes and hear the murmurs of more children. Above us, the rain clattered on the tin roof, and below, a white hen pecked desperately at a few grains of rice in the cracks of the wooden floor. It was growing very dark and the woman lit the wick of an old beer bottle filled with oil. She ordered one of the little girls to prepare coffee. "I hope you like it black," she apologized. "We have no milk or sugar."

We sipped our coffee and tried to carry on a conversation in the few words of Spanish we knew. Irene had a few chocolates in her purse and she offered them to the woman, who passed them to the eldest girl, who in turn distributed them among the children. From the back room we could hear excited whispers, "¡Cocholate! ¡Cocholate!" [sic]. We learned from the man that he had injured his back in an accident in the cane fields and had not been able to work. (There was no such thing as workmen's compensation or insurance in those days.) "Then what do you live on?" Irene asked.

"Well," the woman replied, "people in town sometimes give me laundry to do; the neighbors help out. There are wild fruit trees around and when this old hen decides to give us a couple of eggs, I make an omelette and we share it." Then she added, with a touch of pride, "Nos defendemos, Señora, no se preocupe" (Don't worry, Señora, we take care of ourselves).

By the time the rain stopped, night had fallen. We said our good-byes and got into the car. I turned on the motor and was about to leave when a little boy came running out of the house, calling, "Wait! Wait a minute!" He reached in through the open window and dropped a little paper bag into Irene's lap, saying, "For you, Señora."

Deeply moved by the experience, I drove on in silence. I could see by the light reflected from the dashboard that Irene too was still shaken. Then I remembered the little paper bag. "What's in it?" I asked her. She looked inside and said, "Two eggs."

After three months and almost three thousand negatives, we ran out of excuses for not leaving and, succumbing to Roy's urging, in March 1942 we arranged for our passage back to Washington. The armed forces still had priority on all air travel, but through the influence of the office of the governor of Puerto Rico, we were taken aboard a Pan American Airways seaplane with bucket seats that took off from the Bay of San Juan bound for Miami, with stops in the Dominican Republic, Haiti, Guantanamo, and Havana. From Miami we enjoyed the luxury of a good night's sleep on the overnight train to Washington.

18 ·

*The War Effort
at Home*

To keep us in touch with what was going on in Washington and to let us know the whereabouts of the other photographers, Roy would often send us what he called the gossip sheet. Here are some excerpts:

> *March 3rd, 1942—*
> Russell is in Arizona and will be going to California. John Vachon is in North Dakota getting ready to photograph the inside of a blizzard (if it comes). Jack and Irene arrived safely from Puerto Rico, thanks to the Pan American Clipper. They are both busy now doing the captions on the pictures they took in the Virgin Islands and Puerto Rico. Arthur [Rothstein] is in Brownsville, Texas. He has taken a few days off to go into Mexico, and I suspect he is taking a postman's holiday there.

> *May 2, 1942—*
> We are working to get FBI, Army and Navy clearances for all of you. . . . incidentally, we are going to do virtually all the work for the Foreign Information Service [of the Coordinator of Information]. . . . As regards our picture emphasis, for internal and external use (in and out of the United States) the demand is going to be more and more on statements of our strength.

The first thing we noticed when we arrived in Washington was the great number of barracks-like wooden buildings that had sprouted in various parts of the city. These were temporary offices for the hordes of employees who had come in to work in the newly created agencies dealing with the war effort—the National Defense Advisory Council, the Office of the Coordinator of Information, the Office of Emergency Management, and others.

The whole city was in turmoil. Everything seemed to be focused on winning the war. Our photographs were to be used in exhibits, picture books, slide films, and special layouts in newspapers and magazines in support of our troops fighting overseas. And the function of the FSA was being changed by the war. We were now not focusing so much on the sharecroppers and tenant farmers as responding to the needs of the government's information agencies. Stryker put it this way in one of his gossip sheets:

> You will keep this ever in mind: Lots of food, strong husky Americans, machinery, show it as big and powerful, good highways, spaciousness. Also watch for such things as good schools, freedom of education, church services, meetings of all kinds. . . . Watch out for particularly important nationality groups, particularly in the rural areas. Scandinavians, Swiss, Portuguese, Spanish showing community life, close-ups of people and activities. These will be most useful.

Soon I would be sent out on assignments to get some of this kind of material in response to requests from the Office of the Coordinator of Information. I was not happy with the kind of instructions I was being given as to what kind of photographs were required. These requests came from people who did not understand the kind of freedom we enjoyed under Roy and the confidence he had in us to develop stories in our own way. In a long letter to Roy I wrote:

> What bothers me perhaps more than anything else is not knowing *how* the story is to be used, *what* it is trying to say and *to whom* it is addressed. When I ask for more information about a story, it is not a shooting script I'm asking for, but answers to the above questions. Once I know that, I can work out my own shooting script.

For the rest of the year, my projects followed the same course, all directly or indirectly related to the war effort—sometimes *very* indirectly. For instance, while in Wisconsin, I was asked to do a story on John Stuart Curry, the painter—a portrait, his studio, the painter at work, and so on. Now I had nothing against Curry, but I wrote to Roy, "What the hell has a story on Curry got to do with the war effort?" Also in Wisconsin, one of my main assignments was the Forest Products Laboratory in Madison. Again, I didn't understand what such a place had to do with the war effort, and so I asked for an explanation. An answer came, and it was reasonable: There was fear of a shortage of metals for industrial purposes, and the laboratory was experimenting with new products produced from wood. I was shown an ugly little black ashtray and told that this was a new substance they had just developed, which they called plastic. They predicted it would have a great future.

But many of the assignments did have a direct connection to the war. The Russians were now our allies, and one day I was asked to get some pictures of a Russian war hero who would be arriving in Washington. Oh, great! I thought. A fellow Russian. I'll be able to congratulate him in person. The hero turned out to be a young woman in her twenties. She showed up resplendent in her Red Army uniform covered with medals, one of which was the highest military award of her country—Hero of the Soviet Union. She was being feted in Washington because, as a sniper, she had been responsible for shooting down dozens of Nazi soldiers. I got my pictures at a meeting in her honor at Constitution Hall and then, at the reception that followed, I rushed up to give her the congratulations of a fellow Russian. I shook her hand and opened my mouth to say something in Russian—but nothing came out. I couldn't think of a single Russian word! Seeing my embarrassment, she just smiled and said, "Sank you," while I sheepishly took my leave.

More obviously pertinent to the war effort were my next assignments. At the Edgewood Arsenal in Maryland, I spent several days photographing the production and testing of gas masks. At Fort Benjamin Harrison, Indiana, the subject was the Army Chaplains School, where Christian and Jewish chaplains were straining, sweating, and groaning, doing pushups and learning about military discipline. At Fort Riley, Kansas, I followed the U.S. Second Cavalry Division (horse and mechanized) through maneuvers and simulated combat. Other assignments included the induction process of a young draftee, the meetings and procedures in a Selective Service committee, an army cooking school, and the work of the Red Cross.

Material was frequently requested about the increasing participation of blacks and various ethnic groups in the war effort. More and more blacks and women were entering the labor force and joining labor unions that had previously rejected them. Now I found them working in munitions factories, machine shops, and industrial plants such as the Reynolds Metal Company in Alabama and the Ingalls Shipbuilding Company in Mississippi. The contribution of blacks not only to the economy but also to American culture was emphasized. In New York I was delighted when asked to get a portrait of the poet Langston Hughes and photos of the activities at the Apollo Theater in Harlem. In Chicago I spent considerable time photographing life in the Ida B. Wells housing project, where many black musicians and other artists lived.

The importance of increasing food production was also receiving a great deal of emphasis. I was sent to Iowa State University, where much research was going on to improve and increase the production of all sorts of agricultural products, from wheat to hogs and cattle. Much of my work was focused on students preparing to be agronomists and veterinarians. For a city boy like me, the exposure to such an environment was an education in itself.

In Minnesota and Wisconsin, my assignments had to do with the work of the Scandinavian community—machinists and engineers at the Northern Pump Company, the Olson Iron Works, the Olson Tool and Die Company. The Swedish population of

Minneapolis was represented in all walks of life—defense plants, draft boards, trade unions, the Red Cross, civil defense, and the church. The culture of the "old country" was preserved through a local Swedish newspaper, folk dances, and various social groups such as the Swedish Institute and the Swedish Society.

From Minnesota I went off to Alabama and Tennessee to photograph the Vultee Aircraft Company and Loudon Dam and Chicamauga Dam of the Tennessee Valley Authority.

While I was roaming around the country, enjoying my work and looking forward to more and more interesting assignments, ominous rumblings of change were being heard in Washington. Toward the end of July 1942, a gossip sheet from Roy included the following comments:

> As I have told you by phone or word of mouth or intimated in letters, the Historical Section has been not too safe a spot these many months. If Mr. Byrd and Tydings had found us, I am afraid it would have gone very hard and we might have become the Farm Security Administration's fan dancers.
>
> After the cut in the budget this last budget period, Mr. Baldwin [administrator of the FSA] told me that he simply could not carry the size budget which we now have and suggested we had best begin seriously to search for a new home. . . . The way it now looks, I think we will become part of the Office of War Information.

It took several weeks and months of political maneuvering (at which Roy was an expert) before we were indeed taken over by the Office of War Information—lock, stock, and barrel. I could hardly feel that any change had taken place. Roy was still in charge, we photographers were still doing what we had been doing all along, the laboratory remained intact, and our headquarters—offices, files, and other physical facilities—remained where they were. As far as I could tell, Roy had saved us from extinction.

At Christmas time we all received the following missive from Jonathan Daniels, of the *Raleigh News and Observer*:

> MERRY CHRISTMAS TO STRYKER
>
> or
>
> If you can't be Santa Claus,
>
> It's a good idea to know the route he's traveling
>
> Roy Stryker struck it rich
>
> But I got the dope on the son-of-a-bitch.
>
> You remember his pictures—the New Deal art,

Photographic Memories

The dispossessed family in the broken-down cart,

The tenant's children, the dead-end street,

The cotton row under half-shod feet.

You'd better remember; we'll not see soon

The hound dog baying to the hungry moon.

This poem is written solely in praise

Of Roy Stryker in a nobler phase.

When the sun went down on the FSA

When McKeller turned the cash away

Our agile Roy didn't mope and cry

He shifted his payroll to OWI.

Now his pictures are pretty; his farmers fat

His colored folks gleam like grandpa's high hat.

This is America—so strong—so good!

And Stryker he photographs it as Stryker should.

No labor so hard that our rich will ere welch

And the poor man gets up from his feast with a belch.

Oh Stryker, Oh Stryker, you're the man that we need

In a land all rid of its grief and its greed.

The hell with all the post-war planners, we-must-doers and if-we-canners

All we need for the people's world, is Stryker, a camera, four men and a girl.

With a click of the shutter, the shy little elf

Will show us a world that won't know itself.

With a Wallace speech and a Stryker print

We can save the world—and also the mint.

So Merry Christmas to Stryker—he's the hope of mankind

And he's neither a dope before nor behind.

19 ·

Riding the Rails

Just as my photographs in Greene County, Georgia, represented one of the high points of my work for the FSA, so did the coverage of rail transportation seem to me to be the most exciting part of the work I did for the OWI.

Armed with credentials from the FBI, the Association of American Railroads, the Headquarters of the Western Defense Command, and the War Department Office of the Chief of Transportation, I set off with Irene for Chicago, the rail hub of the nation, to begin a photographic story of American railroad freight transportation. According to the letter sent to district managers by the Association of American Railroads, I was to

> get striking photographs of Chicago as a railroad terminal, showing yards, tracks, handling of trains, hump and retarder operations, inspection and repair of trains, signal systems, roundhouses and repair shops, as well as photographs of train and yard crews, and other railroad workers, not overlooking the work that goes on in the offices. From Chicago Mr. Delano expects to go to Milwaukee, St. Paul, Minneapolis and Duluth, to get similar photographs of railroad operations in and around these centers, and especially pictures of the car ferry operations at Milwaukee, the grain handling in the Twin Cities, and the iron ore movement in Duluth. From that area he plans to go to the Pacific coast.

End of letter.

That's all? The credentials I carried would allow me not only to photograph anything I wished in the Chicago area but also to spend a month riding freight trains, sometimes in the caboose with the conductor and brakeman, other times in the locomotive with the engineer. I even had the authority to stop the train for a particular shot I might want (with the consent of the engineer, of course). I would share the living quarters of the railroad men and learn some of the intricacies of managing a huge railroad system. How could I ask for a more exciting assignment?

Irene and I rented an apartment in Chicago as our headquarters, and I went to work. First I did an extensive coverage of Union Station, then the Indiana Belt Railway and other small railroads that served to connect the railroad system of the East with that of the West. It was bitterly cold in January and February 1943, and the railroad yards were covered with ice and snow. Once I took shelter in an idle caboose, joining a group of railroad men warming their hands at the potbellied stove and swapping stories. One of the men told of getting off a freight car in below-zero weather and noticing a figure lying on the ground. He went over and saw it was a man there frozen stiff. "He was frozen so solid we had to use a board to pry his hands apart. At first we thought he was dead, but then we decided to take him into a caboose and warm him up. We laid him down on a bunk, but none of us could stay there because we had to go back to work. We figured we'd go back in a little while and see how he was coming along. A little later, we returned to the caboose thinking that we'd better call an ambulance and get the stiff to a hospital. We opened the door and there was our stiff, sittin' up straight with blankets all over him and yelling, 'Shut the goddamn door! There's a f———g draft in here!'"

While in Chicago, we received a call from Roy asking us to look up and interview a young black photographer by the name of Gordon Parks, who was applying for a Rosenwald Fellowship that would allow him to work at the FSA. Would we meet with Gordon, take a look at his photographs, and see if we thought he should be recommended for the fellowship? We had a very cordial luncheon meeting with Gordon and were impressed with him as a person and by his talent as a photographer. I called Roy and told him of our impressions. I don't how much our recommendation was worth, but shortly afterward, Gordon's fellowship was approved. (Gordon worked for a while at the FSA and later went on to join the staff of LIFE magazine as that publication's first black photographer.)

Union Station was always bustling with activity—passengers buying tickets for overcrowded trains, servicemen taking leave of their girlfriends or wives and children, porters lugging baggage, and people crowded around the information booth and at the taxi stands. The baggage department was originally built to handle 2,500 pieces a day; now it was handling almost 10,000. Behind the scenes, I was able to meet the men working in the interlocking tower, where inbound and outbound traffic was controlled, and also the people in the office of the inspector of watches. I had not realized how important it was for a conductor to have his watch working perfectly and for the trains to be running exactly on time. In my ignorance, I asked a foolish question: What happens if a train comes in a little early? The watch inspector gave me a paternalistic look of mixed scorn and pity and replied, "Young fella, trains don't come in early *ever. Not ever!*"

But most of my work was done in the ice and snow of the Proviso Freight Yard—the busiest in the country. Nearly all of the photographs were in black and white, but I did experiment with some color shots taken at night. The ice made it difficult to get around, and I slipped and went sprawling on my back more than once. Fortunately, my bones suffered more than my cameras did, although one camera was damaged and had to be sent back to Washington for repairs. Irene sometimes accompanied me to the yard and made a charming series of drawings of the hand signals used by trainmen to communicate. (This was long before cellular phones.) The drawings now form part of my railroad coverage in the OWI collection at the Library of Congress.

After our work in Chicago, I started out on my 2,000-mile trip to California on the Atchison, Topeka, and Santa Fe Railroad. Since I would be traveling on freight trains and sharing living quarters with railroad workers, Irene could not come along. From my seat in the caboose, I watched as we left Chicago proper and went through the industrial area on the outskirts of the city. The railroad followed the deep waterway that connects Lake Michigan with the Mississippi River. We passed several intersections with other railroads and headed out to Joliet, Illinois, where the train went through another inspection and took on coal and water.

For the rest of the trip, I learned, stops would be made every hundred miles or so—to change shifts, to pick up or deliver freight cars, and to take on coal and water. I also learned some of the trainmen's jargon: a "reefer" was a refrigerator car, a "hogger" or "pigsnoot" was the engineer, a "zoo" was a cattle car, and the "ox" or "foreman" was the conductor of the freight train. At every stop, I would hop off the train and photograph whatever I could, depending on the time available—the work in roundhouses and repair shops, where many women were employed, in switching towers, and in the trainmen's living quarters.

I wrote to Roy about some of my tribulations:

> One of the first things I learned was that I couldn't be in two places at the same time, that is, at the caboose end and at the engine end. The distance might be anything from a quarter of a mile to over a mile and it was impossible for me to be running back and forth because the stops were often very short and the train would start before I could get to either end. So I learned to hop on the caboose while the train was in motion. After many clumsy starts I got over the fear of being left behind and was able to get off and take some shots when the train stopped for short intervals. (I still need *both* hands to hop on and let the brakeman get on with my camera.) Once in the caboose I learned another lesson from bitter experience: don't stand up in a caboose unless you hold on to something, otherwise you and your camera might go flying out through the rear of the train. . . .
>
> I could take with me only a limited amount of equipment—just what I could carry in my arms and *on my back*. Railroad yards are usually far from train or bus stops

and walking is the only means of transportation. . . . Trying to stand in a caboose and take pictures is worse than in any rocking boat.

There followed many days and nights in the caboose and intensive work at every stop. But on the long stretches across the vast plains of Kansas and Missouri, there was plenty of time between stops to catch up on paperwork. To the accompaniment of the *clackety-clack* of wheels on the rails, I kept a detailed diary of my activities and of the distances covered, the names of the train crews, the contents of the cargo we carried, and my impressions, to be used later in a general caption about the entire trip. There was also time to catch up on correspondence. In a letter to Irene I wrote:

Dearest I:

It's 7 a.m. in Amarillo right now and we're sitting in the caboose waiting to get started out of the yard. I got down here at 6:30 this morning hoping to take a few shots before we pulled out. It was still dark then and the first streaks of dawn showed on the horizon. There were a couple of small elevators on the siding and the floodlights in the yard were on. The whole thing looked swell and I took a couple of shots. Now the sun is beginning to come out, the lights have been turned out. The horizon is a bright straight line and the black streaky clouds hang low over it. The light is swell but impossible for pix.

The conductor is giving the "high-ball" and in a minute or two we'll be on our way. I've been watching the air pressure gauge go from zero to eighty, that means there's air in the brakes. Everything is set now and I am braced for the jerk of the train that will come any second now. There it is! We're off.

We pull out of Amarillo past the back yards of the slums I've seen in every town so far. It is not the Negro section, it's where the Mexicans live; not segregated by law as the Negroes but segregated nevertheless.

Now we leave Amarillo and are out on the plains. Looking back the city looks like an oasis in this limitless land that's as flat as a sheet of glass as far as the eye can see. It's rich fertile land. Off on the horizon are little clusters of homes and an occasional windmill. Droves of cattle are grazing in the fields and green grass and the stubble of last year's wheat stretches out in every direction. We are heading due west and behind us the sun is blinding. Shiny rails go off in a straight line as far as the horizon. As we round a curve I can see the crazy shadow of the entire train bouncing along the side of the tracks.

We are going up a "hill" right now and the train has slowed to a crawl. (A hill, for a train, is any slight deviation from the level.) This one is hardly perceptible to me. . . . The conductor is at his desk working on his bills, the brakeman is up in the cupola watching the train. Of my assistants, the trainmaster is up in the cupola too and the company public relations man has gone to sleep. . . . We're still going uphill and the thump-thump of the wheels below is very slow, but the little squeaks and rattles of the caboose are still the same. As soon as we reach the crest we'll begin rolling down and going 50 or 60 miles an hour. The first half of the train will go over the crest then back here we'll feel a lurch that will throw us off our feet if we're not holding on to something and—down the hill we go. . . .

    Darling, I've tried to give you a little idea of what it feels like along here now. But I'll have to wait till I see you to really tell you all about it. . . .

    Good-by, my dearest—see you soon.

And later, in a note to myself in my diary, I wrote:

Things I cannot photograph:

The warm darkness of the caboose

The constant throbbing of the train

Two men sitting in darkness of cupola looking out windows

The passing of signal lights

Lonely looking farmhouses

Isolated interlocking towers,

The crazy moon in the sky with one lone star above it

The lazy rocking to and fro of the brake wheel on the car ahead of us

No wind.

The dark smoke in one long line

The smoke becomes silver-lined

A train is approaching us!

The glare of the headlight

With a WOOSH of thunder it flies by us.

The brakeman gets down from the cupola and watches it go by

Two red lights and a white one pass us

The white one waves up and down.

We answer

Then back again to the drone

I throw a cigarette out of the window

It whirls off in the backwash scattering sparks wildly like fireworks

The blackness again.

For part of my trip through Arizona, I rode in the locomotive with the engineer. We were hauling a long train of more than a hundred cars and going up a slight hill, with one engine up front pulling and another behind pushing. We were carrying, among other things, tractors, bombs, trucks, electrical equipment, steel, mines, military tanks, engines, and other military goods. From the window of the engine cab, I could see the whole train in a great arc behind us. Relying on the authority of my credentials, I asked the engineer to stop the train so I could get off to take some photographs. He looked at me as if I were crazy and said, "Young man, if I stopped the train here we could never get started again but would go rolling down the hill backward!" Undismayed, later on, when we were on a flat Nevada desert, with a different engineer, I tried again. We were going around a great curve with a train of more than a hundred cars. I looked out the engine cab window and thought what a great picture it would make. I asked the engineer to stop and let me off with my camera and tripod. As he applied the brakes I could hear the *clackety-clack* go from car to car through the entire length of the train.

I quickly hopped off and set up my view camera on the tripod. When I looked at the ground glass I found that the composition was not quite right—I wanted the engine a little more to the right. So I shouted to the engineer, "Move her up just a little bit." Again heard the *clackety-clack* as each car of the mile-long train began to inch forward. Never had I had such a sense of power! I felt like Hercules. Wow! To think that I could move that whole train with just the wave of my hand! When I was satisfied with the composition, I gave the engineer an OK sign and he stopped the train. I got my picture, gathered up my equipment, and hopped back on the train, with the help of the conductor, as the caboose went slowly rolling by.

Everywhere along the route, workers of many racial and national groups were employed in a variety of tasks. In the West, there were many Indian and Mexican workers, men and women. In the Albuquerque shops, about half the workers were Mexican Americans. In the Chicago area, they were mostly Russians, Poles, and other Slavic groups, as well as Italians. In every city along the route, newspapers were filled with want ads soliciting switchmen, train dispatchers, telegraphers, signalmen, boilermakers, machinists, car inspectors, and car repairmen.

But all good things come to an end. After a month of travel, I reached the end of my journey in San Bernardino, California. From there to Los Angeles I went by passenger train and then—what luxury!—on the Santa Fe *Super-Chief* to Chicago, and back to Washington on a train with Pullman sleeping compartments and delicious meals in the dining car—a tired but happy photographer.

20 ·

*The Army Tries
to Make a
Soldier of Me*

My flat feet were not sufficient grounds to disqualify me from serving in the army, and Roy's efforts to keep me out of the draft proved ineffectual. On August 27, 1943, I received a communication from Selective Service that read: "GREETING: having submitted yourself to a local board composed of your neighbors for the purpose of determining your availability for training and service in the land or naval forces of the United States, you are hereby notified that you have been selected for training and service therein." I was duly inducted and sent to the Corps of Engineers at Fort Belvoir, Virginia, for basic training. Why the engineers? I don't know, but I suppose that according to army logic that's where a photographer belonged. I had never had any ambition to become a ferocious warrior, but at camp the drill sergeant kept reminding us that he was going to make us "tougher than the Marines." I was taught to build bridges and blow them up with different kinds of explosives, to handle a rifle and pistol, and to march for ten or fifteen miles with a full pack on my back. I took most of the training in stride, but the marching landed me in the hospital with swollen feet. Ed and Louise Rosskam brought me special orthopedic shoes, but nothing helped. Even to take a few steps was excruciating. I thought that I would surely die. But the army knew better: I didn't die. I became a tough, hardened soldier like the rest of my buddies. On the rifle range, where I could shoot lying down, I was outstanding and won a medal as a sharpshooter.

At the end of three months, elevated to the lofty rank of corporal and thirty pounds lighter than when I arrived, I finished my stint at Fort Belvoir. Someone in the army hierarchy decided (maybe it was Roy's influence) that I had the makings of an officer, and I was shipped off to the Army Air Force Officer Candidate School in Miami Beach, Florida. If I had known what I was getting into, I probably would have gone AWOL.

The training began the first night, when we were subjected to the kind of hazing and harassment typical of a college fraternity initiation. From then on, as long as we were "freshmen," we were required to perform all sorts of demeaning tasks and given to understand that we were the scum of the earth and that the upperclassmen were gods to be worshiped—this in the name of "discipline." The whole experience at the school had such a surreal and nightmarish flavor, I could think of no way to describe it except in a series of caricatures that I produced shortly afterward. The captions to the drawings convey some of my feelings at the time:

> The charge of quarters is an IMPORTANT MAN.
> He wears a pink tag to show he is in the UPPER CLASS.
> Reporting to him is a great event.
> At the table one eats with ONE HAND.
> Fire drills come after one goes to bed.
> If it rains there is no parade. Best you pray for rain.
> At a "song" fest you sing real loud how good your squadron is.
> A bivouac is a place where you get lost at night.
> The 26th day is "Black Friday"—that's when you do to them what they did to you.

My impressions of Officer Candidate School.

In my brand-new uniform after graduation from Officer Candidate School as a second lieutenant, on April 28, 1944.

After completing quickie courses in administration, chemical warfare, small arms, military sanitation, camouflage, map reading, voice and command, first aid, supply, infantry drill, regulations, and lots more, I finally got my coveted certificate of graduation on April 28, 1944. Dressed in my new, natty, tailor-made uniform and sprouting lieutenant's bars on my shoulders, I went out into the street to watch the lowly enlisted men snap to attention and salute as I went by.

I was now classified as a still photography officer and shipped off to the public relations department of the army air force base at Wright-Patterson Field in Dayton, Ohio. No assignment could have suited me better, because Irene was already working at the base in a civilian capacity as assistant to the director of a huge army printing plant that produced magazines, training manuals, posters, and other visual material for the air force. (I don't think it was mere coincidence to find myself stationed at the same base as Irene; it seemed suspiciously like the Machiavellian hand of Stryker at work.)

We rented an apartment in the city and set off to work every morning together, she to her office at the printing plant and I to the photographic laboratory at the base. My work was dull and uninspiring: photographing visiting dignitaries, organizing training sessions, supervising the laboratory, and providing photographs as required by the public relations office for press releases. Irene, on the other hand, was having a great time. Her supervisor had been a brilliant graphic designer with an important Chicago advertising agency and was commissioned a major in the air force to take charge of the printing plant. Irene learned a great deal from him. He was a kindly, cordial man, but he had a serious problem—alcohol. Almost every morning he would arrive with a hangover, unable to work. As a result, Irene often had to run the entire establishment of 250 employees on her own.

Some of the fighter planes at the base were intended for shipment to the Soviet Union, and the Russians had two officers, a captain and a lieutenant, stationed in Dayton as military observers. The captain was a woman and the lieutenant was her husband. They spoke very little English and kept very much to themselves. I met them one time on the train coming back to Dayton from Washington. Trying to strike up a conversation, I asked them how they liked living in Dayton. They shook their heads and said, "Nyet." What was it they didn't like? I wanted to know. "No opera," they replied in unison.

Irene and I somehow managed to survive without opera until October 9, when I received orders to report to Brookley Field at Mobile, Alabama, for a special ninety-day temporary assignment with the First Aircraft Repair Unit (Floating). The ARU was a ship (a seagoing ship, not an airship) that had once been a freighter called the *Daniel E.*

Garrett but was now converted into a floating machine shop equipped with every conceivable kind of tool and machine for the repair and servicing of our aircraft at remote island airfields in the Pacific. My orders said I was to act as the ship's public relations officer and produce a series of picture stories about this unique branch of the U.S. Army Air Force. To assist me I was assigned a young sergeant, Amos Landman, who had been a newspaperman in civilian life.

Leaving Irene behind in Dayton, I sailed out of the harbor of Mobile, heading for the Panama Canal and on to the South Pacific. The next three months, while war was raging furiously in Europe and the Far East, were, for me, the most boring time of my life. After the first week at sea, I had photographed most of the facilities and activities aboard the ship and had set up a makeshift darkroom (which could not be used when the seas were rough because the liquids would all spill on the floor). After that, there wasn't much to do except watch the waves lapping against the side of the ship and hope for something interesting to happen.

The only thing of interest that did occur during the first ten days was that one of the enlisted men had to have a tonsillectomy. It lasted twenty-five minutes, and the doctor did a fine job. I did too, recording the whole operation on film for posterity. The tonsils also were preserved for posterity, in a glass jar. Another time we all rushed out on deck when we heard shouts of "man overboard." There was a small flight deck aboard the ship for two helicopters. Several times a week they would practice taking off and landing. One of them had been caught in a downdraft on the lee side of the ship and went plunging into the sea. The pilot was quickly rescued, but the helicopter was a complete loss.

Most of the time there was not much to do while waiting to arrive at our destination. I developed a gorgeous suntan walking the decks in my shorts and spent many hours writing mushy, passionate love letters to Irene, as well as some purely informative ones, such as this:

> Thursday, Oct. 17. [1944] At sea.
> Darling:
> I wish you could see me at this moment. I'm sitting on the top deck next to a life boat, dressed in khaki pants and a T-shirt getting myself a beautiful sun tan while I type. The sun is warm and the water calm, a gentle breeze is blowing on to my face and the boat is rocking only very slightly from side to side. Off on one side of the deck the Andrews Sisters are sounding off with "Ender bender abee gesund" over the radio loudspeaker. All along the railing men stripped to the waist are sunning themselves. The water is a deep blue and the sun is reflected harshly on it. A little dog the Navy boys brought along is yapping at a piece of rag the wind is blowing about the

deck. All is calm, warm and soothing. The lazy pace of the ship is reflected in the slow motion movements of everyone on deck. This is just after a noon meal and most of the men are in a siesta mood. Even the waves seem to have got the siesta spirit—they lap gently against the side of the ship and bounce slowly back to rub shoulders gently with another wave. The radio has now changed to a lazy melancholy cowboy tune. Outside one of the hatches a sailor is sitting crosslegged in a shady spot washing his underwear in a bucket of water.

What a way to go to war.

Darling:
It's been several days since we lost sight of land and the voyage is beginning to get monotonous. . . . Blackout regulations go into effect quite early in the evening but darkness comes very quickly and soon after seven-thirty it is quite dark. We generally go out on deck and spend several hours just sitting in the wind talking or staring out into the blackness and thinking. Last night it was cloudy and the night particularly dark. It was very quiet. All we could hear was the swishing of the water against the side of the ship and the gurgle of waves we could not see. Occasionally the voices of men talking would come up faintly from below decks. Several hundred yards off in the distance we could just barely make out the form of another ship following us—as black and as silent as we were. Looking down over the rail we kept watching the phosphorescence—the seamen told us they were jelly fish. From time to time the whistle of our ship would bellow a series of long wailing calls in a deep hoarse voice that would go off into the night to whisper a secret message to the other ships. Across the deck, lining the rail, were the black forms of other men, talking quietly or just thinking and looking.

Here is a brief sample from the "mushy" letters:

Darling, my darling, oh my darling:
I love you, I love you, Love you—all of a sudden I've fallen for you all over again. Yep, absolutely. I don't really know why this sudden urge, but it came to me right out of the blue (while I was shaving, of all times). I was just finishing my chin when I says to myself, "Gosh, what a pip! I think I'll tell her so." So here I am telling you. I wish you were here so I could look at you and fall in love all over again. . . .

But to get back to business—in a closet-size cubbyhole barely large enough to accommodate one person standing and one sitting, I established my headquarters, painted the floor black, and hung a sign on the door reading, "Public Relations Office." To minimize the risk of claustrophobia, I painted pastoral scenes on the walls and false perspective lines on the floor, which made the tiny room look much bigger. Here Amos and I would interview servicemen, get "human interest" stories, and write out reports to my superiors. Spending so much time aboard ship, I couldn't help picking up the seamen's language. My conversation was full of "port" and "starboard" and "topside" and "belowdecks," and "for'ard" and "aft" and "galley" and "fo'c'sle."

When we started out, we didn't know our exact destination; it was supposed to be secret and couldn't be mentioned in our letters. But after going through the Panama Canal and heading northwest, we realized that we must be on our way to the Hawaiian Islands. Arriving in Honolulu under blackout conditions was an eerie experience. But the following morning was a joyful day when we were all given shore leave. After six weeks at sea we were finally on dry land!

When we were in Panama, we had sent our first batch of films and stories back to the States. Now after leaving Honolulu, we would continue to send material back from every island we passed on our way to the South Pacific. I never got to see any finished prints of all the negatives I sent back. They must be somewhere in the National Archives or the files of the army air force. I do have a few contact prints ($3\frac{1}{4} \times 4\frac{1}{4}$) that look like they are from my days with the First Aircraft Repair Unit, AAF. My ninety-day special assignment completed, I returned to Dayton by military air transport in twenty-four hours.

21 ·

A Secret Mission to Peru

As soon as I had arrived from the South Pacific, I received orders to report to Washington to leave on a secret mission for somewhere. Eight of us were to travel in an old, unarmed twin-engine DC-3 on a route known only to the pilot, and for purposes to be explained to us only when we arrived at our destination. We were told nothing about where we were going—not even whether to take winter or summer clothes. And of course we were not to breathe a word of the mission to our wives. The crew consisted of the pilot (a veteran of many years with a commercial airline and now a captain in the air force), a copilot, a navigator, a radio operator, an engineer, two enlisted men, and me—the official photographer.

Bright and early on an August morning, we took off from Washington National Airport and headed south. The DC-3 was a cargo plane and had no facilities for passengers. We sat in bucket seats or took naps in sleeping bags on the floor. Of course, there was no air conditioning, and oxygen for high-altitude flying came from little portable tanks that were available for anyone who felt a little dizzy. We suspected that we were going south when we landed first in Mobile, Alabama, and then in Panama.

After such a long, tiring flight we needed some rest and entertainment, so we headed to a bar for some beer. The entertainment was provided by a young man who sang and played the organ. I couldn't understand the words because they were in Spanish, but the plaintive, haunting melody moved me deeply. As the singer repeated stanza after stanza, I jotted down the tune on the back of an old envelope, hoping to find out later the title of the song and the name of the composer.

After Panama, we landed in Quito, Ecuador, and finally in Lima, Peru. What in the world were a beatup cargo plane and her air force crew doing in Peru while the war was raging in Europe and Asia? We would learn soon enough.

When we opened the door of our plane to get out, we were greeted by an extraordinary sight. A regimental band played martial music, a platoon of soldiers marched in formation, an envoy from the presidential palace stood by with two limousines to greet us, crowds of people lined the fence along the runway carrying banners reading,

"Bienvenidos, Americanos" (Welcome, Americans). Newsreel cameramen and radio reporters were everywhere. So much for the secret mission!

We were escorted in royal style to our hotel and then, the very same evening, to a banquet at the presidential palace, where an enormous feast had been set out on a long table. The seating was arranged according to rank; the president, of course, sat at the head of the table, and I, as a mere second lieutenant, sat at the tail end, while the enlisted men sat at a separate table. The food looked succulent, but I didn't get much of it. The president was served first, and then the rest of us, according to rank. By the time I got my food, the president, who was a fast eater, had finished his, and the dishes were quickly scooped up, starting with me, before I could gulp down my first mouthful. (Just like in a Charlie Chaplin comedy.)

There was much toasting of Peruvian-American friendship with *pisco* (the local firewater) at the banquet, and some of us got up the next morning with hangovers, but we woke up quickly when the pilot called us to a briefing session to explain the purpose of our mission. The war in Europe seemed to be drawing to a close, and there would be many DC-3s to be disposed of as surplus. We were to show the Peruvian government that our plane could land and take off from any airport in the country and that the DC-3 would make an excellent plane for a Peruvian airline in the future. My job was to photograph airfields, navigational aids, and the general terrain around the airports. The following day we took off from Lima and began hopping from airport to airport through every part of the country—traveling salesmen on a demonstration flight.

Some of the airports, used by the military, were in fairly good condition, but others were merely cow pastures or simply flat, grassy meadows. In order for me to get my pictures, the cargo door was left open and I, with a rope tied around my waist, would lean out as far as possible and try to keep my camera from blowing away. Sometimes, such as around the volcano Mount Misti, we flew at altitudes of 18,000 or 19,000 feet with no oxygen except what we could sniff once in a while from the little portable tank we carried aboard. When we landed at the city of Puno, on Lake Titicaca, I couldn't resist taking a picture of the altimeter of the plane indicating 13,000 feet with the plane on the ground! From airfield to airfield we went, crossing the Andes to land in the Amazon jungle at the town of Yurinaguas on the Huallagua River, one of the sources of the Amazon.

The president of Peru was an amateur pilot and insisted on flying the plane himself as we wove through the Andean valleys. Unfortunately, he was not much of a navigator and could fly only by following the railroad through the mountains. The only time we were scared was when we found ourselves zigzagging above the railroad tracks through the mountains at an altitude of about two hundred feet. I, from my position at the open cargo door, was getting close-ups of shepherds' faces looking up at the huge plane. The shepherds were not unaccustomed to seeing airplanes, but they had not seen monsters such as ours. There was a local operation, Fawcett Airlines, that everybody used to go from town to town. Fawcett's little cloth-covered planes carried passengers and chickens, pigs, produce, and general merchandise all over the Andes.

We couldn't leave the city of Cuzco without visiting the famous Inca ruins of Machu Picchu. Then we were given a royal send-off at the city hall as guests of the mayor and the bishop. The *pisco* flowed freely at the reception, and every toast was followed by a long, flowery speech. We ate and drank as never before and felt as if we were floating sky-high in the rarefied atmosphere of the Andes. Finally, almost at daybreak, when everyone was sated and groggy with sleep, the bishop bade us farewell and Godspeed—in Quechua, the language of the ancient Incas—which no one present understood.

Back in Lima, we packed our bags and prepared to leave. But there was one more ceremony awaiting us. We were to be decorated by the Peruvian armed forces. We lined up in military fashion, and to the sound of rolling drums, each member of our crew received a citation. I was presented with a gorgeous diploma and proclaimed honorary lieutenant in the air force of Peru.

I don't know if our mission was a success, or if the Peruvians decided to buy the planes. But we returned to Washington on our trusty DC-3 carrying with us the air attaché of the Peruvian Embassy in Washington. He had diplomatic immunity, and therefore we had no difficulty in getting through customs loaded with our souvenirs—a baby monkey, a parrot, Indian blankets, hats, and all sorts of trinkets. I later described this journey in a series of picaresque drawings called "The Journey of the Leaping Llama."

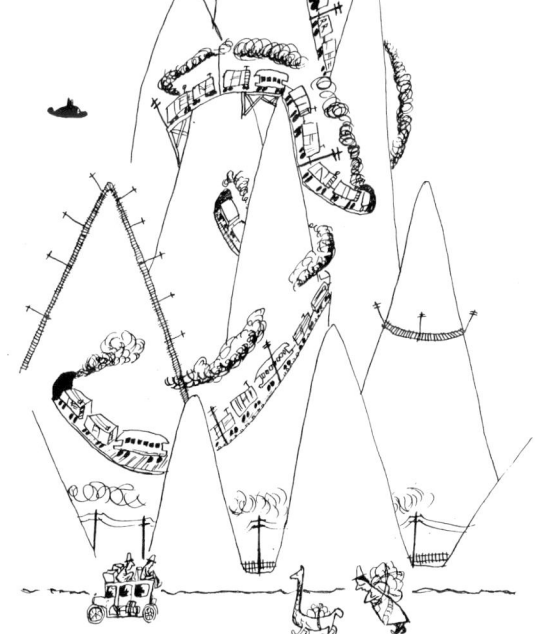

My impressions of our secret mission to South America.

22 ·

*B-29 Bombers
and Bloody
Bodies in the
South Pacific*

Little did I know, when I returned from Peru, that I would soon be going on a much longer journey. Pare Lorentz, the documentary filmmaker I had met during my FSA days in Washington, was now a lieutenant colonel in the air force in charge of a group called the Overseas Technical Unit of the Air Transport Command. The group traveled all over the world photographing, in still and motion pictures, routes and airfields used by our air force. American pilots were often required to land at foreign airfields or at airfields captured from the enemy. They needed good visual materials showing them navigational aids and safe approaches for landing. The purpose of the Overseas Technical Unit was to fly the routes our planes would be following and produce documentation to be used in briefing sessions for flight crews before combat missions.

Colonel Lorentz was familiar with my work for the FSA and arranged for my transfer to his unit. Imagine my delight at finding that my friend Russell Lee (now a captain) was also a member of the group. The Overseas Technical Unit held a unique position in the Air Transport Command. It was directly responsible to General "Hap" Arnold, commander of the U.S. Army Air Force. But that did not imply any special privileges. The entire unit consisted of eleven men and an old, obsolete four-engine B-24 bomber that had been stripped of all its armament, the guns replaced with movie cameras and special windows installed to facilitate taking still pictures. (We learned just how obsolete the plane was when we tried to get spare parts and were greeted with laughter.) In this ancient retired bomber, we were to go to the South Pacific and take a look at the airfields just recaptured from the Japanese.

On June 3, 1945, we took off from Washington, D.C., at 7:15 P.M. and flew nonstop to Los Angeles, arriving at 12:30 A.M. Early the next morning, with extra gas tanks attached to the wings, we started the twelve-hour flight to Hickam Field in the Hawaiian Islands. During the long, uneventful hours in the air, we got a chance to know one another a little better. The pilot, with the rank of major, had spent many years in civilian life with United Airlines, flying commercial passenger planes. His copilot had also come from commercial aviation. They handled the huge plane gently and with ease, as if it were a school bus full of children. The navigator and radio operator were career air force men, and the rest of us were draftees or volunteers in for the duration. All except me were veterans of many flights on this same plane to airfields in all parts of the world.

The drone of the engines and the monotonous seascape were conducive to sleep, and we all took turns napping on the floor. We arrived at Hickam Field at one-thirty in the morning. The landing lights had been turned on for our approach but were immediately turned off when we touched the ground. There was blackness everywhere, and an eerie cloud of silence enveloped the field. After all, Pearl Harbor, with all its devastation, was only a stone's throw away. A sergeant in a military truck drove us to our sleeping quarters. The field was completely deserted, but in the light of the pale moon we could make out the ghostly shapes of aircraft lined up alongside the runway.

After two days for servicing our plane and making arrangements for

The crew of the B-24 bomber of the Overseas Technical Unit in front of the plane that took us to the South Pacific, in 1945. That's me on the far left. Pare Lorentz is second from the right.

the rest of our journey, we took off from Hickam Field and headed south. Five hours later, we landed on a tiny spit of land called Johnston Island. This was simply a landing strip surrounded by a fringe of beach and palm trees. How the navigator ever found it in the middle of the Pacific Ocean I'll never know. Its most outstanding feature was a row of oil drums on the beach that the servicemen had equipped with propellers to serve as wind-powered clothes-washing machines! After spending the night in a Quonset hut we left the next day for Kwajalein, Eniwetok, and Guam. It was during this leg of our trip that we had our first scare.

Somewhere in the Pacific, before we reached Guam, one of the men in the rear of the plane noticed a suspicious-looking black spot in the sky behind us. "It looks like a Zero," he said. (That was a type of Japanese fighter plane.) "I think he's following us." A fine state of affairs, and our old B-24 with absolutely no armament aboard! "Look under that pile of blankets in the back," said the pilot. "There's supposed to be a case of rifles back there. At least we'll have something to shoot back with." We all rushed to find the case and pry it open. Everyone was shouting, "Hurry, hurry, he's getting closer!" But instead of rifles, we found the case filled with cans of beer. Fortunately for us, the Zero seemed to get tired of the chase. It banked abruptly to the right and turned back.

With Guam as our headquarters, we photographed airfields and approaches on all the islands to the south, as far as Palau in the Caroline Islands basin. During our stay in Guam and the Philippines, I had the opportunity to do some photography on the ground. In Manila, the destruction wrought by the Japanese invasion was appalling—bomb-scarred buildings everywhere, worthless paper money lying in the streets, and beggars hoping for a handout. At our base in Guam, I did an extensive picture story on a B-29 bomber crew going out on a bombing mission over Japan. I also photographed wounded men from the front, brought in to be transferred to hospital ships or sent back to hospitals in the States. As we watched the macabre scene—men with arms or legs missing, or complete basket cases—a member of a B-29 crew remarked, "That doesn't happen to us. In our racket, you either come back whole or you don't come back at all." The Guam photographs were published in 1996 by Motorbooks International in a book titled *Superfortress over Japan.*

On the night of a bombing mission, the movie theater at the base carried a sign that read, "No Movie Tonight." It was during one of these missions that we suffered our first casualty. Late one afternoon, we were all resting on cots in our Quonset hut while the bombers were lined up, ready to take off. We could hear them roaring down the runway, one after another, minute after minute. Suddenly the earth shook and a thunderous explosion filled the air. The whole sky seemed to be afire. One of the planes with a full bomb load had crashed at the end of the runway. As sirens screeched and wailed and men from everywhere rushed toward the scene of the crash, a rain of bomb fragments and pieces of human beings began to fall from the sky. One ugly piece of shrapnel came crashing through the roof of our hut to land on the legs of our radio operator, who was lying on the cot next to mine. He survived, although never to walk again without crutches. As for the crew of the bomber that crashed, they bore out the truth of the remark "Either you come back whole or you don't come back at all." By the end of July, we had spent nearly two months on our photographic assignment in the South Pacific, and it was time to go home. The surrender of Japan was imminent. So off we went, island-hopping back to Hawaii. What a surprise met us at Hickam Field: The airport was ablaze with lights and bustling with activity. Over the loudspeaker came announcements of planes leaving for and arriving from destinations such as Los Angeles, Manila, Singapore, New Zealand, Samoa, and Australia! Gone were all signs of blackouts or security precautions. The place had become a busy commercial international airport.

But not for us the luxury of a commercial airliner; we went home in our own B-24 on another twelve-hour flight to San Francisco.

23 ·

We Win the War but Lose a President

In Washington many changes had taken place while I was overseas. The OWI had ceased to exist. Our photographs, along with those of the FSA, had been transferred to the Library of Congress, thanks to the efforts of Roy. (As far back as 1936, he had written a long memorandum to Archibald MacLeish, Librarian of Congress, urging him to establish a photographic collection at the library.) Roy himself had left Washington and started a collection of industrial photographs at the Jones and Laughlin Steel Company in Pittsburgh. When that didn't work out, he moved his operation to the Standard Oil Company (N.J.), with headquarters in Rockefeller Center, New York City. Irene had left Dayton, Ohio, and was now working for Roy, producing exhibits and a photo magazine called *Photo Memo*. The magazine served as a showcase for the photographic collection that Roy was developing for Standard Oil by sending some of his former FSA photographers to the far-flung installations of the company's worldwide empire. Through Roy's connection with Standard Oil, we came to know Robert Flaherty, the noted documentary filmmaker, who was doing a feature film about oil in the state of Louisiana. One evening, at a party at Flaherty's apartment in the Chelsea Hotel in New York, he learned of my interest in filmmaking. I confessed that I didn't have any camera equipment of my own. Taking me by the arm, he led me to an adjoining room filled with movie equipment of all kinds. Reaching out, he chose a Kodak 16mm camera and handed it to me, saying, "Here, take this. Use it as long as you like and bring it back when you're finished."

Roy was now living in New York. Pare Lorentz's Overseas Technical Unit was getting ready to close down operations. Its headquarters had been established in Manhattan to be near film-editing facilities, and all of us were looking for places to live. As for me, I was now a captain, on terminal leave waiting to be discharged from the army.

Irene and I found a little basement apartment in Greenwich Village, on Christopher Street. The subway trains ran underneath our building and whenever a train passed by, we heard the tinkling of chinaware in the kitchen, but otherwise the place was quite comfortable. Irene saw Roy every day at his office, of course, but we were also often invited to visit him and his family at their apartment near Columbia University.

One day while I was at my office in the OTU headquarters, I heard a commotion in the street below. Newspaper boys were shouting, "Extra! Extra!" I picked up my Rolleiflex camera and rushed out into the street. President Roosevelt had died! In Times Square a dazed, solemn crowd had gathered in front of the New York Times Building to watch the news displayed on the electric news bulletin. I took many shots of the anxious faces of people watching the words "Roosevelt Dead, Roosevelt Dead" flashing by. Everyone seemed so stunned by the event, they paid no attention to my sticking the camera in front of their eyes.

People's thoughts seemed to be concerned only with the great tragedy. They talked in low tones, remembering the Roosevelt years and asking the question, What's going to happen now? Irene heard the news on a taxi radio on her way to meet me at the OTU office. We went to a nearby cafeteria for some coffee and sat there for over an hour, speechless. Overwhelmed by the calamitous events of the day, we just couldn't seem to find anything to say.

There was not much for me to do at the Overseas Technical Unit, and I welcomed any chance for some extracurricular activity. I was glad of the opportunity to do some work for an organization concerned about the danger of the proliferation of atomic weapons. The words "Hiroshima" and "Nagasaki" still struck fear into the minds of people throughout the world. I was asked to produce a slide film, in drawings, on the urgent need to establish controls over the use of atomic energy. The result was a filmstrip called *How to Live with the Atom.* It consisted of about sixty frames of humorous drawings, produced with the cooperation of the National Committee for Atomic Information. A selection of twenty-three of the drawings was reproduced in the *New York Times Magazine* on June 9, 1946, in conjunction with an article on the atom bomb by J. Robert Oppenheimer. Then, perhaps stimulated by this project, I produced a fanciful booklet of drawings on my own, about a Chaplinesque little man who has the ability to create atomic energy simply by reciting a string of complex mathematical and scientific formulas. Free atomic energy for the people! Naturally, he is looked upon as a menace by the atomic energy industry.

At Roy's urging, I had submitted some of the photographs from Puerto Rico to the John Simon Guggenheim Memorial Foundation in New York in the hope of getting a fellowship. As the day of my discharge from the army came ever closer, Irene and I began to be concerned about what the future would hold for us. There was no FSA to go back to, and we had no job offers anywhere. Our old FSA friends were scattered around the country—Russ Lee was going back to Texas, Arthur Rothstein and John Vachon were at LOOK magazine, Gordon Parks was at LIFE magazine, John Collier was teaching in New Mexico, Marion Post was married and living in California, and Ed and Louise Rosskam were in Puerto Rico working for the government. During our first visit to Puerto Rico, in 1941, Irene and I had become fascinated by the island and its people, and we had always hoped to return someday. Now, at the urging of Roy, whose friend Henry Allen Moe was the head of the Guggenheim Foundation, we submitted a proposal for a grant to go back and do a book of photographs about the social conditions on the island. We included some of the most dramatic images taken in 1941 as samples of my work. There followed nerve-racking weeks of waiting anxiously for a reply. Meanwhile, we had been receiving encouraging letters from the Rosskams, who were in San Juan, about the possibilities of work in Puerto Rico, both for me as a photographer and for Irene as a graphics designer. Finally, I don't know if it was Roy's influence or not, but imagine our joy when the grant was approved! It would support Irene and me for a year in Puerto Rico to work on the book. It was only the second grant in photography awarded by the foundation—the first had gone to Edward Weston just a year earlier. Now that we would have an assured income for a year, we sublet our apartment in Greenwich Village and left on the first Pan American flight we could get for Puerto Rico, a nine-hour trip in a twin-engine propeller plane.

24.

Back Where Sugar Is King

We landed at the old San Juan airport of Isla Grande, in the heart of the city. Ed and Louise Rosskam met us and escorted us to a new hotel that was still under construction, the Normandie. One of the first things I did upon arrival at the hotel was go to the desk clerk and show him the piece of paper on which I had jotted down the song that had affected me so much in Panama. I whistled the tune for him and asked if he recognized it. "Why, of course," he replied. "Everyone knows that song. It is the 'Lamento Borincano' [Borinquen, or Puerto Rican, Lament], by Rafael Hernández," and he translated the words for me. The song is the lament of a poor farmer who comes down from the mountains singing happily on his way to the market to sell his produce, but the whole day goes by and no one buys his wares. Sadly he trudges back home lamenting his fate, singing:

> Que será de Borınquen
> Mi Dios querido?
> Que será de mis hijos
> y de mi hogar?
> [What will become of Borinquen (Puerto Rico)
> my dear God,
> What will become of my children
> and of my home?]

Puerto Rico was still an impoverished island depending almost entirely on its sugarcane industry. There was almost no middle class. Society was divided into the rural and urban poor and the well-to-do merchant class. Much to our dismay, we found a certain disdain among intellectuals for the folk art and music that we admired so much. Puerto Rican products were looked down upon in favor of anything imported, especially American goods. Big, juicy, locally grown tomatoes were known as "Tomates Americanos."

Rexford Tugwell was still governor, and from the Rosskams we learned that an

Office of Information had been started at La Fortaleza to serve as a public relations agency, but with a historical outlook such as the FSA had emphasized. Tugwell, having had the foresight to select Roy to create the Historical Section of the FSA in Washington, was well aware of the importance of establishing and maintaining a historical photo file. When he became governor of Puerto Rico, he asked Roy to send someone down to set up a similar file on the island, and Roy recommended Rosskam. Ed's experience at the FSA was extremely useful in his new position. He prepared a detailed plan for a historical photo file to be established (he was very good at planning) and began recruiting personnel. To set up a laboratory, he obtained the services of Charles Rotkin, a young man who had been stationed in the army in Puerto Rico and decided to stay on after the war. Charlie not only set up the laboratory with the necessary equipment and personnel but was also very good at aerial photography in his own right. A Puerto Rican photographer was hired as well; the photographic staff, including Ed and Louise, now consisted of four people. Soon the photographs they produced of social conditions in the cities and the countryside in all parts of the island began accumulating, to be filed according to a system devised by Ed Rosskam.

When I was asked to join the group, I immediately accepted. Irene and I both looked forward with great enthusiasm to continuing the work we had started for the FSA in 1941. We could hardly wait to start traveling throughout the island, renewing our acquaintance with country people we had met years ago. I looked forward to focusing my camera again on sugarcane workers, on elements of health, education, housing, religion, and transportation.

The late 1940s were years of experimentation and implementation of a number of new government programs. From the U.S. came an army of experts—in agriculture, economics, planning, engineering, education, merchandising, geology, and business administration. (The local press had a great time playing on the words *perrito* with two *r*'s, meaning "little dog," and *perito* with one *r*, meaning "expert.") All Americans were, by association, included among the "experts." The government had leased the second floor of the Hotel Normandie in San Juan as housing for all of us. Every morning, Irene and I would come down to have breakfast at the open-air cafe next to the swimming pool to find the tables occupied by men and their wives reading their hometown newspapers—the *Whitestone Bugle*, the *Hicksville Call*, the *Mapletown Reporter*, and so on. Outside of their own specialties, none of them seemed to have any interest in Puerto Rico.

A group of documentary filmmakers stayed there for a while, on a contract to produce a promotional film about Puerto Rico. I had met one of the men, Benji Doniger, in New York when I had been invited to a reading of the script for the benefit of Don Jesús T. Piñero, Puerto Rico's resident commissioner in Washington. The meeting took place at Ed Rosskam's New York apartment, which boasted the extraordinary address of number 10 Downing Street! Don Jesús was a jovial, pleasant man. He listened attentively as the script was read, smiling and nodding his head from time to time. Then he said, "Very good. Very good. I like it very much." Everyone was delighted. Then he added, "Yes. Very good. But there is one thing missing—a very important thing." Suddenly we were all ears. What could it be? Then he smiled and said, "Love. There is no love in this movie, and in Puerto Rico there is *lots* and lots of love."

I was glad to see the film crew at the Normandie and presumed that they had settled the "love" problem. We all became good friends during their stay in Puerto Rico. There was a pleasant, homey atmosphere about the hotel, and the friendly switchboard operator kept tabs on everybody by listening in on telephone calls. One time, when I was spending the night at a guest house in a mountain town, I needed to make a call to Irene at the Normandie. It was one-thirty in the morning and I had an urgent message for her. The hotel operator kept ringing her room, but there was no answer. No answer? Where could she be at that hour, I wondered. The operator responded, "Let me try Mr. Doniger's room," she said. "I think that's where she is." In Mr. Doniger's room? At one-thirty in the morning? Sure enough, that's where she was. The film crew was having a party! "It's a great party. We all wish you were here," Irene said.

The builder of the hotel lived on the top floor with his flamboyant young French wife. Every now and then, at night, we would find her enjoying a dip in the huge swimming pool in the lobby, stark naked, accompanied by her little white poodle.

The Rosskams were also staying at the Normandie. We met often socially and to discuss our work at the Office of Information. One day they introduced us to Luis Muñoz Marín and his wife Doña Inés. Muñoz was a liberal of the New Deal variety. He had been brought up in the States and educated at Georgetown University in Washington, D.C. He was completely bilingual and published poetry in both Spanish and English. He had started a new political party in Puerto Rico, the Popular Democratic Party, that had just won the elections (by a slight margin) and made him president of the Senate. In her youth Doña Inés had once been a fiery supporter of independence for the island. As a schoolteacher at Central High School in San Juan, she had been dismissed for refusing to teach her class in English, although she herself spoke the language fluently. (English was the mandatory language of instruction in the public school system, directed by a secretary of education appointed by the president of the United States. All major public officials were presidential appointees.)

Muñoz and Doña Inés were highly intelligent, motivated people, deeply committed to the struggle against poverty in Puerto Rico. In addition, they had a wide range of interests—in people, in politics, in poetry, in philosophy, in history, in music—in everything. One time, after a Casals Festival concert, Muñoz said to me, "Tell me, what is it about the music of Bach that Don Pablo finds so inspiring?" He said it in all sincerity, I am sure. He really wanted to know what made the music great so that he too would feel inspired. Muñoz was a big man with a great lust for life. He enjoyed good literature, good company, good conversation, good food, and good wine. Sometimes on weekends he would go along with a few friends to a beach near the town of Luquillo to spend an evening around a bonfire, discussing the poetry of Walt Whitman, the political situation in China, or the latest Puerto Rican novel. Then, after an abundance of seafood washed down with several glasses of wine, he would lead the assembled company in an improvised imitation of Italian opera, to the text of a menu from an Italian restaurant. On the campaign trail, he once started the day by stopping at a little country store to consume a breakfast of six scrambled eggs and an equal number of soft drinks. His driver and the bodyguards, who were always served first, at his insistence, could only sit and gape in astonishment. Doña Inés, although busy with official duties as first lady, would nevertheless sometimes go off to the countryside in a government car, with Irene beside her, to visit rural schools in search of children with special artistic talent.

In meetings Muñoz and Doña Inés expressed their deep concern for the sad state of the educational system in Puerto Rico. Illiteracy was extremely high, especially among the rural population. The people's knowledge of the world around them came almost entirely from the radio. Those few who could read and write had no more than a third-grade education. As Muñoz put it to us, "Even if we used the entire island budget for traditional methods of education, the effect would hardly be noticeable. We must invent something new, a new way of teaching." After many such sessions with Muñoz and Doña Inés, the idea was born to create a new government agency that would use audiovisual techniques of education—films, photographs, posters, profusely illustrated booklets, and the like. These materials would be used by group leaders in rural communities to provide the basic education that was lacking and to help people organize to solve some of their local problems without expecting the government to do everything for them.

Muñoz was well aware of the experience that the Rosskams and Irene and I had in the visual media. Eager to get the new plans under way as soon as possible, he arranged to have a Division of Cinema and Graphics established in the Commission of Parks and Recreation. Why in this particular agency? Simply because the commission already owned and operated a fleet of Jeeps equipped with portable generators, film projectors, and screens that were used for showing sports films in the baseball parks of the island. I was charged with organizing a documentary-film production unit, Irene with establishing a graphics workshop for producing posters and illustrated booklets, and Ed Rosskam with supervising the entire operation and taking charge of the editorial work.

I had spent almost the entire past year traveling around the island, delving with my camera into the many aspects of Puerto Rican life—sugarcane, tobacco, coffee, the role of women, children in school, the hospital system, religious services, village fairs, and the new industries just established by the government. But sugar was still king. Every day during the harvest season, the cane fields were crawling with oxen and men drenched in sweat, swinging machetes from dawn to dusk. An endless line of railroad cars carried the cane to the nearby sugar mill. A song I often heard went like this:

Puerto Rico, Puerto Rico,	[Puerto Rico, Puerto Rico,
tanta caña tiene sembrá.	you have so much cane planted.
Todavía no se ha visto un rico	No rich man has ever been seen
trabajando ganando el pan.	working to earn his bread.
Caballeros, la cosa no está bien	Gentlemen, things are not good,
cada día poniendose peor.	getting worse every day.
Las mujeres muriendose de hambre	The women dying of hunger
y los hombres jartandose de ron.	and the men besotted with rum.]

As part of my coverage of transportation on the island, I had photographed a trip on the passenger railroad that ran from San Juan to Ponce. According to the timetable, the train was supposed to leave at 7:00 A.M. and arrive in Ponce at 4:00 P.M. We did leave San Juan at 7:00 A.M., but arrived in Ponce at 7:00 P.M.—normally a four-hour ride by car in those days. Then I noticed an announcement in the published timetable. It read: "The company is not responsible for the prompt arrival or departure of the trains." I did a complete coverage of the trip, which was later published as a book by the University of Puerto Rico Press under the title *De San Juan a Ponce en el Tren* (From San Juan to Ponce on the Train).

This intense period of traveling and photographing added about two thousand new negatives to the picture file. Now I resigned from the Office of Information to devote myself to filmmaking. Irene and Ed Rosskam also resigned to work for the new agency.

25 ·

*Producing and
Directing Films*

Since we knew no Spanish, one of the first people we hired was a bilingual administrative assistant, Aida Passalacqua. She not only did much of the translating for us but also was in charge of our purchasing department. She was ever conscious of economizing, and I once heard her make a call to an electrical supply house to purchase a pair of electrician's gloves that had to be safe up to 20,000 volts: "What?" she said. "So much money for a pair of gloves? Don't you have something with less volts for fewer dollars?"

To establish my film production unit, I began searching for trained technicians and filmmakers, but only one person on the island was making films—Juan Vigüe Sr. He and his three sons produced occasional newsreels and documentaries for the government and for private industry. I would have to look elsewhere for my staff. There was no alternative except to find young people interested in becoming filmmakers and to train them. A friend at the University of Puerto Rico drama department recommended a student of his who seemed to have a passion for films. The American film crew told me of their truck driver, who was fascinated by what they were doing and kept asking all sorts of questions about the camera. A young man at one of the radio stations heard that we were looking for a sound engineer and applied for a job. None of these people had any film production experience, but they wanted desperately to learn.

Bit by bit, we formed a cohesive film department. The drama student eventually became a director, the truck driver a good cameraman, the radio operator an excellent sound engineer. In the same way, we trained a film editor, script girls, gofers, and all the other personnel. For the training program, I used some of the books on film production that I had brought with me and showed a series of great film classics that we rented from a company called Brandon Films in the States. Before we acquired much of our equipment, I made arrangements with a circus that performed each year in a park across from our offices to allow our trainees to produce short films using my own personal 16mm Kodak camera. Soon the equipment we had ordered began arriving, and before long, our facilities included a small film studio, an editing room, a sound recording studio, and Moviolas, microphones, lights, and laboratory equipment for processing 16mm film. Ed Rosskam had to go through the same process to create a competent group of writers to produce film scripts and booklets, and Irene started her graphics workshop with youngsters from the neighborhood who had never had anything to do with the graphic arts. So we began, in the basement of the Sports and Recreation Building, to produce illustrated booklets, documentary films, and posters, while up above us, on the first floor, baseball players, boxers, karate students, tennis stars, swimmers, and runners were discussing plans for all sorts of athletic events. We all got along just fine.

We decided it was important for us to learn Spanish so as to communicate more easily with our staff. Although some of our employees did know some English, many did not. Irene found that one of her young silk-screen workers was spending his lunch hour every day trying to memorize an English dictionary. We took Spanish lessons three times a week and asked all our employees not to hesitate in correcting our mistakes. Irene kept a blackboard in her office and asked everyone to write down the mistakes she made. One day I found the words "*el* problema" (the problem) on the board. That was the word we used more often than any other. She had been saying "*la* problema."

Our Spanish teacher was a lady from the States who had come to Puerto Rico many years ago to teach English in the public schools. She had studied Spanish in the States and knew her grammar perfectly, but her accent was atrocious. Three times a week we met to translate articles from the Puerto Rican newspapers and to read our Spanish compositions to her. I felt very proud when she gave me a high grade for writing, in perfect Spanish, "The cow is a very useful animal. The cow produces milk and more cows."

At the beginning, I found myself acting not only as the director of the whole film production unit but also as the producer, director, cameraman, editor, and—sometimes—composer of the music for the first films we produced. As word of our unit began to spread, artists, writers, composers, and filmmakers who were working or studying abroad began returning to Puerto Rico to join our staff.

I wrote to the Guggenheim Foundation requesting permission to change my grant from photography to filmmaking. Permission was granted.

When Irene and I had first arrived on the island, we were pleasantly surprised to find very little evidence of racial prejudice. Later we learned that it was not entirely absent. It did exist, but on a level far, far below that of the southern United States. There was no segregation in buses, trains, trolleys, public housing projects, or schools. When we first came to a school assembly to take photographs, Irene whispered to me, "Look! Technicolor!" It was true. The room was filled with children of all colors.

In public life, there were many prominent black men and women. After Muñoz,

The movie truck of the Division of Cinema and Graphics of the Parks and Recreation Commission during the filming of the inauguration parade of Governor Jesús T. Piñero in 1948.

the most outstanding political leader was the president of the Puerto Rico House of Representatives, Ramos Antonini, who was a black man. A brilliant labor lawyer, he delighted in entertaining his guests at the piano during musical soirees in his home. And now Irene and I found ourselves working in a government agency headed by a tall, handsome black man, Julio Monagas, a former baseball hero. Although he was, in theory, our superior, in practice he never had anything to do with our work. As a matter of fact, he never even came down to our facilities to see what we were doing. Monagas was passionately devoted to Muñoz and the Popular Democratic Party. He accepted our unit into his agency only because that was Muñoz's wish. Although he pretended to be a rough, tough, ignorant muscle man, he was actually highly intelligent, well-read, and cultivated. He detested any form of pretension and what he called "fake intellectuals." Apparently Irene and I did not fall into that category, because he soon came to accept us as good friends.

One of my early films was a biography of Jesús T. Piñero, who had been appointed by President Truman to be the first native-born Puerto Rican governor of the island. (All previous governors were either Spaniards or Americans.) Don Jesús had been a landowner in the town of Carolina, and much of the film was shot on his land. Carolina was a predominantly black community, and naturally the film included many faces of the black people who worked on the farm. As I was editing the film one day on a Moviola, I noticed a young secretary looking over my shoulder at the monitor screen. "Why do you have to have so many ugly people in the movie?" she asked. I was shocked. That was not a reaction I would have expected. What did she mean, "ugly people"? Was I doing something wrong? After all, I was a stranger here. What do I know about Puerto Rico? I decided to consult Julio. (We were by now on a first-name basis.)

He took me outside the building, and we sat on the front steps as I told him of my concern about what happened. Should I reedit the film? Should I deemphasize the black presence? He listened carefully and then asked, "What do you think?" I told him I thought the film was turning out quite well and that the people in it, far from being ugly, showed strength and dignity. He slapped me on the back and said, "Well, don't ask me what to do. You're the boss. Do what you think is right."

In 1948, Muñoz became the first *elected* governor of Puerto Rico. (Previously, all governors had been *appointed*.) A few days after being sworn in, he invited Irene and me to join him and Doña Inés for dinner at their new residence, the governor's palace. He had a great sense of humor and took a childlike delight in escorting us around the building, showing off its ostentatious trappings that contrasted so sharply with the simple wooden country house that had served as his home for so many years. He told us that on his first night in the palace, he made the rounds of all the rooms to see if the previous occupant had left anything behind. In one of the bathrooms, he found a used toothbrush. He walked around with the toothbrush in his hand looking for a wastebasket in which to dispose of it but could find none. Then, when he came to an open window, he surreptitiously tossed it out into the street. "I could hear it go *clink* on the cobblestones below," he said. "Suddenly, security guards with rifles appeared on all the surrounding rooftops. Then I knew I was the governor." It was that same evening that Doña Inés, who spoke English very well but was not familiar with some of the niceties of the language, said to me in all candor, "Well, now that Muñoz is the governor, does that make me the governess?"

With control of both houses in the legislature, Muñoz began pushing through much of the social legislation to which his party was committed. One of the bills, passed in 1949, created the Division of Community Education within the Puerto Rico Department of Education. Fred Wale, a specialist in community action programs, was brought from the States as director, and our Cinema and Graphics Unit was transferred, in its entirety, to serve as the nucleus of the new agency. Now, having an increased budget and staff, we searched for a new location. The old San Juan marketplace, a colonial building dating back to the nineteenth century, had been used by the army as a warehouse during World War II. We leased it from the City of San Juan for a dollar a year and transformed it into the headquarters of the Division of Community Education. My film unit now boasted a large, soundproof motion picture studio, several editing rooms, projection rooms, sound-mixing facilities, a laboratory with three motion picture developing machines under the direction of a trained laboratory technician, an emergency power plant, and a 10,000-gallon water tank to protect the laboratory in case of a power failure or a water shortage—problems that frequently occurred in San Juan. Irene's department included studios for artists, a huge silk-screen shop (for editions of up to five thousand), and facilities for mixing paints and drying the silk-screen posters. The rest of the building was occupied by administrative personnel, offices for scriptwriters, and a conference room.

The films produced under my direction were intended for showing not in theaters but out in the open air. I remember once attending the preview of a short documentary about the sugarcane industry. The showing was to be held at a crossroads in front of a country store in a sugarcane field. We used no professional actors in our films, finding plenty of acting talent among the country people. The cane-cutters in our film were just like the men coming to see the movie. To be present at one of these showings was a thrilling and exhilarating experience. On this occasion, just at dusk, miles before we arrived at the country store, we found posters produced by Irene's workshop all along the roadside, announcing the film showing. They were everywhere—on trees, walls of houses, doors of country stores, telephone poles—everywhere. Each poster carried the word "gratis" (free) in big letters, and a line that read, "Film produced in Puerto Rico." The air was filled with music coming from a loudspeaker on the Jeep of the local group leader and his voice announcing that the film was about to start.

In the fading light, we could make out streams of people coming along the mountain trails toward the projector in front of the store. There were children, old people, women with babies in their arms, almost everyone barefoot, to stand in a crowd of about two hundred and socialize with neighbors, exchanging news and gossip while waiting for the film to begin. When it was quite dark, the projector was turned on. A sudden hush fell on the gathering. The people stood openmouthed, transfixed by the images flickering on the screen. Sometimes they would point at the screen and laugh in delight at the familiar faces and scenes they recognized. This was no Hollywood movie with gorgeous, otherworldly ladies and gentlemen. They were looking at people just like themselves. That evening, no sooner had the film started than a little steam locomotive hauling cars of sugarcane appeared on the nearby narrow-gauge tracks. The bright beam of the headlight fell on the screen and obliterated the image. Immediately an angry chorus of shouts rose up from the audience: "Turn off the headlight! Turn off the headlight!" The engineer not only turned off the headlight but kept the train standing there so he could watch the movie too. Never had the people seen such a film as this. As a matter of fact, some of them had never seen any film at all.

As I stood in the darkness, watching the faces illuminated by the light reflected from the screen, I was reminded of an incident told to me by a doctor in the medical corps during the war. He had been traveling from island to island in the South Pacific on an educational campaign to eradicate malaria by teaching the native populations about the danger of the anopheles mosquito. On one small island, the village chief had gathered his people to watch a film that showed graphically just how malaria is transmitted. In huge close-ups that filled the screen, the mosquito was seen landing on the skin of a malaria patient, probing for blood, and flying off to transmit the disease to another person. When the film was over, the village elder thanked the doctor profusely and said, "Now we understand why you people are so afraid of the mosquitos. Out there where you come from, they are so *huge*, but here they are just tiny little things that don't harm anyone."

At the Division of Community Education, I produced and directed a total of seven films, and for some of them I composed the music as well. When we produced what I think was the first animated film in Puerto Rico, based on a children's story, "La Cucarachita Martina," I wrote the music, which later became a ballet. Our films were widely shown, not only throughout the island but also at several international film

Directing little boys in the film *Los Peloteros* in 1952.

festivals, including those in Mexico, Spain, and Edinburgh, Scotland. The films were acquired by UNESCO, which showed them in foreign countries interested in starting community development programs. My last (and best) production for the division was a feature-length film with two professional actors—the first time I had used professionals. One was a comedian of radio and theater, Ramón Rivero, who went by the name of Diplo. He was known and beloved as a blackface character in the theater but appeared without such makeup in our film. The other was a young drama student from the University of Puerto Rico, Miriam Colón, making her first appearance in a film. She later went on to become a highly acclaimed actress and the founder of the Puerto Rico Traveling Theatre in New York. Ed Rosskam wrote the script for the film, which was titled *Los Peloteros* (The Ballplayers) and was based on the childhood experiences of one of our employees.

The film begins with a group of people seated in front of a little store at night discussing the need for a school in their neighborhood. They have sought help from every government agency, but to no avail. A young man in the group suggests that they build the school themselves. "Impossible," everyone says. "We're all starving. Nobody has any money." To which he replies, "Let me tell you a story, about when I was a little kid."

His story is about a group of urchins in a slum area of a mountain town. They are obsessed with the idea of joining the junior baseball league but find it impossible because they have no money to buy uniforms and equipment. One of the boys suggests that they raise the money themselves. For help in making such an important decision, they go to their coach, Don Pepe, a kindly but lazy former baseball player married to an ambitious young woman, Lolita, who constantly castigates him for not getting a job. The boys decide to collect and sell junk, shine shoes, wash cars, sell homemade candy, and put on an amateur circus to raise money for their team. When Lolita hears of their plans, she offers to be their banker as they raise the money. The high point of the film comes during the "circus," in which I let the boys improvise all sorts of acrobatics. The result is hilarious. But the circus is interrupted by the news that Don Pepe's wife used their money to buy clothes and furnishings for her house. In the end, Don Pepe repays them by selling the pig he had been raising for Christmas. The boys get their uniforms and everything ends happily. We come back to the group of neighbors in front of the country store. They agree that they can raise the necessary money for the school. "But," says one man, "we must be very careful about choosing our leader."

All the outdoor scenes of the film were shot in the mountain town of Comerío, and the interiors in our studio in San Juan. The little boys who were the principal actors came from the local public school, and dozens of townspeople served as extras. The premiere took place in the baseball park of Comerío, with two projectors running simultaneously. The field and bleachers were filled to capacity with almost the entire population of the town.

During the shooting of one of the final scenes, an incident had taken place that almost had fatal consequences. Our station wagon, loaded with equipment, was parked on a steep hillside in the slum area of town where we were filming. One of the boys, the lead actor, while waiting for his scene, sat down in the driver's seat and began playing with the controls of the car. He released the emergency brake, and the station wagon began rolling down the hill, directly toward a group of boys playing marbles in the street. In a panic, a group of us rushed to the car and managed to stop it. We gave the boy such a severe scolding that he ran off crying. The next day, when we expected him for the filming of his last scene, an extreme close-up, he showed up with a new, very short haircut! Since we couldn't wait for his hair to grow back, the lighting and camera technicians were required to call upon all the resources available to them to film the scene so that his hair would not show.

It was while we were filming *Los Peloteros* that the nationalist uprising occurred. A small group of armed revolutionaries, inspired by their fiery leader, Pedro Albizu Campos, started an armed revolt and tried to set up an independent Republic of Puerto Rico. Sporadic attacks on police stations and some government buildings took place. The police station of the town of Jayuya was seized and the Republic of Puerto Rico proclaimed. A group of armed gunmen tried to penetrate La Fortaleza, where Muñoz had his offices. In the resulting shoot-out five nationalists were left dead. The National Guard was called out and began patrolling the streets and the roads and protecting government buildings. There was a jittery atmosphere, and the newspapers and radio broadcasts were filled with exaggerated, sensational accounts of the fighting. Nervous, trigger-happy young National Guardsmen stood watch at the capitol building, eyeing every suspicious-looking vehicle that passed. I drove by one evening with some friends in a little convertible, just to see what was going on, and as we passed the capitol building someone in the backseat, seeing the soldiers standing guard, began shouting hysterically, "Don't shoot! Don't shoot!" The uprising, although violent and deadly, did not last long and did not spread throughout the island as the Nationalists had hoped it would. Though completely lacking in popular support and quickly suppressed, it did put a scare into the government, and what followed was a mass crackdown on all supporters of independence.

In Comerío, we were so busy with our filming that we were hardly aware of these occurrences. Only the radio kept us informed. Nothing disturbed the tranquillity of the town, and only occasionally did we pass an armored vehicle loaded with National Guardsmen while we were on the road taking our exposed film to San Juan.

Los Peloteros has been shown widely on television, in the schools, at film clubs, at universities, and at film festivals. In 1993 it was shown at the International Film Festival in Nantes, France. Although the French know nothing about baseball and the film had no French subtitles, it had to be shown twice in response to popular demand.

Working with film, I became accustomed to running the musical sound track back and forth on the "sound reader." Intrigued by the strange sounds produced by music played backward or at speeds other than normal, I wrote to the Guggenheim Foundation requesting permission to change my grant from filmmaking to electronic music. Permission was granted.

In an improvised studio, with tape recorders modified to record and play back at many different speeds, I, with the aid of a sound technician, recorded musical instruments and nonmusical sounds at varying speeds, forward and backward, to produce new musical effects for our films. The results were somewhat primitive, since this was 1950, before the days of the transistor, and re-recording on sixteen-inch plastic discs inevitably produced a great deal of background noise. Nevertheless, although we didn't know it at the time, we later learned that we were among the first in the world to conduct experiments of this sort. I used short pieces of these musical effects in the film *Desde las Nubes* (From the Clouds).

After my experience with *Los Peloteros* I felt capable of producing a feature film on a Puerto Rican subject for commercial distribution. In 1952, Irene and I resigned from the Division of Community Education. We resigned partly because we wanted to make our feature film and partly because we felt that we had fulfilled our commitment to Muñoz and Doña Inés. The film and graphics departments were functioning well and were in the hands of competent Puerto Rican artists and technicians. With our friends Benji Doniger and Pete and Ellen Hawes, we formed a film company called Cine Alba.

The following year was devoted to trying to produce a script for a feature film. We traveled all over the island taking pictures of possible locations, collecting stories, interviewing people, and pounding away at the typewriter—all to no avail. We agreed that the finished script was not good enough. In desperation, we hired a professional scriptwriter from the States. He knew nothing about Puerto Rico but had worked in Hollywood and had written plays that were produced on Broadway. When he began work and wrote that a farmer "parked his horse at the curb," we realized that he would need a lot of coaching. A month passed, and the script he produced was not at all what we needed. We then decided to abandon the project for the time being in the hope of reviving it sometime in the future. Looking back after all these years, I think we failed because we never really had a clear idea of what we wanted the film to say.

26 ·

*Embarking on
New Ventures*

During our search for talent, we one day came upon Doña Sara. She was about sixty years old and had strong Indian features. A thousand wrinkles covered her face and multiplied when she smiled. I was taking pictures of some sugarcane workers in a field next to her tiny wooden house, and when she noticed Irene with me, she called out for us to come in out of the sun and have some coffee. As we sat on a rustic bench sipping our coffee with hot milk, she bombarded us with questions. The most important one was, How many children did we have? When Irene said we didn't have any, Doña Sara was shocked. "What? No children? A young woman like you and no children? What are you waiting for? Before long you won't be able to have any. No children? Don't you realize what you're missing? Look at me, I have *fourteen* children. They are all fine and I love them all." And on and on she went, in a good-natured way.

When we took our leave, she presented Irene with some tangerines to take home and invited us to come back. Come back we did—the very next week—with some candy for the children. No sooner had Irene stepped in the door when Doña Sara went after her again about having children: "Well, are you pregnant yet?" For the next several months, every time we visited the family, Irene was subjected to the same lecture. Then one day, lo and behold, our son, Pablo, was born! Doña Sara was elated by the news. She felt responsible for the extraordinary event and insisted on having a picture of the baby. I brought her one, and she immediately tacked it up on the wall of the living room. Many years later I would find it still there, flanked by two other images—on Pablo's right was Governor Luis Muñoz Marín and on his left the pope!

Doña Sara was convinced that Irene didn't know anything about taking care of babies, so she sent one of her daughters, Ana, to spend the first month with us. Ana certainly did know about caring for babies. She could have taught Dr. Spock a thing or two. In her sweet and gentle way, she took charge of everything, ordering me about and giving Irene lessons in baby care as if she were a professor of pediatrics. When her month was up, she came to Irene to take her leave and said that if we agreed, she would be very pleased to be Pablo's godmother when he was baptized. "That's very kind and generous of you, Ana," Irene said, "but you see, we are Jewish, and Jewish people don't baptize their children." Ana, a good Catholic girl, was not at all taken aback. She simply replied, "Oh, that's all right. But I'm sure you want Pablo to grow up to be a good Christian boy. No?"

Our dream of producing a feature film now put aside, Irene and I decided to dedicate ourselves to other pursuits. Our friend Dr. Tomás Blanco had been asked by the government's public radio station to write a Christmas story for broadcast on the eve of Epiphany. Tomás had graduated from medical school in Spain but never practiced medicine. Instead, he became a poet, a folklorist, and a historian. He called us to say that he had an idea for the story and would like to discuss it with us over lunch. We sat enthralled as he told us his version of the Three Wise Men making their journey to Jerusalem in search of a very special Child. We told him of our enthusiasm for the story, and he said he would write it but only on the condition that I compose the incidental music. I immediately agreed.

Part of Irene's silk-screen poster workshop at the Division of Community Education.

The music, partly original and partly based on medieval Spanish melodies, was scored for viola and harpsichord. The recording session was held at the San Juan Cathedral, with Irene on the harpsichord that our friend Pete Hawes had built, and me on the viola. Tomás, waving a large handkerchief, had to play the part of a scarecrow during the recording, because every time the harpsichord sounded, flocks of little birds would fly in through the open windows. The program was broadcast on January 5, 1955, and was so highly acclaimed that Tomás decided to publish it as a book. Again there were conditions—that Irene design the book and do the illustrations.

Irene decided that the bilingual text of the book would be printed in the States but the illustrations would be done in Puerto Rico, in silk screen, because of the rich colors of the medium. We both worked on the designs, with Irene making the major decisions, and I cut the stencils of the separate colors. In a rented space in San Juan, she organized a temporary silk-screen shop and, with help from the young men she had trained at the Division of Community Education, working on weekends and in the evenings, she produced the two thousand sets of illustrations for the first edition of the book. Then she recruited a group of young women to paste the illustrations in the blank spaces that had been left for them by the printer.

The book was an extraordinary success. The whole edition sold out immediately. Governor Muñoz sent many copies as Christmas gifts to influential members of Congress and to Supreme Court judges, and he received effusive replies of praise and appreciation. When we sent a copy to the copyright office in Washington, we received a request for an additional copy for their rare book collection. When the second edition came out, with illustrations again in silk screen, printed by a shop in San Juan, the United Nations Children's Fund (UNICEF) requested permission to use one of the images as a Christmas card. They wanted to know how much it would cost to have three million cards printed in silk screen in Puerto Rico. Irene called the young man who ran a silk-screen shop in San Juan and asked for a quote. Two days later he called back and said, "Three million cards? Irene, do you realize that there are five colors and it would take us four years to print each color?" The card was eventually printed in offset in Switzerland and sold out completely the first year. In the years that followed, two more illustrations from the book were used as UNICEF Christmas cards.

In the same year as the publication of the book, a full-page notice appeared in the newspapers announcing a musical composition contest sponsored by the government radio station. I decided to write a sonata for viola and piano, based on elements in the musical folklore of the island, and dedicate it to Tomás Blanco. The sonata was awarded first prize in the chamber music category and was later recorded by the Institute of Puerto Rican Culture for commercial distribution.

During this period, in addition to the Tomás Blanco book, Irene was working on annual reports for various government agencies. Whenever she needed photographs taken, I would be sent out on assignments. At the same time, in New York, Edward Steichen was organizing the photographic exhibit called "The Family of Man." I was pleased to learn that he had included my photograph of Mr. and Mrs. Lyman laughing in front of their tobacco barn in Connecticut.

Here in San Juan I had composed a ten-minute work for alto voice and harpsichord, called "La Oración de Jimena" (Jimena's Prayer), after taking a course in medieval Spanish literature at the University of Puerto Rico. The text was from "El Poema del Cid" (The Poem of El Cid), a medieval ballad about the legendary Spanish hero. In the story, when El Cid is exiled from Spain, Jimena, his wife, offers a long, passionate prayer for his safe return. ("And she sure knew how to pray," commented Don Federico de Onis, the Spanish professor.) She reminds the Lord of all the miracles He has performed, not leaving out a single one, and asks for only one more—that her husband be returned to her safe and sound. I wrote the piece as a gesture of gratitude to Don Federico, who had allowed me to sit in on his classes in medieval Spanish poetry. I couldn't find an alto to record the song, and so I used the voice of our friend David Jackson McWilliams, a high tenor, while I played the harpsichord accompaniment. We delivered the recording to Don Federico on his birthday. In later years I would arrange the piece for soprano, chorus, and organ, and for symphony orchestra, which is the way it was performed at many concerts.

Don Federico had come to Puerto Rico after his retirement from the Spanish Department at Columbia University in New York. He had graduated many years earlier from Salamanca University in Spain, where he had studied under the great author and philosopher Miguel de Unamuno. He often mentioned the fact that at the graduation ceremonies at Columbia he always marched first in the academic procession "because I came from a university that was founded more than four hundred years before Columbia existed!" In addition to Spanish literature, he was passionately interested in folk music, and while in New York he recorded a great collection of folk music of Spain and Latin America sung and played for him by members of the Latin community in the city. One of the singers was Federico García Lorca, the Spanish poet and dramatist. The recordings were made on plastic (wax) discs. When Don Federico came to Puerto Rico, he brought the discs with him with the intention of donating the collection to the University of Puerto Rico. But before doing so, he wanted to have all the discs transferred to tape. I was interested in the music too and offered to do the re-recording for him.

We arranged to meet several times a week at my house to make tape copies of all

Educational poster designed by Irene Delano and produced by her graphics workshop for the Division of Community Education, Puerto Rico. Silkscreen, 1949.

Poster designed by Irene for the Division of Community Education, Puerto Rico. Silkscreen, 1949.

the discs—for him, for me, and for the government radio station, WIPR. He would arrive with his charming wife, Doña Harriet, and a stack of discs under his arm. Irene prepared refreshments, and we would spend the evening recording the songs and listening to Don Federico's comments. There was one song that particularly interested him—a *velorio*—a song for the wake of a dead child, who would surely go to heaven as an angel. It was sung by a Puerto Rican woman from the town of Patillas. To a doleful melody the woman sang:

> The mother wept, the mother wept,
> the child died, the child died.
> Weep no more, mother, weep no more.
> Look, you're getting his wings wet with your tears.
> The child died for want of a doctor,
> the neighbors went to fetch him.
> The doctor arrived as far as the steps,
> as far as the steps he came,
> and the child was dead.

Don Federico knew a lot about folk music, but he did not know musical notation, so he asked me to transcribe the melody. With him sitting beside me at the piano and disputing every note when I played it for him, we finally reached an agreement about the melody that the woman sang. The music and words were later published in an article Don Federico wrote for the quarterly magazine of the Institute of Puerto Rican Culture. We saw Don Federico and Doña Harriet frequently. We admired them both and considered them our friends. Later, we were horribly shocked to learn that Don Federico, fearing that he had an incurable disease, had shot himself. Doña Harriet could not bear to live without him. About a year later, she invited many of her friends to a party at her house. She greeted us cheerfully and we didn't realize it was to be her farewell party—the next morning she was found dead of an overdose of pills.

Some of what I learned from Don Federico bore fruit in my next musical work, *La Bruja de Loíza* (The Witch of Loíza). Ana García, the director of the repertory company Ballets de San Juan, knew of my interest in Puerto Rican folklore and asked me to compose the music for a ballet based on a folktale recorded by Ricardo Alegría in the predominantly black town of Loíza. The story, probably of African origin, is about a beautiful girl who "takes off her skin" at night while her lover is asleep and turns into a horrible witch, to spend the night in a frenzy of wild dancing. At daybreak she returns to put on her "beautiful skin" before her lover awakes. There was no money for an orchestra, so I was asked to write the piece for two pianos. In this version, it was recorded for the Institute of Puerto Rican Culture and issued as a commercial disc. The piece is full of Caribbean rhythms and sounded much better several years later when I was able to arrange it for full symphony orchestra.

In 1955 Pablo Casals, the world-famous musician, paid his first visit to Puerto Rico. Casals had fled to France from Barcelona after the Spanish Civil War and had been living in the town of Prades, where an annual music festival was held in his name. Many friends, including the violinist Alexander Schneider, had urged him to come to the island, the birthplace of his mother, and perhaps establish a Casals Festival in San Juan. The person perhaps most responsible for his visit was his Puerto Rican student, Martita Montañéz. Doña Inés was immediately aware of the importance of having Casals on the island, and she arranged for me to do a documentary film of his visit. So there I was, on the docks of San Juan with my 35mm newsreel camera, filming Casals coming down the gangplank of the liner *Isle de France* to be greeted by a multitude of friends and admirers, including Doña Inés.

Words of wisdom from Pablo Casals, in 1962.

Posters of the Division of Community Education, produced by Irene's graphic workshop, pasted on the outside of a farmer's house.

Above: Plate from Tomás Blanco's book *Los Aguinaldos del Infante*, designed and illustrated by Irene. Silkscreen, 1954. This book was a by-product of a radio program that I produced.

Left: Plate from *Los Aguinaldos del Infante*. Silkscreen, 1954.

Don Pablo was at first not at all interested in having a film made. He had apparently been involved in an unfortunate experience with lights and cameras in France and didn't want anything to do with films. But I explained that I, too, was a musician and understood his concerns. Doña Inés also urged him to consent. He finally agreed when I promised to do the camera work myself, as inconspicuously as possible. Every day I would call his apartment and find out his schedule for the day from Martita, who was acting as his secretary. I planned to film all his daily activities in Puerto Rico—answering mail, going for walks, attending concerts and receptions, going sight-seeing, and so on—and then edit the material after he left. We got along well and he was quite cooperative, until one day we reached a crisis.

It was all very well to follow Casals around with a little portable camera, but how can one do a film about Casals without the sound of him playing the cello? We knew that he liked to spend the weekends at a government-owned guest house on the beach, so I assembled a crew of technicians who had worked with me at the Division of Community Education and we set up our sound equipment in the house—microphones, recorders, cables, cameras, and, of course, lights. After everything was in place, the crew and I sat around a little table on the beach waiting for Casals to come out. He greeted us warmly and sat down at the table next to me. "You know," he said, taking a puff on his pipe, "I have something to say to you. I have been watching you work and I don't understand what you are doing. To tell the truth, I think *you* don't understand what you are doing either." I knew him well enough by then not to take offense and realized he was trying to tell me something important. "Look," he continued, "I have heard some of your music and I know you have some understanding of musical form, of the structure of a musical work, its architecture, the interrelationships of themes, the beginning, the middle, and the end. Well, *in films it's the same thing.*" And he repeated, "In films it's the same thing. Now here on the table is some paper and a pencil. I want you to write out for me a brief outline of how this film is to be constructed, how it begins, how it develops, and how it ends. Then we'll know where we're heading. I'm going in for a little siesta now. When I come out, I'll look at what you've done and if it's all right we'll go right ahead, but if it's not all right we might as well stop right now and we'll still be friends." Faced with such an ultimatum, I realized that he was perfectly right. I sat down to write, my mind cleared of doubts, and in ten minutes I had an outline for the film. When he came out, he looked at it, slapped the table, and said, "Good! Now we can go ahead." We never had another problem after that.

I have since come to believe that what he said about music and films is true of all works of art. There seem to be some basic rules of composition—order, balance, contrast, tension, climax, resolution—that apply equally to every work of art, whether it be a poem, a film, a painting, a photograph, a play, a piece of sculpture, a symphony, or a cathedral. (What is the Taj Mahal if not a symphony in marble?)

The documentary, *Pablo Casals en Puerto Rico*, was made on 35mm black and white film. Because we had no equipment for editing 35mm film (all of our films at the division were 16mm), I went to New York, rented a fully equipped editing room at 1600 Broadway, and edited the film myself. When it was finished, several copies were made in 16mm. Don Pablo was about seventy-five years old at the time, and every subsequent year, he liked to have the film shown at his birthday party. On his ninety-second birthday, he said to me after watching the film, "How nice it is to see myself in those days when I was young and full of vigor!" The closing scene shows Casals walking along the beach, looking out toward the sea, as we hear his voice declaring his intention to return to Puerto Rico and organize an annual music festival in San Juan. The film can now be seen by the general public at the Pablo Casals Museum in San Juan.

While working on the Casals film, I was also doing a cartoon of social satire, under the pseudonym of Joaquín, for a weekly English-language newspaper called the *Island Times*. The cartoons were often used to fill the entire front page and sometimes used in a smaller size, as part of a series called "Signs of the Times." I continued to produce a cartoon every week from 1955 to 1968, sometimes finishing a drawing at five o'clock in the morning to meet a deadline.

The Department of Education had for years been operating a radio station, WIPR. In the early days, the programs were recorded on discs and delivered by messenger to local stations for broadcast. By 1955 the government had applied to the Federal Communications Commission for a license to operate an educational television station. Just before the station was to begin broadcasting, I was offered the job of assistant program director. On the eve of Epiphany, an important holiday in Puerto Rico, January 5, 1957, Governor Muñoz pressed a switch in the control room of the station, and the first program went on the air.

Casals kept his word and returned to Puerto Rico in

One of my cartoons from the newspaper the *Island Times*.

Plate from *The Conquest and Settlement of the Island of Boriquén or Puerto Rico* by Captain Gonzalo Fernández de Oviedo y Valdés. Irene and I prepared these illustrations for the Limited Editions Club of Avon, Connecticut. Silkscreen, 1975.

Above: Plate from *The Emperor's New Clothes*, illustrated by Irene and me, and published by Random House in 1971.

Left: Plate from *The Emperor's New Clothes*.

Photographic Memories

1956. With the full support of Muñoz and Doña Inés, the first Casals Festival was organized by the government's Industrial Development Company, the only agency empowered to take such action without waiting for new legislation. When the Casals Festival Orchestra was organized, the finest musicians of the world came to join it because Don Pablo was to be the conductor. The musical world was shocked when he suffered a heart attack at the first rehearsal and could not go on. Alexander Schneider, his friend and concertmaster, took over, and the festival continued. Once the government TV station was on the air, it was decided that all the Casals Festival concerts would be broadcast.

I happened to be the only person at the station who was trained to read an orchestral score, so it fell upon me to direct the broadcasts of the concerts on television. At the first broadcast, when I asked a cameraman for a close-up of the first horn and was given a shot of a trumpet player picking his nose, I realized that the cameramen and other technicians were not at all familiar with symphonic music and didn't know one instrument from another. I had to teach them to identify the various instruments and to locate them in the orchestra. The first recordings were made on Kinescope using 16mm film. Later we received our first videotape recorder. It was a monstrous machine that used radio tubes and had to be kept in a special air-conditioned room. It recorded on two-inch tape.

Directing a Casals Festival television broadcast with technicians of station WIPR-TV, Channel 6.

Casals rehearsing in the studio of WIPR-TV during a recording session for CBS.

A woman and child aboard a train near Lajas, Puerto Rico, in 1946. Photograph by me (train series).

Passengers aboard a train near Mayagüez, Puerto Rico, in 1946. Photograph by me (train series).

Don Pablo recovered from his heart attack and went on to conduct and play at subsequent concerts. To be thoroughly familiar with the music, I often went to rehearsals with a score and my Nikon camera to watch him conduct and sometimes to take photographs. I knew him quite well and took every opportunity to photograph him. (Several of my photographs were used on the covers of the Casals Festival programs.) Irene and I sometimes visited him at his home. Once we came with the painter and photographer Ben Shahn, who had come to Puerto Rico with his wife to spend a month vacationing at our house. Don Pablo did not know that Ben was recognized as a great American painter, and when they were introduced, he said, "Oh, so you paint, do you? Well, let me show you this book a friend just gave me, about a really great American painter." The book was about the work of Andrew Wyeth.

The Columbia Broadcasting System (CBS) sent a television crew to Puerto Rico to do a program about Casals. They needed a studio in which to record him playing the cello, and so they rented our sound studio for the purpose. The young woman producer of the program asked Casals if he would please say something about the music to introduce the work he would play. He said he would prefer not to. She persisted and became annoyed. Finally she said, "But we just did a program with Segovia, the guitarist, and he spoke about the music." Casals replied, "No, no, young lady. I don't talk about music. I make music. Now, if you would like me to talk about *peace*, I'd be glad to." "No, thank you," she said, and walked away in a huff. And that was the end of that.

Our house was not far from the University of Puerto Rico, where the Casals Festival concerts were then held. Sometimes, after a concert, musicians would come to the house for drinks and to socialize. The house came to be known as a place where all sorts of artistic activities took place. A friend of ours who was studying to play the bagpipes decided that our house was the perfect place to practice. (He had been banished from his own neighborhood.) One day I found him marching up and down on the terrace in his kilt, to the thunderous blast of his bagpipes, while a ballet dancer was practicing in another part of the house and a fashion photographer was taking some shots of models in wedding gowns on the lawn.

My work at the TV station was not limited to the Casals Festival broadcasts. As assistant program director, I was responsible for all the programming—news, a children's program, dramas, opera, interviews, and strictly instructional programs. I arranged for Don Federico to do a series of thirteen programs about *Don Quijote*, which he had taught so successfully at the university. I promised him that I would direct the programs myself. He was an extraordinary teacher and had the gift of being able to mesmerize his audience. We recorded all his programs on videotape. One evening I was watching him at home on TV when we had some guests from the States in the house.

They were so spellbound by his personality that they remained glued to the image on the screen through the entire half-hour program, although they understood not a word of Spanish.

In addition to programming, I had not given up writing music. I continued to compose songs, chamber music, orchestral pieces, and ballets in my spare time, which usually meant on weekends or at five o'clock in the morning before going off to work. Irene was not idle either. She gave birth to a beautiful baby girl we named Laura. Early mornings seemed the most appropriate time for me to copy out parts of some of my music. It was very quiet, I was unmolested, and everyone was asleep. Everyone, that is, except Laura and her mother.

For several months now, all this work had been building up a feeling of frustration in both Irene and me. We were becoming touchy and sensitive about inconsequential matters. One morning at about five-thirty I was sitting at my table correcting the parts for some complicated orchestral music when Irene appeared in the doorway in her nightgown, holding the baby and saying, "Would you mind warming up the baby's bottle that's in the refrigerator?" Furious at being interrupted, and oblivious to the fact that Irene was just as frustrated as I with all her work, managing the house, and looking after the children, I thought only of my own immediate, vexing problem. Boiling over with exasperation, I blurted out, "I didn't get up at this hour to get the baby's bottle!" She was shocked. It was the first time I had ever spoken to her in anger. Surprised by my own fit of temper, I meekly went to warm the baby's bottle and then returned to work on the music, overcome by a feeling of shame for my ridiculous outburst.

Another time my work was interrupted when a tremor went through the house and the hanging lamp over my table began swinging like a pendulum. Suddenly Irene appeared naked in the doorway, saying, "What in the hell is going on?" "I think it's an earthquake," I replied softly, so as not to wake the children. "Well, aren't you going to *do* something?" she shouted at me.

The earthquake produced no serious consequences, but another shock, shortly afterward, really shook me up—with good results. I was offered a trip around the world with all expenses paid! I don't know how it happened, but UNESCO became interested in the social programs taking place in Puerto Rico and the role that our TV station was playing. Many people from all parts of the world, on fellowships from UNESCO, had visited the Division of Community Education to explore the possibility of applying its methods in their own countries. I was offered a fellowship to study the educational techniques used by TV stations in Asia and Europe and to see how they could be applied to Puerto Rico. In February 1960 I set off for a ninety-day trip around the world under the auspices of UNESCO.

Above: Directing some kids in my film *Los Peloteros*, 1952.

Left: In this scene from *Los Peloteros*, I played a priest.

27.

Around the World in Ninety Days

My first destination was Tokyo. It was a long, long journey. From San Juan we went to New York, then to Los Angeles, then to Honolulu (how different the airport was from my previous trip during the war), and then to Tokyo. The office of UNESCO had arranged for my stay at the Dai-Ichi hotel. Here is an excerpt from one of my first letters to Irene:

> February 4th:
> Have done nothing today except catch up on sleep and go for walks. The first thing that struck me here was the *size* of things: everything seems scaled down a little to the size of the Japanese people. The cars are smaller, the houses, the doorways etc. Here in my room the chairs are lower, the wash basin is lower and the bathtub is just the right size for Pablito.

> February 5th:
> We went over for a short visit to NHK, the Japanese equivalent of the BBC. What a huge enterprise it is! Ultramodern studios and equipment (all made in Japan, of course), a huge music hall for television and radio concerts and Radio Japan, which sends short wave radio broadcasts to the whole world in dozens of different languages. The technicians wore natty uniforms and everything seemed to work with perfect precision.

My hosts, representatives of the Commission for UNESCO of Japan, took me for a prolonged visit to the TV studios and to meet with producers, actors, and writers. In one studio, a production of Shakespeare's *The Taming of the Shrew* was under way, and in another, a puppet show for children was being produced. I was told that the studio and its repertory group of actors were devoted exclusively to the production of programs for children. In addition to the TV programs, I went to see the extraordinary productions of live theater at the Kabuki theater, the Noh theater, and the puppet theater (Banruku).

Photographic Memories

From a letter to Irene:

Imagine going to a puppet theater with a capacity of 1500 people at 12 noon and finding the place sold out! I finally managed to find a seat at the last minute. The show is done on a regular theater size stage and the puppets are very large. (These are hand puppets, not marionettes.) Each puppet is handled by three people in black and they are visible on stage. But the whole production is so compelling that you forget about them and are aware only of the puppets. (I took some pictures which I'll send you.)

In the city of Utsunomia, I was taken to a school where a group of youngsters was meeting to discuss community problems much as rural people in Puerto Rico did through the Division of Community Education. Then I visited a showing of a UNESCO-sponsored TV special program for young people who work for a living. There were about ten kids between the ages of sixteen and twenty assembled in the large but freezing-cold library of a school.

At a Japanese-style guest house in the town of Utsunomia during a UNESCO fellowship trip to study educational techniques used by television stations.

This is what I wrote to Irene:

It was 8 o'clock in the evening. The teacher had just started the little pot-bellied stove in the middle of the room and was heating up a kettle of tea. We were welcomed in (three people from the Department of Education and me) and seated with the kids in a semi-circle around the stove (we kept our coats on). The TV set was on a table, alongside. The subject of the evening's program was "The Apprenticeship System of Japan" and how it affects young people. It was obvious that the kids were very absorbed as they watched. In his introduction the narrator talked about the traditional system of apprenticeship and how young people often suffer in so many ways. He showed a film of a young boy who works in a "sushi" restaurant. It would be years before he can be a "sushi" maker in his own right. In the meantime he does all the hard work, all the cleaning up. He works a 12 hour day and sleeps in a little room over the restaurant and gets one day off a month. He earns $11.12 a *month* but gets his food and lodging free. Another film showed a carpenter's apprentice in the same circumstances. In the next part of the program the commentator interviewed the same two boys. They spoke frankly about themselves and their work. . . .

After the program we sat sipping our tea and discussing the subject with the group. Almost all the kids faced situations similar to those shown in the film. The discussion was on a high plane of understanding and had the kind of humor only poor people have about their own misery.

I spent a month in Japan, not only meeting with people in educational television (and exchanging the mandatory greeting cards) but also taking advantage of my stay to visit museums, galleries, and shrines, as well as do a little shopping, which gave me a bit of insight into a culture that was new to me. Walking against the biting wind on a crooked side street, I found a tiny shoe store where I thought I could warm up a little and perhaps get a pair of sandals for Pablo. It was bitterly cold inside, and the place was heated only by a small charcoal brazier. The first thing the old woman attendant did was to bow and offer me a cup of hot tea. Then she gestured for me to look around and choose what I wanted, while she sat sipping her tea. When I had made my choice, she showed me samples of the beautiful little colored straps for the sandals, for me to choose the ones I preferred. Then, with another bow she offered me more tea while she fastened the straps to the sandals. Next, she wrapped my purchase in beautiful wrapping paper. Then, as I was leaving, she bowed again and presented me with a lovely decorated fan as a parting gift. I had never been treated so royally in any store before!

After Tokyo my next stop was to be All-India Radio in New Delhi. After an overnight stay in Hong Kong, I arrived in Calcutta and was received at the airport by the director of the local radio station. Driving though the streets of the city to his offices, I was appalled by the poverty and filth everywhere. As we tried to force our way through the busy streets seething with humanity, meandering cows and goats blocked our path. Our car was mobbed by beggars, crippled and maimed. People with outstretched hands swarmed over us, holding mutilated children, wailing pitifully for alms. Our driver responded by shouting and beating them back with vicious blows of a stick and the incessant sounding of his horn. I was glad to leave the next day for New Delhi.

From a letter to Irene:

February 26, 1960, New Delhi

I walked around the streets today to get acquainted with this place. What a poverty stricken place this is!—It glares at you even in this "modern" capital city. Talk about economic problems! It reminds me a little bit of our visit to Haiti. Remember the Iron Market where even old bottles and empty tin cans were for sale? Well, it's a little like that here, where scraps of paper and bits of string are important economic assets. And everything seems to be going to pieces—the clothes people wear, the cars, the street cars, the buildings, everything. Maybe I am so aware of all this because of just having come from Japan where everything was so efficient and clean and organized and booming. Where the Japanese seemed so correct and precise the Indians seem like lovable *schlumps*. The ones I have met so far love to laugh, to converse, to argue endlessly, to do all sorts of things at the same time—all of them not quite right—and to have tea. . . .

Yesterday I called All-India Radio to inform them of my arrival. The secretary of the Director General sounded a little surprised, didn't know anything about me or UNESCO but said he would inform the Director General and call me later. He did not call, so I went over and just presented myself. After lots of telephone calls from the reception desk, I was finally received by a beautiful, cultured lady who was in charge of "P." Again I had to explain who I was and what I wanted. More phone calls and conversations in Hindi and finally she said that Mr. Mathur, the Director General, had been called away for an important meeting. But he was *very* anxious to meet me and would be back at 5 o'clock. In the meantime, would I like to meet the gentleman in charge of experimental television? Yes, I would.

From this gentleman, I learned that they broadcast only one hour on Tuesdays and Fridays. A dance rehearsal was in progress when he took me into their tiny studio (the only one). The dancers and singers were wonderful but the technical equipment was pathetic. They had practically no money and no staff to work with but lots of enthusiasm. Volunteer assistants were plentiful, getting in each other's way. They were a motley crew dressed in every conceivable kind of costume, from bearded Sikhs in turbans to students in long white robes. At 7 o'clock in the evening, we watched the program go on the air. There was a half-hour comedy-farce followed by spectac-

In India a whole village is enthralled by a television program. From a letter to my son, Pablo.

ular folk-dancing. Then came a 10 minute film to give time for changing sets. A short illustrated talk followed about the nutritional value of vegetables, and the program ended with more folk-dancing. I asked how many TV sets there were in New Delhi and was told 150! A few of the sets were used by community centers in some of the villages, where children and their parents would gather to watch programs on health, agriculture and the importance of good manners while standing in line for a bus! I watched one of these village broadcasts and noticed that among the audience were three peacocks and several monkeys in the trees and on the nearby rooftops, all spellbound by the flickering image on the TV screen.

One morning I came into the hotel restaurant for breakfast and noticed a couple of familiar faces at an adjoining table. Sure enough, they were a man and his wife whom I knew as neighbors in Puerto Rico. What were they doing in India? Following the trail of a famous Hindu guru, that's what.

I could not be in India without going to see the Taj Mahal. In a shared rented car, two Australian tourists and I drove the 350 miles to the city of Agra, site of the great architectural gem. In a letter to Irene I wrote:

28 Feb. 1960. India

Dearest:

Well, I have seen it and now I can die in peace. Today I went to see the Taj Mahal and it far exceeded my wildest expectations. In spite of what I had been told and what I had read, I was not prepared for the shock of anything so beautiful. I am quite incapable of even trying to describe it, but just to sit there and contemplate its exquisite perfection is almost all that one can bear. The only time I have had the same sort of feeling about a work of art was the first time I saw Giotto's murals in Assisi. It doesn't seem to be a manmade thing at all, but rather like a wondrous thing of nature—a great waterfall or a perfect tree.

Having been to a concert of traditional Hindu music in New Delhi, I became interested in some of its effects. On my free evenings in my room at the Janpath Hotel, I had been working on a sonata for solo violin. Now I wrote the slow movement based on the kind of drone, so characteristic of much Hindu music, that I had heard at the concert.

I would have liked to stay longer, but my schedule allowed me to spend only a week in India, so on March 28 I set out for Rome on a night flight that took nine hours, with stops in Karachi and Beirut. On March 9, I wrote to Irene:

I arrived in Rome at 10:30 a.m. and found a message for me at the airport saying that a room had been reserved for me at the Hotel d'Inghilterra by Madame Peronetto, the head of the Italian Commission for UNESCO. By the time I cleared customs, drove into the city, got to the hotel and registered it was one o'clock. I had intended calling UNICEF but was told that office hours were from 10 to 1 and 3:30 to 7:30! . . . Promptly at 3:30 I called and was told that Madam Peronetto had not arrived yet. At 7:00 I called again but there was no answer. . . . Naturally I don't expect people to drop everything just because I am here but I had hoped that by arriving in the morning I would have the afternoon to get together with the UNESCO people and work out a program. But maybe I have been spoiled by the Japanese who had a typewritten tentative schedule waiting for my approval when I checked in at the hotel in Tokyo.

I had been running short of funds while in New Delhi, and now in Rome I was becoming desperate. I was to receive another payment on my fellowship when I arrived at the offices of UNESCO in Paris, but in the meantime I had to be very careful with my expenses. My ticket for the entire trip had already been paid for, but in my letters to Irene I sounded in dire need of money. "I arrived in Rome with only $80.00 in travellers checks! Then to cable you cost $9.00!" I was worried that I would not be able to pay my bill at the Hotel d'Inghilterra. "The hotel here is $7.50 a day, without meals. I'm going to see if I can find a cheaper place." And then, "I'm afraid I'm going to have to ask you to send me another $50.00, I guess we must still have a couple of hundred dollars in savings you can draw on. (I hope!)" I am by nature a great worrier, and saw myself rotting away in an Italian prison for nonpayment of bills, but nothing dire occurred. Finally, "There was just a knock on the door and your cable was delivered telling me that you had sent the money. Thank you, baby."

When I finally got through to the people at UNESCO, they were extremely helpful. They arranged for me to visit the studios of RAI (the official Italian radio and television service). After the well-intentioned but primitive attempts at TV production in India, what a shock it was to walk into the immense facilities of RAI! I wrote to Irene:

> Two of their projects are very impressive indeed: the dramas and their "telescuola" (read tele-escuela)—once a month they put on a full drama from the classics—Moliere, Shakespeare, Pirandello, etc. I attended a rehearsal of one of the plays and was amazed at the amount of care, preparation, detail, and work put into the production. Each play is rehearsed for *three weeks* (full time) and toward the end of that period (the last 5 or 6 days) they rehearse *with cameras!* Each shot, each step, each line of dialog is worked over as in a film. . . .
>
> The "telescuola" is run by a very dynamic woman who had been a schoolteacher. Now she is in charge of all the planning, production and evaluation of these school programs. . . . (I saw a magnificent production of Sophocles' "Antigone"). . . . "Telescuola" is a complete 3 year junior high school course available to all those who have finished grammar school and have, for any number of reasons, not been able to continue. The students follow this course not in school but in clubs, community centers, etc., wherever 20 or so of them can get together. I am told there are about 2,000 such groups following the course—roughly 90,000 students. I think Inés would be interested in this project and I'm collecting all the material I can for her.

There was an American woman working at UNESCO who was running sort of a Division of Community Education project in the Abruzzi Mountains. But the project had no materials production unit and had to depend on whatever films, books, and graphics could be borrowed from other agencies. She had been in Puerto Rico and admired the work of the division and was eager for me to visit the project, which was sponsored by UNESCO. Furthermore, in a letter from the office of UNESCO in Paris, I was specifically asked to visit the project and study what was being done. It would be a five-hour trip to the town of Abruzzi, so I arranged to go and spend the night there and come back the next day. I later wrote to Irene:

> There was only one train from Rome and it left at 6:20 a.m. I left a call at the hotel desk for 5 a.m. and warned the clerk several times to be sure and call me. But I was worried he wouldn't call so I kept waking up every hour during the night. Suddenly I awoke and saw by my watch that it was a quarter to six. They *hadn't* called. I got my

things together without bothering to shave and dashed down the stairs. The desk clerk was half asleep. He greeted me with a surprised "Buon giorno!" "Why didn't you call me?" I asked. "Oh, yes. Well, I just forgot. But you're up now so what's the difference." "But I didn't sleep all night waiting for your call," I protested. "Oh, you shouldn't have done that," he said, and seemed genuinely sorry. "Why didn't you come down here if you couldn't sleep, and keep me company playing cards. You know it gets awfully lonely being behind this desk alone all night long." So—how could I be angry with a man like that? Anyhow, he got me a cab that drove me to the railroad station—in the rain.

There were no restaurants open at that hour and no diner on the train so breakfast had to wait. The station where I had to get off was quite high in the mountains—the second highest railroad station in Europe, the first being in the Brenner Pass in Switzerland. We began climbing as soon as we left Rome on the express train. Soon the snow-covered mountains began to appear. At a town called Sulmona we changed to another train, a one-car mountain-climbing train. In about six hours after leaving Rome we arrived at our destination, the station for the two towns of Pezcoconstanza and Rivizondoli. As soon as I opened the door to my compartment, the icy wind penetrated to my very bones. Only two passengers got off here, an elderly blond lady and I. Both of us were bound for the special UNESCO project and a car had been sent to meet us. The lady was Polish and also spoke some French and Italian. My English and Spanish were incomprehensible to her, so there wasn't much conversation as we bounced along in the ancient, unheated Fiat that looked like it had once been a taxi. . . .

As we drove into the main square I felt as if I were entering one of those good Italian films. Here were those wonderful faces of the Italian peasants, the women in black with their heads wrapped in shawls, the cobblestoned streets that went either up or down, the fountain in the square with young girls drawing water and the ruins of the buildings on all sides—monuments to the war

The headquarters of the UNESCO project was just off the main square. I was greeted warmly by Florita Botts, the American lady in charge of the project, and she turned me over to Miss Zuconni, head of the Social Workers School here. From her I learned that this project is modeled after the Division of Community Education and both she and Miss Botts had been in Puerto Rico to study the work of the Division. . . . At 6:30 I was taken to a "teleclub" where youngsters were going to see a television program. The teleclub was in a monastery. A little hunch-backed monk, his face and hands purple with cold, showed us through the bleak, echoing halls to the "centro sociale." A television set on a high stand faced a low-ceilinged bare room where the only furniture was a series of rough wooden benches.

. . . Soon a gang of boisterous youngsters came bouncing in. One of the boys switched on the TV set and and they settled down to see the show—"Fathers and

Sons" by Turgenev. This was a dramatization of the famous book, prepared by RAI in the Rome studios. The kids sat spellbound through the program. I later learned from the social worker that they have a reading circle in which the same youngsters are reading and discussing the book. . . . After dinner at the only hotel in town I was invited to a showing of a film at the UNESCO center. Imagine my surprise when the film turned out to be "Los Peloteros"! They had prepared an Italian translation of the film and at appropriate places, they lowered the sound track and read the Italian translation.

. . . I couldn't help thinking how wonderful it was that here in this tiny Italian village, high up among the snow-covered mountains, thousands of miles from Puerto Rico, people could still laugh at the antics of the kids in the circus scenes and enjoy the film from beginning to end. When it was announced that I was the director of the film, I was pelted with questions about Puerto Rico. Why wasn't the film commercially released? Were the kids professionals? Was there a film industry in Puerto Rico? etc.

The next day I returned to my hotel in Rome to find that the money Irene had sent me had arrived. No more worries about going to jail. On March 19, my work in Italy complete and the memory of my success in Abruzzi still fresh in my mind, I left for Paris.

Pierre Navaux, of UNESCO headquarters in Paris, met me at the airport, took me to my hotel, and, almost immediately, to his house for dinner. (Pierre was one of the two people I had met in Puerto Rico who arranged for my fellowship.) I met his wife, their two delicious children, and an Indian filmmaker and his wife (friends from UNESCO). The dinner was great—*paella valenciana,* in my honor. Pierre told me that he had taken the liberty of arranging for me to give a lecture on my trip at UNESCO. (Now I'm a lecturer!) The next day I saw some of the films the Indian filmmaker had produced. They were not very good, and when I voiced some mild criticisms, he smiled and said, "How can you make a film that has to be approved by eighty-two countries?"

At a business lunch with Henry Casirer—the other person responsible for arranging my fellowship—we made plans for the rest of my stay in Europe. It was decided that I would spend a few days in Paris, then go to London for a week, then return to Paris before going back to Puerto Rico.

From a letter to Irene dated March 23:

Well, I gave my lecture today. It went off quite well. The material I had accumulated on the trip was so voluminous that it was a bit of a job to boil it down to a short talk. I had also brought with me a Kinescope of one of the Japanese programs. It was in

Japanese of course but that was no problem here at UNESCO. They simply got a young Japanese interpreter to provide a translation into French while the film was being shown. (I had spoken in English.) Since my audience was composed of people who spoke either French, English or Japanese the only person who did not understand the film was I!

A few days later I was shocked to receive a cable from Irene in my room at the hotel. It read simply: "Dearest Pop died in his sleep. They are burying him today Sunday. Love love Irene." He had been living in retirement in Miami, Irene was in Puerto Rico, my brother was in New York, and I was in Paris. I could not possibly arrive in time for the funeral and had to leave the arrangements in the hands of my brother and Irene's mother.

Here is the letter I wrote to Irene:

Darling: Got up this morning to find your cable about Pop's death under my door. You can imagine how I felt. Poor, sweet little man—how much he suffered and how lost and bewildered he was. The news was of course an awful shock to me but really not altogether a surprise. I suppose that in the back of my mind all along on this trip was the fear that it might happen while I was away. But then I've been traveling with my share of fears and worries for all of you—wondering about the things you don't put in letters.

How did you learn about it? Did your mother wire or phone? Was Solly [my brother] able to get there? Had Pop had another attack or what? Where is Mom now? Your mother must have had quite a time on her hands. I can see that Mom would be quite helpless under the circumstances. I keep seeing Pop—lonely even on his death bed. No wake for him—no friends, no family. Just Mom, and your mother.

I feel so far away and so useless here. Please write, dearest.

Love.

My father had never been able to adjust completely to being a factory worker or even a laborer in his own shop. He always yearned for the company of musicians, writers, and other people with whom he could discuss music, literature, and politics. He expressed some of these yearnings in letters to us, always in the neat schoolteacher script that he never lost, and sometimes in his self-taught Spanish, full of hilarious grammatical mistakes. In spite of adversity, he never lost his sense of humor. After he retired he wrote us: "It is a little monotonous for me stay idle, but it does not do me any harm. I feel very good when I think that I have nothing to do any more with customers and the upholstering business. I was offered a job for a few hours a week, but I don't want to work with a hammer again and lifting furniture. . . . Mom is in town. She went to cooking school to take a few lessons in cooking. Does she need cooking lessons? I think she can teach *them* how to cook and bake." On another occasion he wrote: "We are collecting $127.50 in Social Security, which is enough for both of us to live. . . . Darlings: I am enclosing a check for $300.00, which you will use whenever you will make up your mind to write to us. Please, do not send it back!" And from another letter: "It is now Sunday, Fathers Day. Solie [my brother] just called up to wish me a happy Fathers Day. I don't mean to remind you why you did not do the same. Positively not!"

My father, William.

My parents were always supportive of anything my brother and I did. They had no objection to the careers we had decided to pursue. On the contrary, they were willing to make any sacrifice to help us achieve our aims. Even when I decided to leave for Puerto Rico, they felt it was all for the best and asked only that I write often. As long as they had each other, they seemed quite content and self-reliant, but now with my father gone I knew my mother would not be able to stay in Florida alone. We would have to bring her to Puerto Rico to stay with us. This preoccupation weighed heavily on my conscience as I thought of the days still remaining before I could go home.

Before going off to London, I was invited out to visit a "teleclub" in a village of some three hundred families about a two-hour drive from Paris. We arrived at eight o'clock in the evening. It was cold, the streets were deserted, and only here and there did a light shine in the window of a house. We drove up to a small building that turned out to be the town hall, the schoolmaster's house, and the village school, all in one. The schoolmaster, a man in his early thirties, welcomed us in and introduced us to his wife and two teacher friends. Suddenly they all burst into guffaws of laughter. It was the first of April (April Fool's Day), and they weren't sure if our visit was just some April Fool's joke that somebody in Paris had decided to play on them! I soon learned how seriously April Fool was taken in France.

At eight-thirty, the teleclub members began to arrive and the TV set in the classroom was turned on. The program was a riot. Everything was done wrong. All possible technical errors were committed. Credit titles appeared backward, pictures came in upside down, the microphone showed in all the scenes, actors forgot their lines, directors were shown whispering instructions, and strange people kept stepping in front of the camera, always with a sudden awareness of the audience and an embarrassed "Oh! Pardon!" But best of all was a series of parodies of their own serious programs: a dramatization of *Camille* in the style of the worst soap opera, an excited sports announcer showing a football match upside down, an interviewer sweating blood trying to interview a famous author whose only vocabulary was "Oui" and "Non." (The title of his famous book was *Oui et Non*.) It was all very funny and we nearly died of laughter. There was supposed to be a discussion afterward, but nobody was going to discuss *that* program, so we talked about Puerto Rico and France. After the audience left, the teachers wanted to talk some more, so I stayed on. They were intelligent and highly motivated people. Their fathers had been teachers and probably their fathers' fathers too. This gave them an assurance and confidence that was admirable. I enjoyed them immensely. We talked and talked far into the night and I got back to the hotel at four in the morning.

I had been told that because of my interest in music I must not leave Paris without visiting the studios of RDF, the French national TV network, where they were working on what they called *musique concrète*. This is what I wrote to Irene about my visit:

> As you know, this stuff is quite the rage in Europe now and is used often in films. It is, of course, nothing more than the experimental "tape music" I worked on years ago, carried to fantastic lengths. This "concrete" seems to me to be neither "music" nor "concrete." The young men working in the studios have every imaginable sort of gadget at their disposal for distorting simple musical sounds into completely unrecognizable forms. In this they succeed admirably. What comes out has no relation to *musical* sounds, though there is no denying that they are *sounds*, usually ear-splitting ones. The high priest of this movement is even working on a system of identifying sounds on punched IBM cards so that some day you will be able to feed the cards into a sort of UNIVAC and presto! out comes a musical composition. It's all very scientific-mathematical, you see. (Shades of our old friend Jonathan Swift!) The best I can say for it is that it produces some sensually interesting effects of the sort the movies have taught us to associate with horror films, visitors from Mars and other science fiction.

I suppose I should add, looking back on that experience, that I am not against innovation or technological experimentation with music. But what I heard there was terribly imitative (everybody using the same weird sounds) and although intellectually interesting, emotionally not very satisfying.

Letter to Pablo from London.

The flight from Paris to London took only an hour, but what a dramatic change in culture! For me, of course, it meant that I was in the first country of my trip where I could understand the language (although the British speech I was hearing sometimes did sound like a foreign language). In Paris I had become accustomed to the monetary system of francs, old style and new, but now I was stumped by tuppence, thruppence, shillings, and guineas. And I was fascinated by the broadcasts of the BBC.

While staying at the Royal Regent Hotel near Piccadilly Circus, I wrote to Irene:

4 April, 1960

Darling:

All the rooms at this hotel are equipped with radio direct from the studios of the BBC. I came into my room today and switched on the "Third Programme." This is what came out: ". . . my dear Ashbury, I was very fond of you, we have been friends since boyhood, I shall always be fond of you, but what you have just said is the worst, most unspeakable rot and drivel I have ever heard in my life! I should prefer to use much stronger words but they are by some strange hypocrisy forbidden on the air. . . ."

It turned out to be sort of a quiz program called "The Brains Trust." The "rot and drivel" man was trying to defend his opinion that in 100 or 200 years books will be entirely displaced by electronic devices. I heard the program to the very end because of the delightful wit and easy command of language of the three participants.

. . . Maybe I'm so struck by the facility for language because of my own chronic problem of trying to find the right words for what I want to say. . . . I shall always remember my first contact with the British facility for expression on this trip.

It was when we were about to leave Hong Kong on a British plane (BOAC). The passengers had been seated for several minutes, waiting for the plane to take off, when the steward's voice sounded over the loudspeakers: "I'm terribly sorry, ladies and gentlemen, but we seem to have a *fault* in our radio. It is being *mended* and we shall take off *shortly.*" It struck me at the time that on an American plane we would probably have heard "Ladies and gentlemen, I'm terribly sorry but there seems to be *something wrong* with our radio. It is being *fixed* and we ought to be taking off *in a little while*. . . .

And the British commentators are, I am sure, a breed apart. Describing a magnificent fireworks display I heard one of them say, "This is certainly the greatest display we have had here since the one about a hundred years ago celebrating a military victory over the French but perhaps it would be more prudent not to go into that tonight."

The British Commission for UNESCO made arrangements for me to visit the studios of the BBC. For many years, the BBC had been using remodeled old movie studios scattered all over London. Now they were moving into a new production complex designed specifically for television, with seven huge studios. The scenery workshop alone was larger than all of WIPR in San Juan. Their school broadcasts were quite different from those of France or Italy. Since the British had great regard for the independence of each school district to decide its own curriculum, there were no nationwide broadcasts of any teaching series required in all the schools. Rather, the programs were of a general educational nature, produced with the masterly technique for which the British documentary tradition is noted, and school systems would choose those programs that best suited their needs. Educational programs were produced not only by the BBC but by the independent TV (commercial) network as well. I met two young men at the independent network and talked to them about their school programming. This is what I wrote to Irene:

We had lunch together and they started off by pointing out that they were not Englishmen—one was Welsh and the other was from New Zealand, and our waiter was from Cyprus. The Welshman, who was in charge of school broadcasts, was passionate on the subject. He was convinced of the value of TV for schools but only if it is used *in addition* to the teacher. They spend a great deal of time preparing each program after having thoroughly discussed precisely what they expect the program to accomplish. In a series to stimulate the reading of books, they would dramatize a scene from the book and leave it hanging, unfinished, at the most exciting moment. The children were urged to read the book for themselves and find out how it came out in the end. The public libraries were forewarned so they were not unprepared when all over Britain children came requesting the book. . . . "You are dealing with the minds of children—a very delicate and sensitive territory, where you constantly run the risk of doing irreparable harm," he said. He was very much against using the run-of-the-mill teachers on television and preferred actors who had had some teaching experience. An "education officer" works along with the producer and director during all the preparatory work and rehearsals to ensure the correct educational point of view. . . . He kept telling me, "Whatever you do, avoid duplicating what a teacher can do. If your program can't bring the children something beyond the means of the teacher you might as well *chuck it*."

I was about ready to "chuck it" myself after being away from home almost three months, traveling more than halfway around the world, and meeting with so many people who didn't speak my language. But I still had to return to Paris for more meetings with Pierre and Henry to discuss the work I would have to do in Puerto Rico to comply with the requirements of my fellowship.

Back in Paris, I had a big, elegant office all to myself in the UNESCO building. Outside the windows was a breathtaking view of the city and the Eiffel Tower. I had the impression that the UNESCO people didn't quite know what to do with me now that all my work was practically finished. Just the same, they were determined that I should use up the ninety days called for in my contract. I wrote to Irene:

> So we sat around discussing whether I should like to visit so and so or see such and such visual education program. What I'd really like to do is *go home*. Actually, there is not much more I can accomplish here but since I am here I'll do my best to see what interests *me*. (By the way, I have yet to meet a Frenchman at UNESCO—they've all been Belgians, Englishmen, Brazilians, Mexicans, Russians, Italians, etc.)

In meetings with Pierre and Henry we did agree on the project that I would direct when I returned to Puerto Rico. The theme was to be "the effect of rapid industrialization on the Puerto Rican family." WIPR would agree to produce thirteen half-hour programs on the subject. Half of each program would be devoted to a dramatization of a problem, and the other half would consist of an interview with the people affected by the problem. For example: What happens in a male-oriented society such as that of Puerto Rico when the woman of the house earns more money working in a factory than her husband does cutting sugarcane? What effect does such a situation have on the children? On the husband's self-esteem? We discussed possible themes for the thirteen programs, and I explained that our agreements would have to be tentative, pending the approval of my superiors when I returned to the island.

There was not much to do until the date of my departure, so I did some wandering around town. To Irene I wrote:

Photographic Memories

Letter to Pablo from Paris.

It is certainly a pleasant feeling to recognize some of the familiar landmarks—l'Opéra, the Arc de Triomphe, L'Etoile, Les Invalides, le Madeleine, and others. . . . Paris is such a beautiful city and all the corny things that have been said and written about it I am sure must be true—the broad boulevards with their endless rows of trees, the delightful spacious parks, the smells of delicious pastry and men and women rushing home from work in the early evening with those long French loaves of bread in their hands, munching on a piece or two they've already bitten off. And how refreshing to stroll down the Boulevard San Michel, crowded with students from the University—boys and girls with arms around each other's waists, stopping to kiss and then to continue their conversation where they had left off, or youngsters sitting in the cafes arguing passionately about this and that.

. . . I'll be leaving all this soon for I have my reservations for New York already. I leave Paris on the 17th of April at 1 p.m. via Air France flight 0707, and should arrive in New York at 3 p.m.

(Yes, two hours later!) Of course that's local time in New York. Actually the flight is 8 hours non-stop. Incredible isn't it? To think that that's what it used to take to go from New York to Puerto Rico not so long ago.

28 · Managing a TV Station—and Political Turmoil

What a joy it was to be home again! And how wonderful to see Irene and the children! And what a surprise to walk into the house and see all the changes that Irene had made—walls knocked out, arches squared off, a second bathroom added, and so much more remodeling! She must have worked constantly with builders and contractors to finish everything before I returned.

And this was not the last remodeling the house would undergo. A few years later we added more rooms, but this time with the help of our friends, the architect Tom Marvel and his wife, Lucilla. Lucilla taught planning at the University of Puerto Rico and was the niece of Buckminster "Bucky" Fuller, the famed inventor (geodesic dome), mathematician, and all-around Renaissance man. I shall never forget the time she arranged for him to come to Puerto Rico and speak to the architects and engineers at the Puerto Rico Planning Board. The hall was filled to overflowing, everyone eager to hear what he would have to say. He was a short man, his bald head and huge eyeglasses barely visible above the rostrum. His opening words were, "Is there anyone here who can tell me how much this building weighs?" There was a hushed silence in the auditorium. Again he said, "Is there no one here who can tell me how much this building weighs?" Silence. What was he trying to say, everyone wondered. What he was trying to say soon became quite clear. Having been a naval architect in his younger days, he always knew how much his buildings weighed and how much stress they could take. He went on to give a brilliant talk, in which he compared a ship at sea to a building in a constant earthquake. He emphasized the importance of using building materials that were light but just as strong as the customarily heavy and cumbersome ones.

I didn't have much chance to enjoy my newly remodeled house because I still had a lot of work waiting for me at the TV station. My obligation to UNESCO to produce thirteen programs was part of my agreement for the fellowship. The plan for the programs as agreed in Paris with Pierre and Henry was readily approved by the general manager of the station. The program director of the station had just resigned, and I was appointed to replace him. It was now up to me to see that the thirteen programs were produced.

With a well-known dramatist as the scriptwriter and the technical staff of our news department as the production unit, filming began almost at once. We used no professional actors. Each half-hour program began with a fifteen-minute dramatization of a real situation, with real people, of some aspect of the problems created by rapid industrialization in Puerto Rican society. The second half of each program consisted of interviews with people who had actually coped with the problems. The programs were aired weekly, and the viewer response to them was excellent. A copy of the entire series was sent to UNESCO.

Just as the programs were finished, I received a plaintive letter from my mother, who was staying at a retirement home in Miami. It read in part: "I would like to go and stay with you and your dear family. I can play with the children and have a good time. In this hotel everyone is for himself. You can't make friends. . . . Please write to me and tell me if I can come to you." I went to Miami to make arrangements for bringing her to Puerto Rico. I arrived in a taxi and asked the driver to wait while I fetched my mother so he could then take us to the airport. She had packed her things and was ready to leave. I walked into the building and noticed everyone staring at me as I made my way down the hall. A nurse approached me and asked where I came from. "Puerto Rico," I replied. "Well, I suppose that explains it," she said. "You have a black cab driver, sir. We don't do that here." To think that it hadn't even occurred to me!

The little apartment in the basement of our house had been prepared for my mother, but it was very difficult to have her staying with us. Because her mind would wander, she needed constant attention, and both Irene and I were working all the time. Besides, the shock of losing her husband seemed too much for her. She was confused and frightened, and our doctor insisted that she be hospitalized.

Soon I was off on another trip, this time to New York. In 1962 Edward Steichen organized an exhibit of FSA photographs, called "The Bitter Years," at the Museum of Modern Art. It was a big show, representing the work of all the FSA photographers. I went to the opening, eager not only to see the exhibit but also to visit with Roy and the other photographers, whom I hadn't seen in a long time. Roy introduced me to Steichen, whom I had never met. When Steichen heard my name, I saw tears well up in his eyes. He embraced me tightly and kept repeating, "So you're the artist. You're the artist." I don't quite know what he meant, but it was certainly a very moving moment for me. The opening was successful and got a great deal of press coverage. The *St. Louis Post Dispatch* devoted an entire page of its Sunday rotogravure section to the show.

It was wonderful to see my friends from the FSA days—Roy, John Vachon, Russ

Photographic Memories

Friends from the FSA days, reunited in 1962. Left to right: Russell Lee, Roy Stryker, Arthur Rothstein, John Vachon, and me.

Lee, and Arthur Rothstein. After the show we all went out to a fancy restaurant and then to Arthur's studio at LOOK magazine to have a group photograph taken

I took advantage of my visit to the States to stop in at the Library of Congress and take a look at my FSA/OWI pictures. I walked into the Prints and Photographs Division of the library and introduced myself. The reaction of the young woman at the desk was as if she were seeing a ghost. Yes, I really was Jack Delano, and I really had taken all those pictures twenty years ago. (I think the young people working there thought I was dead.) When I asked to see my FSA pictures from Puerto Rico, taken in 1941, nobody knew anything about them. We looked everywhere in the FSA collection and could find nothing on Puerto Rico. At last, a young man—I think his name was Leroy Bellamy—said, "Wait a minute. I think I know where they might be. Let's look on the second floor."

Down we went to the second floor, which was covered with file cabinets labeled with the names of foreign countries, in alphabetical order. And there, lo and behold! together with Panama, Pakistan, Peru, and Portugal was *Puerto Rico*! I opened the file drawer and, sure enough, there were my precious FSA pictures. I brought the matter to the attention of Alan Fern, director of the Prints and Photographs Division, and he ordered the photographs to be transferred immediately to the main body of the FSA collection. But to think that they had lain buried there, separated from the rest of the FSA collection, in effect inaccessible to the public, for more than twenty years!

I had expected to stay in New York for a while and enjoy a vacation, but I received an urgent call from my secretary at the TV station urging me to come back as soon as possible because "things are in a mess here." It seems that some members of the opposition political party had been feeding the newspapers ridiculous rumors of subversive activities at the station. They were joined by a vociferous group of Cuban exiles because we had shown a program we received from the Public Broadcasting System called "Three Faces of Cuba." The program had been shown on PBS stations throughout the United States and had been highly praised for its objectivity, but here in Puerto Rico it aroused the ire of the Cuban exile community and I was accused of sympathizing with the Castro regime for having permitted it to be shown.

I had just been named general manager of WIPR-TV and Radio when a group of about fifteen university students of the pro-statehood party began picketing the station, carrying signs that read, "Why is a Russian directing the TV station of the government of Puerto Rico?" Other signs demanded that I resign. A young man whose contract at the radio station was not renewed alleged political discrimination because he was a member of the pro-statehood party. (The reason for the cancellation of his contract was because the program he was producing was terrible.) The newspapers carried headlines such as "American Flag Desecrated at WIPR." (We had both the American and the Puerto Rican flags displayed in the lobby of the station, where dozens of children assembled every day for our five o'clock children's program. One day it was discovered that some little vandal had snipped one of the stars out of the American flag.) A letter to the editor of a newspaper was given prominence because it complained that our station showed a lack of patriotism by ending our day's programming with a question mark after the American national anthem! I sent the paper the text of "The Star-Spangled Banner" showing the question mark after the phrase "home of the brave," but it was not printed. The newspaper *El Mundo*, in a front-page story, stated that WIPR was being investigated by the Federal Bureau of Investigation "for communist and nationalist infiltration." The police, the FBI, and the Federal Communications Commission all categorically denied that there was any such investigation under way, but the newspaper, now defunct, did not retract the story.

Incidents such as these were obviously similar to the McCarthy hysteria that had previously swept the United States. The House Un-American Activities Committee decided to come down and hold hearings in Puerto Rico. Many witnesses were called and cross-examined, but the general public seemed apathetic and indifferent to the proceedings. Many people considered the investigation an unwarranted interference of the federal government in Puerto Rican affairs. No communist plot was uncovered and nothing nefarious was revealed. A noted Puerto Rican woman lawyer made a practice of attending all the hearings wearing a flaming-red dress and sitting defiantly in the front row facing the investigators.

I was concerned about the disquieting effect that the incidents at the station might be having on the morale of the employees. The picketing never became violent, and the work of the station continued undisturbed, but the situation was nevertheless somewhat unsettling. One of the first things I did upon my return from New York was to call all of the employees of the station together to calm their fears. The meeting was held in our largest studio and was attended by the 150 employees who could leave their posts for a while. When I walked into the studio, they all stood up and greeted me with thunderous applause. I had no doubt about their complete support. We had a thorough, frank discussion of the station's problems (subversion was not one of them, everyone agreed), and the meeting ended on a hearteningly positive note. The following day, 120 employees signed a letter pledging their wholehearted support to me and delivered it to Governor Luis Muñoz Marín.

All this hoopla in the newspapers led the legislature to appoint a committee to investigate alleged subversive activities at WIPR. I was called to testify. I knew some of the legislators personally and the atmosphere was friendly. It was easy to answer all the questions to the satisfaction of the committee. The hearing ended when I stood up and sang, "Oh, say, can you see by the dawn's early light?" Then I said, "You see, gentlemen, that is a question, and in English a question always ends with a question mark." The embarrassed committee members thanked me for my testimony and that was the end of that.

Governor Muñoz, in an unprecedented move, answered the letter of the WIPR employees. His letter, which was published in the press, stated in part: "I have known friend Delano for many years and I know he deserves the backing and affection you have for him. He is a man of creative imagination and devotion to the great things we are trying to do in Puerto Rico. I consider it a privilege that a man of such qualifications should have decided to make his permanent residence among us, serving Puerto Rico with the same love and patriotism as any of us who have been born in Puerto Rico and can dedicate ourselves to that noble purpose."

The turmoil over the TV station quickly subsided and did not affect our pro-

Managing a TV Station—and Political Turmoil

gramming in the least. We continued with some new, innovative programs. One of them was called *The Magic Lantern*. With an anchor team in period costumes, it presented a weekly newsmagazine of events as reported in the newspapers and magazines of Puerto Rico fifty years earlier. Because there had been no newsreels in those days, our program was illustrated with photographs and slides, but the presentation of the "news" was done with the same snap and vigor as a news program of today. It was a lively way of delving into Puerto Rican history, and we learned that many history teachers in the schools were encouraging their students to watch the program.

Politics is taken extremely seriously in Puerto Rico, and at election time we broadcast debates among the various candidates for governor and sometimes also among those running for mayor of San Juan. At one gubernatorial debate there were four candidates. It was a historic occasion when they, political adversaries, all shook hands in our studio. At another debate, between the two candidates for mayor of San Juan, a boisterous mob shouting slogans and insults gathered in front of the station in support of one of the candidates. In spite of the presence of the police, tensions grew to such an extent that when the program was over, the other candidate had to be escorted out through the rear entrance of the station for fear of possible violence.

Governor Luis Muñoz Marín at the government's TV station, preparing to address a television audience on the subject of the annual budget.

During these election periods Doña Inés sometimes asked me to help in a rather strange capacity. When her husband, Muñoz, was campaigning he had no hesitation about speaking to crowds of thousands of listeners. He was a brilliant orator and seemed to enjoy the response of the audience. But when he had to face a television camera, alone, he became a nervous wreck. Doña Inés felt that I had a tranquilizing influence on him. If I were by his side, she felt, he would calm down and lose his fear. So whenever he had to record a political speech (at a commercial station, of course, not the government station), she insisted that I be present to help keep Muñoz under control. I felt uncomfortable in this role because I usually knew the director of the program and didn't want him to feel that I was interfering, but with a little diplomacy, I managed to do my job.

One time, Muñoz came into the TV studio to read his thirty-minute speech. We could all see that he was very nervous, and I calmly explained to him that the program was being taped and that he could stop whenever he pleased and the tape would be edited. He spoke for no more than a minute before he stopped and said, "No. No. That's no good. Let's do it again." So we did it again. And again. And again. And each time he became more and more frustrated with himself. Finally, in an act of desperation, and with tremendous fury, he threw his speech to the floor and stalked out of the studio, roaring, "Why do I have to do this? Who says I have to do this? Who gives the orders here? Who is the governor around here anyway?" In the stunned silence that followed, Doña Inés glanced at me and I knew what I had to do. I went to Muñoz and quietly explained again that we had plenty of time, that he could stop as often as he liked and that we would look at the edited tape as soon as he was finished. After he calmed down we went on with the recording. When it was finished the tape had thirty splices—one every minute. But it was expertly edited by the station's staff and came off quite well. And, Muñoz being Muñoz, he apologized sheepishly to everyone for making such a fuss.

One of the most popular programs at WIPR was our news interview show sponsored by the Puerto Rico Journalists Association. It was the first such television program in Puerto Rico. Each week a panel of journalists would subject some distinguished personality of their own choosing to a one-hour interview. The roster of people who appeared on the show was impressive. One of the first guests whom I greeted when he arrived at the studio was Ralph Bunche, the American representative at the United Nations. Then came the Rev. Martin Luther King Jr., who happened to be passing through Puerto Rico. Another person who faced the cameras and was often in the news in those days was Dr. Christiaan Barnard, the heart-transplant surgeon. James Baldwin, the well-known black novelist, was asked whether he had noticed any racial prejudice during his stay on the island. He replied, "No, but I'm sure it's there somewhere." And when Juan Bosch, the ousted president of the Dominican Republic, was about to go on the air, he received an urgent telephone call from Santo Domingo. There was no telephone in the TV studio, so I stood by him at the switchboard in the lobby as he listened to the report of his military commander describing the battle that was taking place in the streets of the city in an effort to keep the leftist government in power.

I remained as general manager of the government's radio and television service until 1969. During that time, in addition to my administrative duties—budget hearings, reclassification of jobs, construction of additional physical facilities, purchase of equipment, contracting writers and producers, and so on, all of which were tolerable duties but not creatively challenging for me—I had to keep doing some creative work to preserve my sanity. So I sometimes took part in producing and directing musical programs, including opera, theatrical shows such as Molière's plays, and documentary news programs. But what I enjoyed most was spending early mornings, late evenings, and weekends composing music.

In the city of Ponce, a new art museum was to be inaugurated, and I was asked to write a choral piece for the opening ceremonies. I selected three short poems by the poet José Balseiro. The opening line of the first poem read "Me voy a Ponce" (I'm going to Ponce), and that is what I used as the title of the piece. It is a romantic, nostalgic work written for mixed chorus, evoking the pleasures of a ride across the mountains to the city of Ponce, known as the Pearl of the South.

The young woman in charge of our record library at the radio station was an accomplished musician with a beautiful soprano voice. I had always wanted to do something on the theme of the sea, and when I found three little poems in a collection of children's literature that were evocative of the sea, I decided to write the songs and have her do the first performance. The first song was "Los Catañecitos" (The Little Ones from Cataño), referring to the little waves coming across the bay from the town of Cataño to San Juan; the second song was "¡A Navegar!" (To Sail!) about a child's sailboat; and the third was called simply "Cantarcillo Marinero" (A Little Sailor's Song). I also enjoyed setting music to four lovely poems by Tomás Blanco and titled the composition "Cuatro Sones de la Tierra" (Four Songs of the Earth).

I should add that Irene and I considered Tomás not only a gifted writer but also a close personal friend who helped us understand and appreciate the moral and cultural values of the Puerto Rican people. To make it possible for me to learn something of Puerto Rican literature, he willingly gave me Spanish lessons twice a week. When I first attempted to set some Puerto Rican poetry to music I was unsure of how to deal with Spanish words, syllables, or diphthongs. I asked him to write me a couplet to set to music and then criticize what I did. I wrote the music to his words as I would have to English poetry. When I showed it to him, he said, "That's awful! Terrible! Sit down and let me teach you something." Then he gave me a wonderful lecture on Spanish syllabification, which I have never forgotten.

Another poet for whom I had great admiration was Luis Palés Matos, mainly noted for the Afro-Antillean influence in his poems. He had been the narrator when Tomás Blanco's Epiphany story was broadcast. When he was chosen to do the narration, everyone told us that we would have trouble with him because he drank too much, never came to rehearsals on time, and was generally irresponsible. We had set up a rehearsal for him to read the story at my house one day at nine o'clock in the morning. I happened to look out from our second-story balcony at about eight-thirty, and there was Luis Palés, pacing back and forth in front of our house, waiting for it to be nine o'clock! Of course we invited him to come up right away and, while we waited for the arrival of Tomás, I asked him what he had been working on recently. "Oh, just a little poem with the title *El Llamado* [He Who Is Called]," he said. "Would you like to hear it?" When I said of course, he quietly recited the long poem while Irene and I sat in hushed silence, spellbound. In the poem he foresaw his own death. He was the *called one*, called by Death, recalling all the wonderful days on earth and pleading with Death for one more minute, one more moment, of life. When he did die, shortly afterward, I wrote a piece in his memory called *Ofrenda Musical a la Memoria de Luis Palés Matos* (Musical Offering to the Memory of Luis Palés Matos). The work was scored for solo viola, solo French horn, and string orchestra. Still under the spell of his poem *El Llamado*, I wrote the work as a sort of dialogue between the poet (the viola) and Death (the French horn). It was first performed by the Casals Festival Orchestra in the plaza of Guayama, the town where he was born.

By contrast, another work originated in a completely different way. In 1962, I was asked by Ballets de San Juan to write a ballet based on Puerto Rican children's songs. They had no idea of a story line or libretto and left that up to me. It so happened that my son, Pablo, who was eight years old at the time, was having a hard time sleeping at night. Every time I tucked him into bed, he would sleep for a few minutes and then let out a scream for me to come and comfort him. "I can't sleep," he would say. "You know what some people do when they can't sleep?" I asked. "They count sheep. That's what they do. Now you just imagine a long fence with a big flock of sheep on one side. The sheep want to get on the other side of the fence, so, one by one, they jump across. You count them as they jump. I'm sure that before you count to a hundred you'll be fast asleep. You want to try it?" "Okay," he said. I left him lying quietly with his eyes closed. I turned out the light and left the room. No more than a minute had gone by before a bloodcurdling shriek came out of his room. "Papa! Come here!" "What's the matter, Pabi?" I asked. "They don't want to jump," he replied.

We soon learned that what was troubling him was an ear infection. The doctor examined him thoroughly and prescribed an oral antibiotic. But there was no way we could get him to swallow the medicine. All our pleading and cajoling were to no avail. He simply would not open his mouth unless we used brute force. And there was my idea for the ballet based on children's songs. The libretto I wrote was simply this: A little boy is severely ill. He has a high fever and is delirious. But he won't take any medicine. In his delirium he sees all his friends, characters from children's songs. They come to play with him, to dance and sing. But every time he gets up to join them, he collapses for lack of strength. Once again they dance, and again he tries to get up to dance with them, but he cannot. One of the characters, Mambrú (Marlborough, from the song "Mambrú se fue a la guerra" (Mambrú Went to War) takes a bottle out of his pocket and a big spoon and urges the little boy to take his medicine. No way! But after watching all his friends enjoying the dancing, he can no longer resist temptation and says he'll take the medicine. To the sound of trumpets and the rolling of drums, he closes his eyes and swallows the medicine. Strength instantly flows through his body, and he joins the dance with leaps and bounds, together with all the others. Awakened from his dream, he calls his mother and father and tells them he is ready to take his medicine now. As mother and father and little boy all dance together, the curtain falls.

All this composing, and much more, was done while I was busy administering the affairs of the radio and television service. In spite of the difficult times we had gone through, our station received the "Codazos" award for outstanding news programming of the year and a citation from the magazine *San Juan Review* for excellence in television programming.

29 ·

*Designing
Museums
and Books*

After twenty-five years in government service—federal, Puerto Rican, and military—I felt that I had had enough. I decided it was time to retire. Retirement, for me, did not mean that I would devote the rest of my life to leisurely pursuits like golf, fishing, or basking in the sun. On the contrary, it meant an opportunity to work harder than ever, together with Irene, on projects we both enjoyed. At the Division of Community Education we had worked toward a common goal; we collaborated on projects of mutual interest and we saw each other often. But during the past several years, with me at the station all day (and sometimes at night) and Irene at work in the studio at home and taking care of the children, we hadn't seen much of each other. We felt that we were losing contact and drifting apart. So in 1969 I resigned from the TV and radio station and applied for partial retirement pay. (I would have had to put in five more years of government service to be eligible for full retirement, but I felt that I wouldn't be able to bear it.)

Once free of a desk job and administrative responsibilities, I was able to undertake a few freelance projects. Ricardo Alegría, the director of the Institute of Puerto Rican Culture, asked me to design a children's museum in an old building that had been a powder magazine in the seventeenth century. There was no budget except a modest monthly fee for me and the salary of one carpenter. All materials were to be ordered through the institute's purchasing office. That meant that when I ordered three laboratory scales calibrated to show the effect of gravity on the earth, the moon, and Jupiter, I received three bathroom scales ($19.99 each) from Kmart. I did enjoy working on the project, however, because it allowed me to do considerable research on scientific matters that had intrigued me since my high school days. This was to be a "hands-on" museum. How was I to explain, in simple terms, the many questions that had bothered *me* as a child? How do we know that air has weight? What makes warm air rise? Why does the moon always show the same side toward the earth? How do the plants use the energy of the sun to make our food? I made a detailed scale model of the museum, six feet long, and construction began. The building was to be divided into four sections, in accordance with this line from the Puerto Rican national anthem: "Puerto Rico—the daughter of the sun and the sea." The four sections were the universe, the sun, the sea, and humankind. The first two sections were completed and inaugurated in a ceremony attended by many children. It was covered by the press because the ribbon was to be cut by the wife of the mayor of San Juan.

Unfortunately, however, politics being what it is, after the elections were won by the opposition party, the new administrator appointed for the Institute of Puerto Rican Culture was displeased with a project started by the previous administration and now halted any further construction and turned the building into a warehouse. I have never been able to find out what happened to my scale model of the museum. It just disappeared. All I have are some photographs, including the one from the newspaper showing the mayor's wife smiling as she cut the ribbon.

But that was not the end of my museum-designing career. The Casals Festival Organization asked me to design a Pablo Casals Museum in a colonial building in San Juan. I had many of my own photographs of Casals available, and access to many others. An integral part of the museum was to be a videotape library and a viewing room where one could choose to hear any work from any of the annual festivals. In addition to designing the museum, I was to supervise the selection and re-recording of the programs from the masters at WIPR-TV (most of which I had originally directed). The museum includes huge enlargements of the scores of some of Casals' compositions and also has one of the maestro's cellos on display. I remember that when he first came to Puerto Rico and celebrated his birthday in San Juan, friends prepared a huge cake in the form of a cello for the party. When he was handed a knife to cut the first piece of the cake, he said, "Oh, no. I can't put a knife into a cello. Let someone else do it." Then he told about his days in Prades, France, during the Nazi occupation, when he was visited by two young storm troopers who had been told by their parents to be sure to visit the famous musician. "They wanted to see my cello, which I always kept on a bed, covered by a blanket," he said. "They carefully removed the blanket and kept staring at the cello. I stood watching the two examples of Hitler youth, knowing what they represented, and wondering what they would do. Then one of them began passing his hand across the cello, back and forth, as if caressing it. To me, it was an obscene, repulsive sight. I felt as if he were ravishing my loved one."

The Pablo Casals Museum was not destroyed. It still stands, in Plaza San José, near the statue of Juan Ponce de León, and is visited daily by countless people—music students, tourists, historians, journalists, and just plain music lovers, for whom Casals is a name to be revered in the history of instrumental music. Others go simply to pay homage to a man who could not separate his art from his concern for the human condition and the struggle for peace.

I enjoyed being involved with the museum, but what I wanted most was to work on a project together with Irene. When I resigned from the television station, we decided that we would devote ourselves to designing and illustrating books for children. With Irene's brilliant sense of color and design and my facility for drawing and a sly sense of humor, we thought we could make a good team. We were both enchanted by Hans Christian Andersen's version of the story "The Emperor's New Clothes." I knew, from my study of Spanish literature, that this was not an original Andersen story. It had first appeared in another guise in *El Conde Lucanor*, a collection of moral tales published in Spain in the sixteenth century. (That book was also the source for Shakespeare's *The Taming of the Shrew.*) We later learned that a similar tale also existed in Ceylon, with the naked emperor riding off on the back of an elephant. The Spanish version takes place among the Moors. With a multinational background such as that, Irene said, "Let's have our emperor in Puerto Rico."

We began working on preliminary sketches for a dummy in the hope that we could interest a New York publisher in producing the book. Our friend Daniel Melcher, whose father was the founder of Bowker Publications (New York), arranged appointments for us with many editors of publishing houses, and off I went, my dummy under my arm and my hopes high.

Everyone liked the idea, but no one wanted to publish the book. A young woman editor at Random House, however, said she had the manuscript of a book of children's stories and needed an illustrator. Would Irene and I be interested in designing and illustrating the book while our Emperor book was under consideration? Yes, we would. The book was called *Stupid Peter and Other Tales*, by Helen K. Olsen. With Irene in charge of the design, I did all the pencil illustrations. The editors at Random House were pleased with the work and accepted our Emperor story for publication. I say "our" story because it is based on the Andersen version but does not follow it exactly. For example, we added a few new characters, we took many liberties with historical periods (in our story, the weavers-swindlers arrive in a *flying machine*), and the setting of the story is Puerto Rican rather than European. I was particularly pleased with the way we solved the problem of creating a visual representation of an *invisible* cloth. We dedicated the book to our children, Pablo and Laura. It contains twenty-five full-color, double-page illustrations and shows the silly emperor completely naked—no dainty panties around his loins. The reviews in the press were very good, and the book was awarded the Brooklyn Museum Children's Art Book Citation.

I suppose that our interest in children's literature came about because we had two children of our own. Since both Irene and I were working all day, we had a wonderful

Puerto Rican housekeeper, Doña María, who looked after the children most of the time. She spoke no English, so Laura (whom we always called Lali) and Pablo learned Spanish from her before they learned English from us. Doña María sometimes brought her son Jaime with her. Jaime was a few years older than Pablo, and Pablo looked up to him as his idol. Since Doña Maria's children called her Mami, Pablo and Lali also called her Mami and referred to Irene as Mamá. When Pablo was asked in school if he had any brothers, he said, "Yes, one. His name is Jaime." One day when the two boys were playing in the garden, Jaime said, "Pablo, get out of the sun for a while. You'll get sunburnt." When Pablo didn't quite understand, Jaime repeated, "Get out of the sun or your skin will get dark, like mine." Pablo couldn't think of anything he'd like better! He ran up and embraced Jaime, saying, "Really?"

When Pablo was about ten years old, we sent him to a nature camp in New Hampshire. He seemed to be quite happy when we left him there, but it wasn't long before we received the following letter:

Dear Papa:

I want to go home. I want to go home.

I want to go home. I want to go home.

I want to go home. I want to go home.

I must go home. I must go home.

I must go home. I must go home.

I must go home. I must go home.

I must go home. I must go home.

Please Papa

Take me back to P.R. now.

Love

PABLO

Both children participated actively in the musical and theatrical activities at their high school. Pablo designed and executed the scenery for the musical *Fiddler on the Roof*, and Lali was president of the glee club and designed the costumes for the musical *Godspell*. They also spent time helping Irene and me in our work and learning something of graphic design and photographic laboratory techniques. Irene would often ask Lali to cut stencils or to put crop marks on material going to the printer, and I found Pablo helpful as an assistant when I was making prints in my darkroom. Lali loved music, and I would sometimes take her to rehearsals of the Casals Festival Orchestra when she was

Photographic Memories

about six years old. I remember seeing her sitting alone in the empty, air-conditioned auditorium while I was busy photographing the orchestra. When I turned to see where she was, she had changed her seat to another part of the auditorium. A few minutes later she had changed again. During the entire rehearsal she kept moving from one seat to another. To my question of why she couldn't sit still, she replied, "Well, all the seats were nice and cold. When the one I was sitting on got warm, I moved to another one."

Both children were brought up to appreciate all manifestations of nature and to respect the environment. One time, when Pablo was only four years old, we were in the gardens at La Fortaleza (the governor's mansion) with hundreds of guests attending an important celebration of some sort. Pablo wanted a drink of water, but the only liquids being served were alcoholic beverages. We were sitting with the governor's wife, Doña Inés, and she told me to take the boy over to the bar and ask the bartender to give him some water. When Pablo entered the bar, the first thing he saw was a huge, beautiful

Irene and I all dressed up to go to a banquet at the governor's palace.

stuffed swordfish on the wall. Immediately, and in a very loud voice, he began shouting, "That fish should be in the water. That fish should be in the water!" He caused such a disturbance that Doña Inés came over to see what was wrong. She got Pablo his water and led him back into the garden, saying to everyone within hearing, "You know, the boy is right. He's absolutely right." A month later, when we were back at La Fortaleza for another party, the fish was no longer there. Doña Inés had had it removed.

It was at one of these affairs at La Fortaleza that Irene unwittingly became the center of attention. It was a formal event; Irene wore a strikingly beautiful white evening gown and I came in my rented tuxedo (for the first time in my life). During the course of the evening, I noticed Irene surrounded by a group of women guests, who were listening to her animated speech. Irene was speaking in Spanish—the Spanish she had been taught by the young men recruited in the poor neighborhoods of San Juan to work in her silk-screen workshop. General Leonidas Trujillo was dictator of the Dominican Republic at that time, and Irene had launched a tirade against him with all the colorful street language she had learned, oblivious of the meaning of the words she was using. She spoke softly but with great aplomb and in the strongest language of her vocabulary. The group of women around her, wives of diplomats and government officials, stood transfixed, gaping in disbelief. How could such foul language come out of the mouth of such an elegant lady? (Shades of Shaw's Pygmalion!) I, of course, enjoyed every minute of it.

The concern shown by Doña Inés during the swordfish incident was a reflection of her genuine interest in conservation and the preservation of the environment. She was an active member of the board of directors of the Puerto Rico Conservation Trust, and in that capacity she asked me to prepare a booklet for children about the importance of preserving our trees and forested areas in the face of uncontrolled urban development. It was to be a book without words, only pictures, so that even children who could not yet read would understand the message. I prepared the booklet, using simple drawings with Magic Markers. She liked it very much, but the board of directors of the trust felt that it would be better to have some text. So I went back to work and wrote the text (in English), increased the number of illustrations, and cut the color separations. Doña Inés translated the book into Spanish, made some excellent suggestions for changes, and suggested the title *Sabios Arboles, Mágicos Arboles* (Wise Trees, Magic Trees). Before doing the translation, she called me and said, "You have done a very good job. The text is very good, but it is a little too cold and calculated, too *Anglo-Saxon.* I'd love to translate it, but if you don't mind, I might add some of the *love and passion* of Puerto Rico which I think it needs." Needless to say, I didn't mind.

The book was an instant success. The Conservation Trust then wanted an animated film made of the book. With additional funds provided by the Puerto Rico Foundation for the Humanities, I hired a gifted young Puerto Rican artist, Poli Marichal, as my assistant. She had studied animation in Boston and would be in charge of the technical production. The narration consisted of the same text as the book. I did all the drawings and wrote the music for a small chamber group, and the actual filming took place at the facilities of Sacred Heart University in San Juan. The music is sometimes performed today as a little suite. *Wise Trees, Magic Trees*, a fifteen-minute animated film, has been widely shown and has been issued also in an English version. And the book, originally published by the Department of Education, has now been reprinted by the Conservation Trust in a second edition of 10,000.

After the success of *Wise Trees, Magic Trees*, a book of a different sort occupied our attention for a very long time. It was an English version of the chapters referring to Puerto Rico in Gonzalo Fernández de Oviedo y Valdés's book *General and Natural History of the Indies*, first published in Spain in the 1530s. This project came about in a curious way. The president of the Limited Editions Club of Avon, Connecticut, Mr. Sidney Shiff, had seen some of the books designed by Irene that were on display at La Casa del Libro, a book museum in Old San Juan that was directed by our friend David (Jack) Jackson McWilliams. Mr. Shiff determined to get Irene interested in designing a book for the club, on any theme suggested by us related to Puerto Rico. The idea was to have a book on a Puerto Rican subject, designed and produced in Puerto Rico. The book would be printed in an edition of 2,000, exclusively for members of the Limited Editions Club. He wrote to Irene, explaining that the club was dedicated to publishing books of the highest quality, designed by the foremost artists in the field, and printed in the country of origin of the artist. Both Irene and I were busy with other projects at the time, and we replied that we regretted not being able to undertake the assignment. But Mr. Shiff persisted and sent us a brochure listing the names of some of the other artists who had designed books for the club. Imagine our reaction when among the first names listed were those of Jean Cocteau, Henri Matisse, and Pablo Picasso! We immediately wrote back and said we would undertake the project. We chose the Oviedo book because we knew that a professor at the University of North Carolina had been working for years on an English translation.

Irene designed the book based on photocopies of the original manuscript that we obtained from the Huntington Library in California. The book was printed in the States and illustrated with many black and white ink drawings that I made. But in addition, Irene designed eight colorful illustrations that were produced in San Juan in silk screen. The blank pages for those illustrations were sent to us before the book was bound. After being silk-screened in San Juan, the pages were returned to the States to be bound into the book. Irene and I both struggled over the illustrations for a long time. So long, as a matter of fact, that the publisher threatened to take legal action if we did not deliver the work. But Irene was adamant. "I'm not going to deliver the illustrations until I'm satisfied with them," she said. That only meant that I would have to do an illustration over again for the tenth time! When we finally delivered the illustrations, we received a letter of apology and congratulations for a job well done.

But there remained one more detail to attend to—every one of the 2,000 books had to be numbered and signed by the artists! By air mail, we received a carefully constructed plywood box that contained the pages that were to hold our signatures. The box was made exactly to the size of the pages. That evening, Irene and I sat down at our desk and signed as many as we could before going to sleep. In the morning, we went to put the signed pages back into the box, but they didn't fit. The pages had absorbed so much of the Puerto Rican humidity that they were at least one-eighth of an inch bigger than they had been when they arrived! When we finished signing, we had to put them in an air-conditioned, dehumidified environment to get them back into the box and returned to the States.

Irene wanted the signatures to appear in two colors. She had used a brilliant red in the book for the initial letters of the chapters, and a dark gray (instead of black) for the pen and ink drawings. So I gave her a *red* pen for her signature and she insisted that I prepare a special *gray* ink for my signature. That's what comes from being married to a perfectionist!

30 · "Every Forty Years"

I have often been asked to teach a class in photography and have always declined. It is not that I am against the teaching of photography, but I would rather spend my time creating something myself than teaching others how to do it. A workshop is quite another thing; I enjoy working with a student on a one-to-one basis. Besides, I think that most of the technical aspects of photography can be learned from books and catalogs (the way I learned them). What the teacher can best contribute is concepts, encouragement, and, perhaps, inspiration. Irene was very good at that. She and I served as advisers to a camera club for youngsters between the ages of eight and eighteen in a poor area of the city of Ponce. The club had been organized by a Catholic church group under the leadership of a dynamic nun, Sister Isolina Ferré, primarily to give the children something constructive to do and keep them off the streets. The Kodak company had contributed some obsolete, simple cameras, film, and equipment for a good laboratory. I remember that at our first meeting, the youngsters, cameras in hand, asked, "Well, what do we do now?" A good question. Irene immediately had the answer. "First, each of you take a portrait of the other. Then you take pictures of your mother and your father, portraits and at work. Then your brothers and sisters. Then your uncles and your aunts. Then your pets. Then your neighbors. In that way, before long, we will have a fascinating history of this neighborhood." The kids did wonderful work, and Irene started the custom of issuing a calendar every year that included her selection of twelve outstanding photos from the year's output.

My teaching experience was of a different sort. I greatly enjoyed the thirteen-part series that I created on the history of symphonic music for WIPR-TV, the government educational station. One summer I taught a short course in animation for a small group of students at Sacred Heart University, and I spent one semester teaching a class in musical form and analysis at the Puerto Rico Conservatory of Music. I was asked to repeat the course the following semester, but I couldn't imagine repeating something I had already done. It would be like repeating the same photograph or the same piece of music. As George Bernard Shaw remarked, "Those who can, do. Those who cannot, teach."

As soon as I finish one project, I have an irrepressible urge to start something new. Instead of repeating a course at the conservatory, I took on an entirely different, and challenging, assignment that would mean working with Irene again. It was to be a one-hour documentary TV program about Puerto Rico's first newspaper, *La Gaceta*, the official organ of the government, started in 1808. I inherited a collection of original copies of the newspaper from Tomás Blanco. Tomás, a frail man, had been mugged and brutally beaten one night near his apartment in Old San Juan. When he decided to move to a safer neighborhood, he consulted me about the disposal of his library and the newspaper collection. I advised him to donate the books he didn't want to the reference library of WIPR-TV, and when he offered me the newspapers I gratefully accepted.

Tomás never fully recovered from the horrendous attack he had suffered. The blows to the head seemed to have done permanent damage. He continued to work on his series of essays "Inventario de Cosas Nuestras" (Inventory of Our Things)—an "inventory" not in a material sense but referring rather to traditions and values. But he kept to himself and had rather a distracted air about him. We loved him very much, but for some reason he imagined that Irene and I had abandoned him, and he often called Irene and asked plaintively, "What have I done to offend you? Please forgive me. What have I done?" One evening I invited him out to dinner at a Chinese restaurant. As we were driving along, I asked if he was working on anything interesting. He reached into his breast pocket and took out a few handwritten pages. "Here it is, if you want to see it," he said. It was a long poem, written in the style of a sixteenth-century ballad, about an erotic love affair between a damsel and her knight. Though full of passion and ardor, the eroticism was handled with such exquisite delicacy and charm I could hardly believe the language did not come from some great Renaissance poet.

Tomás Blanco died in 1975 and was laid to rest in the ancient cemetery by the sea in Old San Juan. Among the many mourners stood Doña Inés, and Muñoz, noted for his aversion to attending funerals, delivered the eulogy.

Of the newspapers Tomás left me, some had been partially eaten by termites, but most were in good condition. The earliest one was dated 1824. It included a report on the capture of Roberto Cofresí, a notorious pirate, and several of his companions. They were all executed by a firing squad at the fortress of El Morro, in San Juan. In addition to occasional such news reports, the papers carried a wealth of miscellaneous information about doings around the island during the nineteenth century—slave uprisings, epidemics, ship arrivals and departures with a listing of their cargo, hurricanes, fires, and regulations governing horse racing through the streets of San Juan. There were also numerous advertisements and personal announcements—leeches for sale, a French "professor's" cure for corns, horses for sale, slaves for sale, rewards for the capture of fugitive slaves, visits of European theatrical groups, performances by a lady tightrope walker across Plaza Santiago, a story about lightning striking the church of the town of Moca and killing three hogs and four chickens, and a social note on the guests at the governor's ball at La Fortaleza.

When the general manager of the commercial TV station, WAPA, learned of my newspaper collection, he suggested that we do a one-hour TV program based on a selection of news items from the paper, including trivial and ridiculous matters as well as serious and tragic events. I set to work to write the script for the show and, with Irene's help, created the illustrations. I did the shipping news and the tightrope walker in animation; other news was represented by full-color illustrations. Many other events were dramatized by actors in period costume—the execution of the pirates, for example, and a religious procession through the streets of San Juan during a cholera epidemic.

Sponsored by one of the local banks, the program was broadcast in prime time and reached a wide audience. I am told that it has often been used in history courses in the public schools.

I had been away from the States for so long and had been involved in so many activities in Puerto Rico that I was not very aware of the many changes that were taking place in the American art world, especially in photography. During my occasional visits to New York, I was surprised by the growing number of galleries in the city devoted to photography and the prices being paid by museums and private collectors for original prints. I had never thought of photography as a *business*. At the FSA I enjoyed what I was doing and never thought of putting a monetary value on my work, as if it were some sort of merchandise. I remember that the prints were considered to be of so little value that when an exhibit was taken down, we would often find some of the prints of Walker Evans, Ben Shahn, or Russell Lee discarded in the wastebaskets. New prints could always be made for the next show. It was during this period that the term "vintage prints" was coined. I couldn't understand why an old, beat-up print was considered more valuable than a new, clean one just because it had been made at the time the picture was taken. I was so naive that when a New York gallery sent me about twenty of my FSA prints and asked me to sign them, please, I promptly returned them signed, without a thought to the increased price my signature would bring. Imagine my surprise when I received a letter from the Sonnabend Gallery in New York in which it offered to be my representative. I knew that the gallery specialized in avant-garde painting. Why would they want me? But Mrs. Sonnabend did pay for the making of prints for a one-man show in her SoHo gallery. And not long after, Howard Greenberg, of the Fotofind Gallery of New York, visited my studio in San Juan and selected several dozen "vintage prints," which have been selling slowly over the years. Why all this interest in my work? Perhaps it was because although I had not been producing much as a photographer in Puerto Rico, my FSA photographs continued to be published and exhibited widely in museums in the United States and Puerto Rico.

Meanwhile, Pablo and Lali had gone off to college in the States. Pablo spent four years at the Tyler School of Art in Philadelphia and went on to get his master's in fine arts at Yale. Lali went to Goucher College in Baltimore. At her graduation, she sang "Six Songs for Laura," which I had written expressly for her.

Irene, in order to have a dependable source of income, had become art editor of the government's monthly tourism magazine, *Qué Pasa*. In that capacity, she often had me take color photographs for the cover of the magazine, and she arranged for our friend John Vachon to be brought down to Puerto Rico for a few weeks at a time to do some work for the Tourism Department. It was great to have him with us for a while and to share reminiscences of our days with the FSA. I didn't see any of the other photographers again except at the occasional seminars we attended, such as the one in Amarillo, Texas, in 1979, and the one at the Southeast Center for Photography in Daytona Beach, Florida, in 1985. I also remember being with Russ Lee, Arthur Rothstein, John Vachon, and Marion Post at a forum and seminar about Lewis Hine at the opening of a huge exhibit of his work at the Brooklyn Museum in New York. I did keep up a sporadic correspondence with Marion, and we sometimes exchanged prints.

I never thought much about the impact the FSA photographs might be making on the public. I was content to leave to others the decision of what to do with the pictures. Of course, I realized that the images I was recording had historical value (artistic value, too, I hoped), but I didn't expect them to be so meaningful to so many people and in so many ways.

In 1977 a young anthropologist in Charleston, South Carolina, organized an exhibit of photographs I had taken in the nearby Santee-Cooper River Basin of people being forced off their land because of the construction of a government dam. I was invited to lecture at the opening of the show. Then I began receiving calls for interviews from newspapers in the States about the photographs I had taken in their area in the 1940s. They planned to do follow-up stories with pictures taken by their own photographers today to show the changes that had taken place. That happened, for example, with my picture of Thanksgiving Day at the Crouch family's home in Ledyard, Connecticut. (It showed pumpkin pies in the foreground and the family at dinner reflected in a mirror.) A photographer from a Connecticut newspaper located some of the members of the Crouch family, set up a photograph in imitation of mine, and sent me a print. If imitation is the height of flattery, I was amused but didn't feel flattered.

Similar situations, for example, comparing a community in the 1940s with the present, occurred in Portland, Maine, in Allentown, Pennsylvania, and in other cities across the country. I couldn't help asking myself why people were so interested in seeing the changes that had occurred in their lifetimes. Was it because the whole country was changing so much? Was it because they did not want the younger generation to forget what things used to be like? In Puerto Rico I had witnessed profound changes that had altered the very nature of the island. The sugarcane industry was disappearing, industrial parks were springing up in many of the towns, there was an endless flow of people from the farmlands into the crowded cities. A large middle class had developed, and the plague of our century, drugs, was sweeping through the entire society, bringing with it the attendant soaring crime waves and destruction of the family. How different from the days when Irene and I came to the island in the 1940s—when we never thought of locking our doors at night, when we were not concerned about leaving the keys in our unlocked car, when the word "drugs" referred only to prescription medicines, when a little barefoot boy ran after me as I walked down the street to return a ten-dollar bill that had fallen out of my pocket! I had seen and lived through these changes and many more. Wasn't it about time, after forty years, to go back into the field and show the Puerto Rico of the present as compared with my early FSA photographs? I wouldn't need some young photographer to show the Puerto Rico of today. I was still alive and healthy; I could do it myself.

With the help of Sidney Mintz, my anthropologist friend from Johns Hopkins University, I wrote up a project to be submitted to the National Endowment for the Humanities requesting funds for a year for me to go back to the areas I had photographed in the 1940s, with Irene, and show the changes that had taken place. The title of the project was to be "Contrasts: 40 Years of Change and Continuity in Puerto Rico." I shall never forget the huge grin on Irene's face as she came back from our mailbox that day in 1979, waving a letter in her hand. "We got it!" she shouted. "We got it!" The Puerto Rico Foundation for the Humanities gave us a grant to finance an exhibit of about two hundred photographs, which would open at the University of Puerto Rico Museum of Art and Anthropology when we finished our project.

Now, just as in the old days, Irene and I were delighted to be on the road again, perhaps a little less innocent, a little less naive than when we first arrived in Puerto Rico in 1941. We saw things now not with the wide-eyed fascination of amiable young outsiders but with the critical insight that comes from a long, intimate relationship among friends. Off we went into the countryside, our equipment in the car, staying at hotels and guest houses, carrying many of the old pictures along to help us find the places and perhaps even the same people we had photographed in the 1940s.

Wherever we went, people responded enthusiastically and offered their help as soon as we explained the purpose of our project. One little old woman near the town of San Germán seemed especially interested when I pointed out that I had taken pictures in her neighborhood forty years ago and had now come back to see how things had changed. Her eyes twinkled as she listened and nodded her head. But I wasn't sure if I was getting my message across, and I must have repeated the idea of "forty years" too often, because when I asked if she understood what I was saying, she smiled and said, "Oh, yes, I understand. You come back every forty years."

On the outskirts of the town of Cidra, we searched for the little wooden schoolhouse where we had photographed some children long ago when we were planning to do a feature film. I especially remembered a charming little girl in third grade. We had also photographed her at her home, where she was taking care of the house and her little brother and sister while her mother was away in town. The school was now a sprawling concrete junior high school. None of the teachers recognized the portrait of the little girl we showed them. But one of them said, "Let me ask my husband. We live across the street. He has lived in this neighborhood all his life. Maybe he knows." After one look at the picture the man said, "Why, of course. That's Rosín Casillas. She runs that little fruit stand down the road." We found her, just as charming as the child we remembered from long ago. She was now married and had four children of her own. The eldest daughter was at the university studying to be a teacher. Rosín laughed when she told us she had never forgotten the day "the crazy Americans" had photographed her in school and she still kept the pictures we had given her. As for the entire project, Irene tape-recorded interviews with the people I was photographing. We thought the interviews might be useful if we were to do a book in the future.

Driving through the town of Guayanilla, on the south coast, Irene beside me, I stopped by a group of young men in front of a bar to ask if they could help us identify a street in one of our old photographs. Noticing that Irene had more pictures in her lap, one young man said, "Park over there, lady, we want to see the other pictures, too." Soon we were surrounded by a large crowd of passersby, young and old, all eager to take a look at the pictures we had taken in the town forty years ago. As the pictures were being passed from hand to hand I expressed concern about losing some of them. Immediately the word went out, "Careful of those pictures. They're worth a million!" People thanked us for "taking the trouble to photograph the history of our town," and we received invitations to come in for a beer and offers to help locate some of the people in our pictures. One young woman, a schoolteacher, said, "You sure are lucky to be doing this kind of work." We couldn't have agreed more.

One of the people they recognized in the photographs was a sugarcane cutter, ma-

Photographic Memories

Don Toli, a Puerto Rican sugarcane cutter, being interviewed by Irene for the exhibit "Contrasts" in 1980.

chete in hand, working in a field. "Why, that's Don Toli," one of the young men cried. "Really?" I said. "Where can I find him?" "He lives near the San Francisco sugar mill," he replied. "Don't worry, we'll take you there." Then several people jumped into their cars, and in a caravan we went to Don Toli's house.

He was living in a modest wooden building with his only daughter. The furniture was neatly arranged, with a radio and television set in prominent places. When we were introduced, he said he remembered the day we took his photograph. His eyes watered as he looked at the photograph and said, "How young and strong I look in the picture." Now he was old and frail, living on his Social Security check. His health was failing and he could no longer work. He willingly talked about his life in the sugarcane fields years ago, and Irene recorded his words. "Just imagine! As a child, I worked with the oxen in the sugarcane fields and got 25 cents a day—from sunup to sundown! When that picture was taken I was probably getting $1.43 a day." He never lost his sense of humor and could laugh at his own predicament. "Just yesterday I was coming home after cashing my

Homemade altar at Muñoz's funeral in 1982.

Photographic Memories

Social Security check and I was mugged. They took all my money. Imagine! Me, of all people!" And he chuckled at the irony of it.

In 1980 our work was interrupted by the stunning news that Muñoz Marín had died. A grief-stricken cry of anguish seemed to erupt from the entire island. In the towns, the cities, and the countryside, people listened in shocked disbelief to the latest news on the radio. As soon as it was announced that his body would lie in state at the capitol building, thousands of people rushed to take their places in a long line, waiting to pay their respects. I spent all day and all night at the capitol, photographing men, women, and children in the interminable line of mourners that filed past the coffin—members of the cabinet and the legislature, government workers, officials, political adversaries, poor people from the housing projects, the slums, and the countryside. And through it all stood Doña Inés, graciously receiving the condolences of thousands of friends and admirers.

The funeral procession was to leave the next morning from the Cathedral of San Juan at ten o'clock for the town of Barranquitas, a two-hour drive away, where Muñoz was to be

Sign displayed at Muñoz's funeral.

buried in the cemetery that held the tomb of his father. But the roads and the towns on the route were so choked with crowds of people anxious to say their farewells that the procession did not arrive at the cemetery until eight o'clock in the evening. I was there to photograph the arrival and the ceremony that followed. At last, after many emotional speeches, he was finally laid to rest. It was almost midnight. At the entrance to the town of Barranquitas someone had placed a crudely lettered banner that read: "Muñoz; you have gone, but your example and your accomplishments shall remain alive in our hearts." In later years, the Muñoz Marín Foundation published my photographs in a little book under the title *The Day the People Said Farewell to Muñoz Marín* (in Spanish, El Día que el Pueblo se despidió de Muñoz Marín).

He had been governor for sixteen years and had transformed Puerto Rico from "the poorhouse of the Caribbean" to a highly industrialized island with the highest per capita income in the Caribbean. For Irene and me he had also been a good neighbor and a dear friend.

Mourners at the funeral of Luis Muñoz Marín in the capitol building in San Juan, where his body lay in state, 1980.

Photographic Memories

But in our interviews with the humble people in the countryside we learned how much he had meant to them. A ninety-two-year-old retired sugarcane worker put it this way: "The poor people came into their own when Muñoz Marín took over. May God keep him in his glory. He is the one who fixed up the country a little."

One of the people who shared those views was Don Vicente Arroyo. We came to know him because his daughter was working for us as a housekeeper. She was a lovely woman with Indian features, whose portrait Irene had painted. Her name was Luz. When we asked about her family, she readily took us to meet her father, who lived near the town of Guayama on the south coast. Don Vicente was a tall, imposing man with a booming voice that belied a gentle character. He had begun working in the cane fields at the age of twelve, taming wild mules. Sixty-two years of his life had been spent in those fields. Don Vicente was a highly respected leader in his community. Everyone, including his wife, called him Don Vicente. Although illiterate, he was president of the local sugar workers union, and when I asked him how he

Mourners paying their respects at the funeral of Luis Muñoz Marín, as his body lay in state at the capitol building in San Juan, 1980.

could carry out his duties as president he said, "Don't worry, I know the contract from memory." When we got to know him better he always called me Mr. Jack, but Irene was always just plain (and affectionately) Irene. Don Vicente was a man of tremendous dignity and self-esteem. He was quite aware of the difference in our economic and social status but always treated us as his equals. When we invited him to visit us in San Juan, he accepted readily but said, "I come in through the *front* door, you know." (He did come, and he brought us a gift of half a dozen live crabs for dinner. Irene was scared to death of the creatures, but Luz took charge and made a delicious crab stew.)

Don Vicente had a keen mind and was one of the wisest men I ever met. He loved to discourse about philosophy, religion, politics, science, music, poetry—everything. Where he learned so much I don't know. Perhaps it was because he was also a great listener and always asked a lot of questions. Whenever we visited him, we pumped him for information and he did the same with us. I remember his asking me once, "Explain something to me, Mr. Jack. How was it possible for the German people, who produced so many great scientists, philosophers, and musicians, to have also produced such a beast as Hitler?"

Don Vicente, Don Toli, Doña Sara and her fourteen children, Ana with her concept of religious tolerance, Rosín, and so many other people we met in our work—how much they taught us about what it meant to be Puerto Rican! And not only Puerto Rican, but simply decent people. Their personal qualities of character—compassion, respect, tolerance, love of one's neighbor, sense of humor, personal dignity and self-esteem—these qualities that had so impressed us when we first came to Puerto Rico were still evident in the countryside, but they were having a hard time surviving the impact of acquisitiveness, commercialism, violence, drugs, and crime. Whenever we asked the question of how does life compare today with the old days, the answer was always the same: "It is true that today we have more hospitals, schools, highways, cars, factories, and housing projects, but we are losing the most important thing—respect for the golden rule: Love thy neighbor as thyself." That those basic human values were still holding their own, even in the cities, was brought home to me not long ago when I found myself in need of help.

While driving in the city one day I stopped for a traffic light and when it turned green, the car wouldn't go. No matter what I did, I couldn't get the motor started. At that intersection, as at most busy intersections in the city, there was a gang of boys ready to wipe windshields with a dirty rag in the hope of getting a quarter. One of the kids, seeing my distress, came over, stuck his head through the open car window and said cheerfully, "What's the matter, grandpa?" I hadn't expected such an affectionate greeting but readily explained my predicament. He offered to push the car around the corner, but when he couldn't budge it, he called another boy to help. This fellow also greeted me like a grandson. But the two boys together couldn't move the car and had to call a third. Straining every muscle, they managed to move the car around the corner to the curb. But when I saw that it was a dangerous place for the car to be because of traffic, I asked them if they could push me another block down the street to a parking lot at a supermarket. It was too much for the three boys, and they had to call for the help of two more. Now, with five boys pushing, shoving, huffing, and puffing, they finally got me into the parking lot. I was so grateful for their help that I reached into my pocket to offer them a tip. But they wouldn't take any money. Much as I urged them to accept a couple of dollars, they politely refused, saying, "No, no, no, grandpa. It's okay. It's okay." Then it dawned on me that these boys—tough street kids—had been brought up to believe that when you do some work for someone, you expect to be paid, but helping an old man in trouble, that you don't do for money. You do it *por amor al prójimo* (for love of thy neighbor).

It was not our intention for this project simply to set up my camera in exactly the same spot as forty years ago and take another picture. No. We intended to show the basic changes that had taken place in the lives of all Puerto Rican people. That included many aspects of society that had not even existed before: factory workers in pharmaceutical plants, workers in oil refineries, clothing shops, electronics industries; people in centers for the treatment of drug addiction and centers for the care of the elderly; and evidence of technological advances in agriculture (tractors replacing oxen in the cane fields and monstrous machines replacing human sugarcane cutters). We spent a year traveling throughout the island, photographing and tape-recording interviews. Irene sometimes felt weak and a little dizzy but insisted on accompanying me and doing her share of the work—planning our itinerary, keeping track of our negatives, and recording the interviews. We didn't realize yet that she would soon succumb to cancer.

During the course of this project, I didn't enjoy the luxury of having a laboratory like that of the FSA to develop my film. I had to do it all in my own darkroom, in San Juan. I made contact prints of all the large negatives, and 4 × 5 enlargements of the 35mm work. In addition, we selected and borrowed negatives of the 1941 work from the Library of Congress and of the 1946 coverage from the Institute of Puerto Rican Culture. The next step would be to select no more than two hundred images for the exhibit and arrange them in a logical, constructive sequence. It was while we were involved in this phase of the work, one evening in our studio, that Irene had a severe attack of convulsions. It seemed like epilepsy and didn't last for more than a few minutes, but we were both very scared.

Early the next morning, I rushed her to the doctor. After a cursory examination, he immediately sent us to a neurologist. There she was given an electroencephalograph test, which showed the possibility of a brain tumor. We called a niece in New York who was a doctor, and she arranged for Irene to be admitted to the New York University Hospital. Further examinations showed that the brain tumor was a metastasis of a cancer in the lung. There was no choice but to operate on the brain and submit to radiation and chemotherapy for the lung. The tumor was removed successfully and after a short stay at the hospital, we returned home for Irene to continue chemotherapy treatments in Puerto Rico. Our friend Dr. Alandel Castillo was a great help to us at this time.

When the news of Irene's illness spread through the art community of San Juan, a group of friends and admirers organized an exhibit of her (and my) work at the art gallery of the University of Puerto Rico. A large crowd attended, including many of the young men who had worked under her at the Division of Community Education. They came with guitars and *cuatros* (a native stringed instrument), playing and singing country music. Music of another sort was provided by Lali, who sang my "Six Songs for Laura," and by my brother, who played the violin sonata I had written for him. Irene, wearing a turban to hide the loss of hair because of the chemotherapy, enjoyed everything tremendously, overwhelmed by the outpouring of affection and admiration from so many friends.

Despite her illness, sometimes confined to a wheelchair, Irene continued working with me in organizing the exhibit. We selected prints and rejected, compared, and discarded, with Irene always the severe critic. When it came to choosing an image important for its documentary value but lacking in aesthetic qualities, she was adamant. "If it's no good as a photograph, it's no good. Kill it," she would say. There followed weeks and months of taking her to the hospital and watching her slowly wither away. Even when she could barely speak, she never lost her combative spirit and sense of humor. In one of her last sessions with the doctor, he said to her, "I don't understand what's going on with you. You have suddenly gone into remission; you are much better than you were a few weeks ago. And it isn't anything we have done, because the treatment has been the same. The only thing I can think of is that it must be all those friends of yours praying for you." Irene looked him straight in the eye and said, "In that case, what do I need you for?"

To this very day, I often meet people who tell me how much they were influenced by Irene—teachers, graphic artists, printers, or youngsters who still preserve some of the handmade paper she taught them to make when she was a volunteer teacher. (One of her former students is now in charge of Greek and Roman art at the Metropolitan

Museum of Art in New York.) Not long ago, as I was walking toward my house, a man in his mid-fifties approached me and asked if I was Jack Delano. When I replied that I was, he said, "You don't remember me, but I remember you very well. You see, when you were here taking photographs for the FSA, my father was your driver and interpreter. Sometimes he would take me along on your trips to the country. I remember an incident that took place and I would like your wife, Irene, to know about it because it concerns her more than you. One day, in the mountains, you were about to take a photograph of a landscape, when suddenly your wife called out, 'Jack, look at that beautiful woman!' I was about twelve years old at the time and just beginning to get interested in girls, so I quickly turned, expecting to see a pretty young woman. But the only person I saw was a thin old farm woman standing in the doorway of a poor shack. Her face was bronzed by the sun, her hands were covered with wrinkles, and she wore a black dress that had been mended many times. She stood watching us with curiosity but with no animosity. 'Could this be the beautiful woman Irene was referring to?' I asked myself. During our drive home I kept thinking of what Irene had said. I didn't understand how she could consider that woman beautiful. I want you to tell her that now I am fifty years old, I teach at the university, I have three children, and I want her to know that I never forgot her remark. I grew to understand what it meant, and it changed forever my concept of beauty, my attitude toward women and the dignity of work. You tell her." I told her.

Irene did not live to see the "Contrasts" exhibit. She lay for weeks and weeks in our bedroom, unable to move, hardly able to speak, attended by a nurse day and night, while I stood by helplessly, watching her life ebb away. She died on February 4, 1982. Pablo and Lali came down from New York, and the following day, during a gentle tropical shower, she was buried in the municipal cemetery of San Juan, attended by Doña Inés and a group of government officials, friends, and former students.

Irene was gone, but her "beautiful woman," thanks to the power of photography, lives on in the collection at the Library of Congress, to be resuscitated from time to time in publications and exhibits. Irene had never been openly demonstrative in her affection for me (that would have been "improper"), but the last words she said to me when she could barely move her lips were, "I love you. Promise me you won't marry [So-and-so] when I am gone." I still feel Irene's presence in the studio we shared for so many years. When I am arranging photos for an exhibit, or working on an illustration, or designing a publication, I can't help thinking, Is this the way Irene would want me to do it?

31 · New Avenues of Creativity

Facing the future without Irene was frightening at first. Our friend Padre Antonio, speaking of pain, used to say, "When something hurts, I yell." No stiff-upper-lip-grin-and-bear-it business for him. It was really a much more natural and sensible reaction to pain than our tradition of scorning self-pity and being told to "stop whining." I was left to carry on our unfinished work alone and to combat solitude accompanied only by our two dear black Labrador retrievers, Saba and Bambú. I did not "yell." On the assumption that the best antidote for grief was hard work, I simply plunged right into it. There was so much to attend to, so much work to be done.

Waiting for me to get back to work was the "Contrasts" exhibit. The prints had to be matted and framed, and the captions, in English and Spanish, had to be printed and mounted and a poster produced. Consisting of 220 11 x 14 images, the exhibit opened at the University of Puerto Rico Museum in November 1982. It consisted of a selection of FSA photographs from my first visit to Puerto Rico in 1941, and the following series done in 1946 for the government of Puerto Rico, plus recent work done in the 1980s. The images are often shown in pairs, to make a social comment. For instance, a sugarcane worker's barefoot family having lunch in the 1940s is shown next to a scene of a mob of people at a Burger King restaurant in the 1980s. A little girl in the 1940s playing stickball in a school yard is shown next to a little girl in a similar pose in a ballet class in the 1980s.

"Contrasts" seemed to affect people deeply. I was extremely pleased when Doña Inés came to the opening. From the University of Puerto Rico, the exhibit traveled to InterAmerican University in the city of San Germán, to the Museum of Art in Ponce, and to several other educational institutions in Puerto Rico. I always kept a book for comments at the exhibit, and what people wrote was fascinating, highly complimentary, and sometimes very moving. One of the most touching comments I found was this, referring to a photograph of a child's funeral in a small town: "Mr. Delano—Thank you for making it possible for me to witness the funeral of my little sister, who died before I was born."

Photographic Memories

Doña Inés and I at the opening of the "Contrasts" exhibit at the University of Puerto Rico.

Another exhibit that claimed my attention took place in the Virgin Islands. A young teacher from the University of the Virgin Islands had come upon my pictures at the Library of Congress, which I had taken in 1941 for the FSA. On a grant from the National Endowment for the Humanities, he had obtained prints from the library and mounted an exhibit at the city hall in St. Thomas. I was invited to speak, and so was a professor from the University of Delaware who had written a history of the Virgin Islands. There was a great deal of interest in the old photographs, and for me, of course, the show brought back memories of the days when Irene and I stayed at the Penthany Hotel and tried to photograph people who shied away from the camera. The local newspaper published a picture I had taken of a family in Frenchtown, a neighborhood of St. Thomas where white French-speaking fishermen lived. I was told by one of the exhibit organizers that the children of that family had cut the picture out of the newspaper and had it framed because it was the only family picture they ever had. (The miracle of photography!)

As a change from photography, I began designing a book written by our friend Teodoro Vidal, a dedicated student of Puerto Rican folklore. Irene had designed several of his books, and he assumed that I was just as good a designer as she. Not so. The book was called *The Tradition of Witchcraft in Puerto Rico*. Pretending I was Irene, I designed the book and did all the illustrations, some of them quite funny. Of course the book taught me a lot about witchcraft, but I confess that I have not yet had occasion to practice what I learned and I doubt that the spells and incantations I was reading about had anything to do with my next adventure.

The State Department of the Commonwealth of Puerto Rico was preparing a cultural mission to Argentina that would include the "Contrasts" exhibit, to be shown in the main cultural center of Buenos Aires. I arrived a few days before the opening to supervise the hanging of the pictures. Because of delays in clearing customs, the exhibit arrived at the center just three days before the announced opening. That meant the technical crew in charge of hanging the exhibit had to work overtime every day. I noticed that the workmen scrutinized the photographs carefully as they handled them. They had never been in Puerto Rico and apparently felt attracted by the images. One carpenter especially spent a lot of time examining each photograph. When the last picture was finally hung (minutes before the exhibit was opened to the public), the carpenter approached me respectfully and said, "Señor, permit me to say that I think you are a great artist." (The highest compliment I have ever received!)

What prompted him to say that? He was an ordinary man, a carpenter. What did he know about photography? or art? I recalled another time, many months earlier, when a similar question had been raised. A letter arrived in my mailbox from a twelve-year-old boy in El Paso, Texas, asking for my autograph. The letter was written in pencil on school notebook paper. The first sentence read, "Mr. Delano, when I grow up I want to be a photographer just like you." Wow! Flattery like that I couldn't resist. I began a correspondence with the boy, and in subsequent letters I learned that he was interested in photography, that he had had a camera but it had been stolen, and that he was saving up for another one but money was hard to come by (his mother worked in a shirt factory). He had seen some FSA photographs that he liked very much in a book about the Great Depression while he was preparing a report for his history class in school. I sent him not only an autograph but a signed original print. And I asked this question: "What was it you liked about the FSA photographs?" He replied, "I liked them because they make ordinary people important."

Was that why the carpenter was impressed by the "Contrasts" exhibit? It is true that there are no "celebrities" in the exhibit, no "important" people. But I think there is something else, what Paul Strand called "respect for the thing in front of the camera," which is one of the guiding principles of everything I do. From watching and listening to people who have visited the show, I think they too have the same feeling about the pictures. Respect.

Why am I interested in what they think? It's simply because every creative artist needs an audience. Art is created for people to see, hear, and enjoy. Just as there is really no sound when there are no listeners (the tree falling in the forest story), so there is no visual art when there are no viewers. I cannot conceive of working just for the purpose of expressing myself. Why should anyone be interested in what I feel at gut level? When I feel the urge to express my feelings I am fortunate in being able to compose music. And as for photographs—I *take* pictures, I do not *make* pictures. Of course I enjoy working, and I work not by looking into myself, but primarily by looking around me with my camera in the hope that what I find may bring some enjoyment, understanding, or revelation to others (like my friend the good carpenter). To do that, I must speak a language that people can understand. It would be arrogant of me to expect people to learn some strange language of mine in order to understand me. I don't think I have anything so transcendental to say that anyone need make a special effort to understand me. I am reminded of the story of a young art student in a class at the University of Puerto Rico who brought in a painting for her teacher to criticize. The teacher, a kindly man from Spain, looked at the scrawls and blotches on her canvas and asked her to tell him a little about what she had in mind. She said that the painting represented a nightmare she had had a few nights ago. The teacher put his arm around her shoulder and said, gently, "Well, my dear, you know that sometimes nightmares are caused by constipation."

When I was in Buenos Aires, I was surprised to learn how well informed the Argentine photographers were about photography in the United States. They knew a great deal about the FSA and were curious to learn more. The publishers of the magazine *Photo Mundo*, A. Becquer Casaballe and Silvia Mangialare, arranged for me to speak at a meeting of the Argentine Photographers Association, where I was questioned at length about the FSA, the other photographers, Roy Stryker, my various assignments, and the government's support of such a program. The same thing was true in Caracas, Venezuela, when the exhibit was presented at the Rómulo Gallegos Cultural Center. The national library of the city had an extensive photography collection, including some FSA prints, and eagerly accepted a gift of one of mine. People everywhere expected an FSA photographer to speak in English, and they were extremely pleased that I was able to address them in Spanish. I was also interviewed extensively on the radio and in the press, as if I were some important visiting dignitary.

The success of the exhibit stimulated the Institute of Puerto Rican Affairs, in

Washington, to try to arrange for its distribution in the States. Through the efforts of the institute, then directed by Paquita Vivó, a shortened version (one hundred prints) of the exhibit was accepted by the Smithsonian Institution Traveling Exhibit Service (SITES) and began a three-year tour of about twenty museums and other cultural organizations. I was frequently invited to be present and lecture at the openings. My travels took me to the universities of Connecticut, Illinois, and Michigan and to Bradley University in Peoria, Illinois, among others, as well as to such institutions as the Newark Museum, the Milwaukee Museum, the Bronx Museum, Hostos Community College, and the Miami–Dade County Library. I usually interspersed my talks with a few humorous anecdotes. At Columbia College in Chicago, I seemed to have overdone it, for when I finished, a little woman came up to me and said, "I enjoyed your talk very much, Mr. Delano. Have you ever thought of being a stand-up comic?"

No, I had never considered that. But I confess that I feel quite at ease talking about my work before an audience. I was offered a chance to do that when the Meet the Composer Program of New York offered me a grant to spend a week touring community centers in the city with a musical group that was performing my Quartet for Strings. The grant required that I attend each performance to explain the work and answer questions from the audience. We went to high school auditoriums, centers for the elderly, hospitals, and settlement houses. Everywhere we played, the audience was attentive and interested in the music. At one school, in a largely Latin community, the audience consisted of people of all ages, small children and teenagers with their parents and grandparents. After the performance, the children wanted to touch the instruments; they asked how they were played and how did I compose the music—the violin parts first, then the viola, then the cello? An elderly woman said, in Spanish, "The music is very nice, but I don't understand what it says. When I hear a song, there are words and I understand. But here there are no words, so what does it mean?" I was aware of the Latin fondness for flowers and all growing things, so I said, "Señora, do you like flowers?" "I love flowers," she replied. "And I'm sure you like to arrange flowers in a beautiful bouquet, right? Well, think of this music as an arrangement of sounds, just like an arrangement of flowers. The flowers don't have words. They don't say anything specific. They are just beautiful, and they bring you joy just to look at them." The woman stood pensive for a moment and then said, "Yes, I see. Now I understand. Thank you."

One work of mine that had not only words but also scenery, costumes, and a symphony orchestra was a theatrical version of Tomás Blanco's story "Los Aguinaldos del Infante" (The Child's Gifts). Ballets de San Juan and the San Juan Children's Chorus commissioned me to adapt the story for ballet, children's chorus, narrator, and orchestra, with sets and costumes designed by me based on the illustrations Irene and I had done for the book. The work would be presented at the Fine Arts Center as half of a Christmas program; the other half was to be the *Nutcracker* Suite.

I was delighted to undertake the commission. The story seemed so well suited to a visual presentation and children's voices, and the symphony orchestra offered wonderful opportunities for dramatic expression. I used a few themes from the music I had originally composed for the radio version of the story, but most of the score consisted of entirely new material. *Los Aguinaldos* was given four performances at the Fine Arts Center in San Juan under the skillful and imaginative stage direction of Pablo Cabrera. The stage sets were painted exactly like the illustrations in the book. And the horse, the elephant, and the camel of the story were monumental, highly decorated animals, built according to my designs. The audience seemed spellbound by the work and frequently burst into applause for the spectacle and the dancing. A baritone narrator read most of the text, but several sections were sung by the angelic voices of the children's choir. I had written dances for all the principal characters, and marches and processional music using all the resources of the full symphony orchestra. Unfortunately, a dispute developed between the administrators of the children's choir and the ballet company (both of which had shared the cost of the commission), and the work has never been performed again.

However, my *Sinfonietta para Cuerdas* (Sinfonietta for Strings), another musical work produced about the same time, has been performed many times, on the island and in the States. The piece was written on commission from the Puerto Rico Symphony Orchestra. It consists of four movements and is of symphonic length, about thirty-five minutes. It was first performed by the string section of the orchestra in the auditorium of the Puerto Rico Conservatory of Music. It has since been played by small chamber groups and was used as the basis for a ballet by the University of Louisiana at Baton Rouge. As is true of much of my music, elements of Puerto Rican folk themes and rhythms are an integral part of the score.

My brother, Sol, played in the first violin section of the symphony when the *Sinfonietta* was performed. He had been an active member of the Casals Festival Orchestra since the 1970s, when he auditioned for Don Pablo. He was also teaching at the Conservatory of Music and had many private pupils. I had suggested that he leave the high pressures of life in New York and come to Puerto Rico, but it was years before he did so.

My brother and I had never had a very close relationship, although we did keep up a correspondence. We seemed to drift apart as far back as the days when I was studying at the Pennsylvania Academy of the Fine Arts and living away from home, and he was working hard as a scholarship student at the Curtis Institute of Music. Later, when I went off to join the FSA, he lived in New York, where he was recognized as a highly accomplished violinist. After his New York debut concert in 1961, the music critic of the *New York Times* wrote, "A rare and first-rate violin talent was heard yesterday afternoon in a Carnegie Recital Hall debut program." Sol was in constant demand as a concertmaster for the orchestras of Broadway musicals and played in operas, recordings, and symphony concerts conducted by Alexander Schneider. He never lacked for work, he had a good apartment in Manhattan, he had married, and he seemed to be sitting on top of the world. Then suddenly, we received a call from Irene's cousin Philip Field in Maplewood, New Jersey, saying that Sol had been in a terrible auto accident and was in a hospital in New York. It looked suspiciously like an attempt at suicide.

I rushed to New York on the first plane to see what I could do. The doctors told me he was recovering very well and suggested we arrange for psychotherapy as soon as possible. Sol seemed to be in good spirits. When he was released from the hospital, he resumed his busy musical schedule. Soon afterward, I got another call from New York: Sol had slashed his wrists and was in another New York hospital. I rushed to New York again to be by his side and to take care of some of the expenses. By now the psychiatrist was convinced that Sol was suffering from severe manic depression and had to be hospitalized. And by now also, his wife had divorced him. In one of his manic periods, when he felt high, he had bought a house with a swimming pool on the outskirts of New York. Then, when he was depressed, he couldn't keep up the payments and we had to arrange to sell the property. Meanwhile, we were covering most of his expenses and debts with money from a modest inheritance Irene had received when her father died, and the funds were slipping away rapidly. I could not stay with him all the time, so when he was released from the hospital, he stayed with friends for weeks and months at a time.

He was convinced that he would never play the violin again, but while staying at the house of Irene's cousin Olga Field for several months, she encouraged him and insisted that he practice every day.

As a result, he seemed to recover, psychologically and physically, and continued to play beautifully, even spending several years as concertmaster of the New Orleans Symphony Orchestra. But the psychological problems did not really go away, and during his fits of depression he suffered terribly. I urged him to apply for the Casals Festival Orchestra and move to Puerto Rico, where at least I would be available in an emergency. He did so, and emergencies did come up. Members of the orchestra would come to me and inform me sadly that Sol was behaving strangely. During a manic period, he bought two cars. One of his private students was a psychiatrist at the veterans hospital, and he arranged for Sol to be admitted for treatment. But that didn't last long. One night Sol stayed at my house, and when I got up in the morning for breakfast, I found him standing in the kitchen doorway, dripping wet, his face pale. He said, "I tried to drown myself in the pool but I didn't have the guts." He went back to his little studio to teach, and I was at a loss about what to do. He needed constant watching, which I couldn't provide, so back he went to the hospital. When he was released, I made an appointment to see him at his apartment. It was July 14, 1988. I arrived at the second-floor studio and knocked on the door. There was no answer. I tried the door; it was open. I went in and called to him. Again no answer. In the little bathroom I found him—hanging by the neck from a clothes hook, his suffering ended.

When I called down to the landlady of the building to inform her of what had happened, she burst into shrieks of hysteria. I remembered from mystery stories I had read that one must not touch the body or move anything, so I rushed to the police station around the corner and reported what I had seen. The officer in charge must have broadcast the news on police radio, because I returned to the apartment to be confronted by reporters and a TV news crew. An official of the Justice Department ordered the removal of the body, and I had to go to the morgue to identify my brother on a marble slab. The thought that kept running through my mind was, "That's just what happened to my mother's brother in Philadelphia when I was a kid." I made all the funeral arrangements and sat at the funeral parlor steeped in guilt for not having done more to avert this tragedy, while many students from the Conservatory of Music came to offer their condolences, and a small chamber group played the slow movement of a Bach suite.

During the 1980s all sorts of activities kept me from being idle for very long. The film *Los Peloteros* was shown at the Fourth Film Festival in Amiens, France. At the Casa Aboy Museum, in San Juan, I had a one-man show of photographs called "Madres e Hijos" (Mothers and Children). In Daytona Beach, Florida, I attended and exhibited at "The Farm Security Administration: A Fifty-Year Commemorative Symposium." (It was a pleasure to be there and visit again with Marion Post, Russell Lee, and Arthur Rothstein.) I composed two songs for baritone and piano, with texts by Puerto Rican poet José de Diego; "Three Preludes for Piano"; and "Aves" (Birds), ten short pieces for piano that became my tribute to the birds I see every day outside my studio window in Río Piedras.

On assignment for the Florida International Alliance, I traveled to Trinidad and throughout Puerto Rico together with photographer Daniel Biferie, photographing, in color, activities of children for a traveling exhibit in Florida on the subject of children in the Caribbean. The show was then presented at the Organization of American States in Washington under the title "Our Children to the South." I went to Philadelphia, invited by the University of Pennsylvania, to lecture at the 150th anniversary celebration of the invention of photography. Members of the Puerto Rican cultural center in Philadelphia, Taller Puertorriqueño, came out en masse to hear me.

While in Philadelphia, I decided to visit Pablo and Lali in New York for a few days. When I arrived at Pablo's house, he said, "There was a call here for you from San Juan. They said for you to call the office of the president at Sacred Heart University when you get back. They wouldn't tell me what it was about." As soon as I returned home, I called the university and was informed that I was to be awarded an honorary doctorate in humanities. I immediately called Pablo to tell him the news. Pablo, at that time, was going through a frustrating period because his wife, Jeannie, a schoolteacher, was spending all her time working on her master's thesis and had no time for him. "She's always at the library, or at the computer, or studying, or out buying books, and working all day and all night," he would say. When I called to tell him of my honorary degree, he paused for a moment and then blurted out, "And to think you didn't have to do *anything!*" Two years later, I received a similar degree from InterAmerican University.

In order to *do* something, as soon as the "Contrasts" exhibit was on its journey throughout the States, I made a selection of about 150 of those images with the intention of publishing a book. I prepared a dummy, with photographs mounted back to back, and wrote an introductory essay. (Oh, how I wished I had Irene to help me!) Several publishers rejected the book. The reason given was always the same: "The pictures are beautiful, but we don't think a book about Puerto Rico will sell." It was finally accepted by the Smithsonian Institution Press and, once in print, turned out to be one of the most successful photography books in the Smithsonian catalog. The book, titled *Puerto Rico Mío* (My Puerto Rico), is dedicated to the memory of Irene.

I sent a copy of the book to the Guggenheim Foundation and acknowledged my indebtedness to the people there for having made it possible for me to return to Puerto Rico in 1946. I also expressed my gratitude for their having had the patience to wait more than forty years for the book to come out! I was pleased to receive a reply saying the book was worth waiting for.

In the late 1980s plans were already being made to commemorate the 500th anniversary of the arrival of Christopher Columbus in Puerto Rico on his second voyage, to be celebrated in 1993. All sorts of events were being prepared, well ahead of time, from a procession of sailing ships representing countries all over the world to the commissioning of musical works by Puerto Rican composers with funds provided by the Institute of Puerto Rican Culture. Five composers were to be selected by a committee of well-known musicians for commissions. I was one of the five, but suddenly a woman, a relative of one of the composers not chosen, raised a hue and cry claiming a conflict of interest because I was a member of the board of directors of the Corporation for Musical Arts, the agency administering the awards, and therefore was not eligible for a commission. The selections committee insisted that no conflict of interest was involved because the funds came from the Institute of Puerto Rican Culture and I had nothing to do with the selections committee. The incident turned into an ugly affair. Some members of the selection committee resigned in protest, and others were appointed. My commission was withdrawn and awarded to the uncle of the woman who had raised the issue. This was a purely personal matter and had nothing to do with my not being a native-born Puerto Rican.

The whole affair made me furious, though I tried not to show that I was boiling inside. But I summoned up all my self-control and decided not to fight the decision. It was disheartening not to have been chosen for one of these commissions (everyone I knew felt that politics was involved), but the Institute of Puerto Rican Culture did respond to my request for a grant to compose a work for symphony orchestra, chorus, and soloists based on the Luis Palés Matos poem about the Antilles *Canción Festiva para Ser Llorada* (Festive Song to Be Lamented). It was the most ambitious work I had ever composed. Inspired by the sonorous, rhythmical, and flamboyant text, I found that the music flowed easily, and I finished the work of four movements in a few months. I gave it the title *Burundanga*, from the first three lines of the poem:

> Cuba, ñáñigo y bachata,
> Haití, vodú y calabaza,
> Puerto Rico, burundanga.

> [Cuba, boogie-man and revelry,
> Haiti, voodoo and calabash,
> Puerto Rico, hodgepodge.]

Burundanga was given its world premiere at the symphony hall of the University of Puerto Rico. Though I had attended rehearsals and knew that the work was going well, I was still very nervous about the first performance and took a friend along for moral support. The hall was almost entirely full, mostly with young people. At the end of the first movement, which ends with loud chords from the whole orchestra, my friend poked me in the ribs and whispered, "That's great. It's a very good piece." As the music progressed, full of Afro-Antillean percussive and melodic elements, I could feel the tension and excitement growing in the audience. When the work ended, not with a crash but softly, in a whisper, there was no applause, only a moment of silence. My heart pounding, I thought the audience didn't like it. Then, suddenly, thunderous applause broke out and everyone clapped wildly, in a standing ovation that lasted several minutes. I was called to the stage several times, where I bowed awkwardly and felt like some famous rock star.

A year later *Burundanga* was repeated at the Academy of Music in Philadelphia. I was invited to attend rehearsals and the American premiere of the work. It was my first visit to the Academy of Music since my days as a music student sitting next to Miss Finnegan. I found myself, sixty years later, occupying the same seat I had used while trying to stay awake through the Wagnerian operas, but now on the stage were musicians of the Philadelphia Orchestra, the eighty-member chorus of Temple University, and three excellent soloists, and they were performing *my music!* The third performance of the work took place in San Juan in 1993 and was recorded for the first compact disc of the Puerto Rico Symphony Orchestra.

My composition of *Burundanga* sprang partly from my admiration for the poetry of Palés Matos and partly from my interest in the African influence in Puerto Rico. Way back in the 1970s, I had steeped myself in the history of slavery and race relations in Puerto Rico. In my research I had come upon the story of an extraordinary free black man who, during the nineteenth century, had started and maintained a school for poor children in his own home in San Juan, not far from the slave market. He supported the school solely with his earnings as a cigar maker. His name was Rafael Cordero, and during his lifetime everyone knew him as Maestro Cordero.

Both Irene and I had become fascinated by him and wanted to do an illustrated book for children about Maestro Rafael Cordero. But although I had a great deal of historical and biographical material about him, and many sketches for a possible book, we really didn't know how to approach the project. At one point, I did a series of large drawings of scenes from his life and mounted an exhibit of them at the municipal gallery of San Juan on the 200th anniversary of his birth. I had plenty of ideas for a visual representation of his life and even worked out a storyboard as I would for a film, but writing the text was something else again. After several futile attempts, we put the project aside. Then, ten years after Irene's death, I became interested in the idea again and began to see how to construct a decent narrative. The visual and literary ideas seemed to fall in place and I produced a dummy titled "In Search of Maestro Rafael Cordero," with drawings and a complete text in English and Spanish. I intended to submit it to the University of Puerto Rico Press. In preparing the book, I was fortunate to have the assistance of a talented young woman, Mariluz Gotay. Let me tell you about her.

I had been living alone after Irene's death, with a housekeeper coming in once a week to do the household chores. But as time went by, I felt in need of some sort of companionship. I let it be known among friends that I had a little guest house available for any student interested in free housing in exchange for keeping me company and doing a little secretarial work. Before long, a young woman appeared, referred to me by a teacher of photography at Sacred Heart University. Her name was Mariluz Gotay, and she was twenty-six years old.

Mariluz was bright, intelligent, and imaginative. She had some knowledge of English and English literature and was a whiz at the computer. Her help on the Cordero book was invaluable. She not only typed up my English manuscript but also translated it into Spanish and made valuable suggestions on wording and text. And her help was not limited to the book. She was interested in my work and organized my library, took care of my files of clippings and correspondence, and made herself indispensable in many other ways. She lived in her little guest cabin, but we spent most of our time in the studio and the house, working, sharing our meals, watching the news on TV, or discussing the history of the cinema when I would bring home a video of one of the film classics. She was with me for almost two years, and it was a joy to have her around.

She had told me that her uncle was preparing a gallery in Old San Juan and she had promised to work for him when it opened. I tried not to think about that as the weeks went by, but when the day came for her to leave I was brokenhearted. I expressed my feeling of loss in the slow movement of the sonata for violin and piano that I was composing at the time. The movement is dedicated to her and is based on a theme of two tones, like the two syllables of her nickname, Mari.

One day she called from the gallery to say that she was applying for a job in the city of Mayagüez, on the west coast. Would I give her a letter of recommendation? "Of course," I said. "Come over and write it yourself and I'll sign it." When she showed me what she had written, it was so self-laudatory that I burst into laughter and said, "Mari, I don't know how to say it in Spanish, but you sure think you're hot stuff, don't you?" Of course I signed the letter. She got the job.

The Maestro Cordero book was accepted for publication by the University of Puerto Rico Press and came out in 1994. I dedicated it to the memory of Doña Inés Mendoza de Muñoz Marín, who had died in 1990. Doña Inés never really stopped being a teacher, and her heart was overflowing with "love and passion" for Puerto Rico. When I learned of her death, her daughter Victoria (Melo) called me to say that her mother had requested that some of my music be played at the funeral. An electric piano keyboard was made available at the cemetery in the mountain town of Barranquitas, and the concertmaster of the Puerto Rico Symphony Orchestra came with his pianist mother to provide the music. In a simple ceremony, Doña Inés was laid to rest beside her husband as we all stood in mournful silence while the plaintive melody of the Andante from my Sonata for Viola and Piano filled the air.

32 ·

The End of an Era

The passing of Muñoz and Doña Inés represented the end of an era, not only for me but for all of Puerto Rico. It was an era that saw Puerto Rico become a bustling industrial society with the highest per capita income in the Caribbean. It saw the Industrial Development Company proudly promoting locally manufactured products with the slogan "Made in Puerto Rico"; an increased sense of self-esteem developing among the people; appreciation growing for the local arts and culture—music, the visual arts, theater, dance, crafts, and folk arts. Irene and I were privileged to play a small part in these changes. It was an era dominated by the personalities of Luis Muñoz Marín and Doña Inés. Now they were both gone. But Puerto Rico had to go on, and so did I.

In the years that followed, I exhibited my photographs at the South Carolina State Museum, the University of Maine at Fort Kent, the Museum of New Mexico in Santa Fe, and Cornell University in Ithaca, New York, where I had been named Andrew D. White Professor-at-Large. I was invited to attend the Fifth Biennale of International Photography in Vigo, Spain, where I would have a one-man show in a special gallery. When I informed the organizers of the Biennale that I had problems with arthritis in my hip and could not travel alone, they authorized me to take my daughter, Laura, along at their expense. Lali and I stayed in Vigo for a week, enjoying the Biennale, being toasted at my exhibit, lecturing, making friends with photographers from Latin America, and being fed huge meals of seafood—usually at ten or eleven o'clock in the evening—by the hospitable Galicians of Vigo. We took advantage of our stay in Europe to visit friends in Germany. They lived near Nürnberg, where I was thrilled to visit the house in which Dürer had lived and worked.

When I returned home, I continued working on a series of photographs in natural color of activities backstage at the Fine Arts Center in San Juan. I was a member of the board of directors of the Corporation of Musical Arts, a government agency supervising the Fine Arts Center, and had easy access to the backstage activities. There I photographed rehearsals, dressing-room doings, makeup technicians at work, lighting engineers, stagehands, and musicians working on operas, ballets, and theater productions.

As a member of the board, I was required to attend monthly meetings and discuss the affairs of the Puerto Rico Symphony Orchestra, the Conservatory of Music, the Casals Festival, and the concerts of dance groups, ballets, and musical theater. The meetings customarily began with an invocation, seeking divine guidance for our deliberations. Members of the board took turns in leading the prayer. I was excused from such a duty because of my plea that I was not very religious, but I would stand in respectful silence while all the others prayed. I shall never forget the horrified look on everyone's face when I said, at one meeting, with no malice intended, "Look, we've been doing this for months now and it hasn't helped much. Why do we need to go through it again?" I was not struck dead by a lightning bolt, and my fellow board members forgave my blasphemous outburst with the same tolerance that Ana had shown when she learned that Pablo would not be baptized. And the prayers went on.

In 1994 the Puerto Rico Supreme Court ordered the police department to disband the office conducting investigations of political dissidents and to return the dossiers that had been kept for so many years on suspected "subversives." By order of the court, the names of people on whom the police had kept dossiers were published in the newspapers with instructions on how to reclaim the files. Three nonpolitical commissioners were named to supervise the distribution of the dossiers. (They happened to be old friends of mine.) The published lists contained the names of nearly all of the most distinguished artists, writers, and intellectuals of the island. It became almost a badge of honor to be included.

Because of all the accusations against me at WIPR many years ago I thought surely my name would be on the lists, but it was not. One day, however, I did receive a registered letter from the commissioners informing me that my police record, no. 30,410, would be made available to me at the Justice Department at my request. All I had to do was to go to room such and such and present my letter to the woman in charge of the office. Full of curiosity to see just how dangerous a character I was, I went to the Justice Department to claim my dossier.

I presented my letter to a nice little lady at a desk in a tiny office. In the adjoining hallway stood a long line of people with letters similar to mine. When the woman saw my name on the letter she looked at me, a little flustered, and said, "Oh, my goodness. You are Jack Delano. I wish I had known you were coming. I just bought three copies of your book *Puerto Rico Mío*. If I had known you were coming I would have brought them for you to sign. Oh, my goodness. Please do sit down. I must call my son." I heard her make the call. "Felipe, you won't believe who is here with me. Jack Delano. Yes. No, I'm not joking." Then she turned to me and said, "I don't have the files here with me;

they are on the third floor. If you don't mind going down to the cafeteria for a cup of coffee, when you come back I'll have the dossier for you." And so she did.

It was the silliest document I had ever seen: a brief file of three or four pages, containing interviews in which WIPR employees said what a fine fellow I was and including the testimony of one man, known for his efforts to have me ousted so that he could take my job, making all sorts of unsubstantiated allegations. To think of all the time and money wasted on investigations of this sort!

Taking photographs while carrying a cane in one hand and a camera in the other had become difficult. I had to curtail some of my photographic activities and travel also, because walking, even with a cane, had become extremely painful. The arthritis in the hip was giving me a lot of trouble. Luckily, I didn't need to walk to write music.

San Juan boasted an excellent children's choir that I admired greatly. I knew the director, Evy Lucío, and when I offered to write a work for the chorus, she responded enthusiastically and applied for a grant from the Meet the Composer Program in New York. The grant was approved. It provided a commission for me to compose the piece and required that it be performed by three children's choruses, those of San Juan, Ponce, and the city of Caguas. I called the work "Un Pétalo de Rosa" (A Rose Petal), and for the text I chose six short poems from Puerto Rican children's literature having to do with nature. The first poem, which gives the work its title, reads:

> One thing I should like to learn,
> how to make a rose petal
> with my hands.

At first the children thought the songs were difficult. At the initial rehearsal, I could tell by their reactions that this music was quite different from the folk tunes and the baroque music and Renaissance songs they were used to. Here they had to deal with what they called "modern" music and slight dissonances. Although they tried not to show it, their faces looked as if they had swallowed some bitter medicine. But as the rehearsals progressed, the children became accustomed to the harmonies, and what they had thought of as strange and difficult became natural and easy. They began to like the songs and performed them extremely well. I was especially pleased when I found them sometimes humming the songs as they walked along.

The Temple University Chorus commissioned me to write a work about a *rose* for a Christmas concert in Philadelphia. I chose the text of another children's poem, "La

Rosa y el Colibrí" (The Rose and the Hummingbird), and wrote the piece for mixed chorus and trumpet. I could not go to the concert but was informed that it came off very well. Judging by the tape recording I received, I would agree.

There followed a work of large proportions, my Trio for Violin, Cello, and Piano. It is a rather difficult work in four movements and received its world premiere at a concert at the Newark Museum in New Jersey, at the opening of the "Contrasts" exhibit there. At a subsequent concert in Newark, my songs for Laura were performed in the same program as the Trio. A newspaper reviewer wrote: "Not only should the song cycle be taken up by a broader spectrum of performers but Delano's piano trio deserves to be part of the standard 20th century literature." The slow movement of the Trio has been choreographed by Ballets de San Juan and formed part of its repertoire when the company went on tour in the States. Entitled "Tierra" (Land), it has become one of the company's most successful pieces, I have been told.

By early 1995 the pain from the arthritis of my left hip was becoming unbearable, and in March I underwent a hip replacement operation. Lucilla Marvel sprouted wings and became my angel of mercy. She saw me through all the administrative procedures at the hospital and arranged for my nursing care when I was sent home. The surgery itself did not bother me, but the weeks of being bedridden with nothing to do except read were torture. Fortunately, Lucilla, ever the planner, arranged to have friends visit me at home every day. In subsequent visits to the hospital for treatment, I don't know what I would have done if I hadn't had such friends as Flavia Lugo, Héctor Méndez Cavatini, Ada Anglada, Mary McHale Wood, and my neighbors Dotty and Bob Fisher.

Because of the surgery and recovery time, I was forced to cancel a one-man exhibit of my work at the Andrew Smith Gallery in Santa Fe, New Mexico. As soon as I was able to get around a bit (albeit with a walker), I hobbled into the studio and got to work on several projects. One was the composition of "Amor America," a song for soprano and string trio with text by Pablo Neruda, the Nobel Prize–winning Chilean poet. I had always been fond of Neruda's poetry, especially the exaltation of the American continent in his book *Canto General*, and hoped someday to write a big orchestral work (perhaps a tone poem) based on the text. That did not happen, but I did set music to the first poem in the book, which he called "Amor America"—evoking the Americas before the European conquest.

When I had recovered sufficiently to be able to travel, I took off for Dallas, Texas, to lecture at and attend the opening of two exhibits of my work, one at the Dallas Museum of Art and the other at a commercial gallery called Photographs Do Not Bend. My illustrated talk at the museum was followed by a concert of some of my music, performed by students and faculty from the music department of the University of

North Texas. The program included my Sonatina for Flute and Piano, and "Aves" (Birds), beautifully played by a brilliant young piano student. Just as in Newark at the opening of "Contrasts," the music and the photographs seemed to go well together.

The Smithsonian Institution had been asking me repeatedly how I would like to dispose of the "Contrasts" exhibit, now that its tour of the United States was complete. After considering several possibilities, I finally replied that I preferred to donate the exhibit to the Ponce Museum of Art, making that the final depository of the photographs. The museum was delighted to accept the gift and arranged a handsome installation of the show, to be preceded by a concert of my music on opening day. So the inauguration of the show became the occasion for the world premiere of my Quintet for Piano and Strings, and when the ribbon was cut, the public surged in to see the "Contrasts" exhibit in its new home. Both the music and the exhibit were received with great enthusiasm. I was overwhelmed by people seeking my autograph, and by others, with tear-filled eyes, eager to shake my hand.

Another project to which I was committed was a half-hour video production of Tomás Blanco's story "Los Aguinaldos del Infante" (The Child's Gifts), which had gone through so many previous versions. This time it appeared in simple animation using the original illustrations that Irene and I had done for the book, plus many more that I had to paint to fill out the story. The music is the same as the original version I did for the radio broadcast, recorded this time by two talented young musicians of the Puerto Rico Symphony Orchestra.

Toward the end of the year, I received a telephone call informing me that I was to be honored with a concert of my music at Casa Casals, the home where Casals used to live, now occupied by the Rappoport family. An overflow crowd filled the house, and I was warmly greeted by many friends. The program included my Trio, the Sonata for Violin and Piano, three preludes for piano, and the world premiere of "Amor America," in an excellent performance by a young soprano from the Conservatory of Music, Hilda Ramos.

33 · Preserving an Instant of Time

Today when I look out of my studio window, I see a flock of red-beaked finches jostling for position on the perch of a bird feeder hanging from a branch of the little calamondin tree that Irene planted more than forty years ago. The tree is always covered with little orange-like fruit or white blossoms, sometimes with both at the same time. It looks for all the world like an illustration in a medieval illuminated manuscript. The fruit is too sour to be eaten, but it does make good marmalade. The tree never asks for anything, it just keeps producing, producing all the time, bringing joy to all who contemplate its beauty. For me, it is also a living reminder of Irene and the permanence of her presence. I feel a little like that tree, a part of Irene, and want to keep producing something all the time to provide someone, somewhere with a moment of joy, solace, contemplation, curiosity, stimulation, or wonder.

From my long and intimate relationship with Irene as a loving husband and working partner, I learned to admire and appreciate the special qualities of women and their ability to perform on an equal level with men. My sympathy goes out to them when they are exploited. Even the sight of a young mother trudging along the country road where I live, carrying a baby in her arms and pushing another child in a stroller, with still another tugging at her skirt, makes me feel that I should stop the car and offer to give her a ride, but, of course, one can't do that nowadays. Perhaps it is because of Irene that so many of my portraits are of women. Today, most of my closest friends are women.

Irene's influence was crucial to my work. I had great respect for her keen eye for detail, her delicate sense of proportion, and her extraordinary feeling for color. I learned to rely on her judgment greatly—in films, photography, graphics, and music. Perhaps most important of all was the confidence and enthusiasm with which she greeted every project that came our way, whether it involved both of us or me alone.

At the FSA, we all hoped that our work would be seen by a wide audience in exhibits, magazines, and newspapers. Today technology has multiplied that audience to unimaginable proportions—through television, satellites, computers, and all sorts of electronic marvels. When I take a photograph to share my exhilaration about something

Irene and I in a hotel room in Chicago while on the road in 1943.

Photographic Memories

Irene and I in our studio in Río Piedras, Puerto Rico, in 1978.

I see, write a piece of music that speaks of how I feel, make a drawing that brings life to a blank piece of paper, or produce a film that tries to combine these arts in some subtle way, I know that technology now makes it possible for my message to reach someone, somewhere, anywhere in the world.

Technology has also made picture-taking much easier than ever before. Automatic cameras have spawned millions of automatic photographers. The Kodak slogan, "You Press the Button, We Do the Rest," is more true today than it was in George Eastman's time. Easy. Just press the button, leave your film at the corner drugstore, and, presto, photography! No worry about exposure, focus, or lighting. One-hour processing. Hallelujah! Of course, I think it is wonderful for people to fill their family albums with pictures of their children and their loved ones, with mementos of their travels, their adventures, their pastimes. I think it's wonderful because I think all photographs are important historical documents that preserve an instant of time.

Documentary photographs also preserve an instant of time, an instant in our history, just as the wall paintings of ancient Egypt preserved images of that civilization for us to contemplate. But documentary photographs do much more than show us what things *looked* like. In taking a photograph, I have always been motivated not by something inside me that needed to be expressed but rather by the wonder of something I see that I want to share with the rest of the world. I think of myself as a chronicler of my time and feel impelled to probe and probe into the depths of society in search of the essence of truth. What impels me to click the shutter is not what things *look like*, but what they *mean*. The difference comes from the fact that when I am looking through the viewfinder of my camera I am aware not only of what is before me but also of every experience of my life, everything I ever learned about color, composition, light, history, art—everything—focusing like a laser beam on the tip of my finger, ready to say "NOW" and press the button. I don't know if photographs can effect social change in society. At the FSA, we certainly liked to think they could. But the unforgettable images of the Vietnam War and the horrors of famine in Africa showed what a powerful impact photographs could have on public opinion.

Television, radio, electronics, the scientific marvels of today were all unimaginable when I was growing up in Voroshilovka. That is where I was when the Soviet Union was born. Eight decades later, I found myself in San Juan when the Soviet Union collapsed. I can't help thinking of the profound changes and the tumultuous events that the intervening years have seen.

They have seen the deaths of millions of human beings in the most devastating wars in history. They have seen the destruction of entire nations and the painful rebuilding that followed. They have seen the dismemberment of colonial empires and the juggling of political boundaries. They have seen acts of unspeakable atrocity committed by human beings against one another. They have seen the awesome mushroom cloud over Hiroshima, which permeated us with fear and trepidation. But they have also seen a civil rights movement wage a valiant struggle against racism in the United States. And they have seen an increased appreciation of the role of women and minorities in our society. And they have seen the scientific explosion that gave us plastics, electronics, computers, polio vaccine, and organ transplants to save lives. They have also seen the transformation of a bewildered little Ukrainian immigrant boy into an American photographer and a busy Spanish-speaking creative artist in Puerto Rico for the last fifty years.

In spite of the horrendous inequities and injustices that still plague us everywhere in the world, I have never lost my faith in the essential goodness of ordinary people. I am often reminded of the remark attributed to Abraham Lincoln: "God must have loved the common people; he made so many of them." I think it is my lifelong concern for the common people and appreciation of their value that have been the driving force behind everything I have done.

Index

Academy of Music (Philadelphia), 17
advertising, xix, 22
Aguinaldos del Infante, Los (Delano, ballet), 200
"Aguinaldos del Infante, Los" (Blanco), 199, 211
Alegría, Ricardo, 172
All-India Radio, 148–49
"Amor America" (Delano, song), 210
"¡A Navegar!" (Delano, composition), 169
Antonini, Ramos, 118
Argentine Photographers Association, 198
Arroyo, Don Vincente, 190–91
artistic influences on J. Delano, 20, 28–29, 51, 212
Asato, Sono, 18
assignments. *See* jobs/assignments
"Aves" (Delano, song), 202

Baldwin, James, 168
Ballets Russes de Monte Carlo, 17–18
Barnard, Christiaan, 168
Blaine, James G., Elementary School (Philadelphia), 12
Blanco, Tomás: "Los Aguinaldos del Infante," 199, 211; death of, 181; Epiphany story, 126–27; *La Gaceta* newspaper collection, 181; music for poems of, 169
Bosch, Juan, 169
Botts, Florita, 152
Bourke-White, Margaret, xix
Bremen, Germany, 4
Bristol, Pa., 5, 6
Brooks, Van Wycks: *The Flowering of New England*, 53
brother. *See* Ovcharov, Sol (brother)
Bruja de Loíza, La (Delano, song), 130
Buenos Aires, 197
Bunche, Ralph, 168
Burundanga (Delano, composition), 204–5

camera club, 181
cameras: for Casals Festival concerts, 138; 8 x 10, 53–54; for filmmaking, 108; using flash with, 50–51; FSA, xv, 49; personal, 49; Speed Graphic, 58
Campos, Pedro Albizu, xxi
Caña (film), xvi
"Cantarcillo Marinero" (Delano, composition), 169
Canto General (Neruda), 210
Caracas, Venezuela, 198
Caribou, Me., 57
cartoons, as social satire, 135
Casaballe, A. Becquer, 198
Casals, Pablo, x, 131, 134–35, 138, 139, 142; museum, 173
Casals Festival, 138
Casirer, Henry, 153
"Catañecitos, Los" (Delano, composition), 169
CBS (Columbia Broadcasting System), 142
Central High School for Boys (Philadelphia), 12
Charlotte Amalie, V.I., 75
Chicago, 89–91
Christiansted, V.I., 75
Cine Alba film company, 124
Colchester, Conn., 59
Collier, John, 109
Colón, Miriam, 122
Columbia Broadcasting System (CBS), 142
composing. *See* music

Index

"Contrasts: 40 Years of Change and Continuity in Puerto Rico" (photo exhibition), 184–88, 192, 211
Cordero, Rafael, 205
Cresson Traveling Scholarship, xiii–xiv, 19–21
Crouch, Timothy, 56–57
SS *Cuamo* (ship), 70
"Cuatro Sones de la Tierra" (Delano, composition), 169
Curry, John Stuart, 85
Curtis Institute of Music (Philadelphia), 9, 10, 15

Daniels, Jonathan, 87
daughter. *See* Delano, Laura (Lali) (daughter)
Delano, Irene Esser (wife): army printing plant job, 97; book design, x, 127, 174, 178–79; as editor of *Qué Pasa*, 183; illness and death, 192–94; influence, 212; introduction to, 16–17; marriage, 35; photographic evaluations, 50; *Photo Memo* magazine work, 108; trainmen drawings, 91; travel to Virgin Islands, 78–79; work of, 26
Delano, Laura (Lali) (daughter), 143, 175–76, 183
Delano, Pablo (son), 125, 175–77, 183
Dempsey, Jack, 12, 22
Desde las Nubes (film), 124
design: books, 174, 178–79; children's museum, 172–73; Pablo Casals Museum, 173
Diplo. *See* Rivero, Ramón (Diplo)
discrimination, 38. *See also* segregation
Division of Community Education (DIVEDCO) (Puerto Rico Dept. of Education), xxi, 119, 124

Eakins, Thomas, 16
Edgewood Arsenal, Md., 86
Emperor's New Clothes, The, 174
Esser, David (father-in-law), 16, 28
Esser, Irene. *See* Delano, Irene Esser (wife)
Evans, Miss, 9
Evans, Walker, xv, 28, 49
Ezequiel, Don, 73

Fairmount Park (Philadelphia), 13
Fanguito, El (San Juan, P.R.), 81–82
Farm Security Administration (FSA): influence of, xviii, 29; job offer from, 29; reunion of photographers, 163–64; survival of, 59; transfer to Office of War Information (OWI), 87; war work, 84–87
father. *See* Ovcharov, Vladimir (William) (father)
Federal Arts Project (WPA), 23
Federal Theater Project (WPA), 23
Ferré, Sister Isolina, 181
films: *Caña*, xvi; *Desde las Nubes*, 124; experimental, 28; *How to Live with the Atom*, 109; *Pablo Casals en Puerto Rico*, 131, 134–35; *Los Peloteros*, xiv, xvii, 122–24, 153; Jesús T. Piñero biography, 118; producing and directing, 116–24, 159, 162–63; screening of, xv–xvi; sugarcane industry documentary, 120; *Wise Trees, Magic Trees*, 178
Finnegan, Miss, 9–10
First Aircraft Repair Unit (Floating), 97–100
Flaherty, Robert, x, 108
Flowering of New England, The (Brooks), 53
Forest Products Laboratory, 85
Fort Benjamin Harrison, Ind., 86
Fort Riley, Kans., 86
frames, xiv, xv, 21
FSA. *See* Farm Security Administration (FSA)
Fuller, Buckminster "Bucky," 162

Gaceta, La, 181–82
García, Ana, 130
García Lorca, Federico, 128, 130
Gotay, Mariluz, 205–6
Greene County, Ga., 37–40
Grolle, Johann, 9
Guggenheim, John Simon, Memorial Foundation grant, x, 109–10, 117, 124

Harwood, Charles, 70
Hawes, Ducky, 12
Hine, Lewis, 27
hip replacement, 210
Holmes, Oliver Wendell, xi–xii, xx
SS *Homeric*, 4
How to Live with the Atom (film), 109
Hughes, Langston, 86

imagery: picture-within-the-picture, xviii, xxii; using mirrors, 57
Index of American Design, An (book), 23
India, 147–50
Inés, Doña, 113, 131, 168, 177, 206
In Search of Maestro Rafael Cordero (Delano, book), 205, 206
Iowa State University, 86
Italy, 150–53
Ithaca, N.Y., 58

Japan, 18, 145–47
jobs/assignments: author, 177–78, 205; book designer, 174, 178–79; documentary-film production unit, 114–15, 116–24; Federal Arts Project, 23; *La Gaceta* television show, 181–82; in Georgia, xv, 37–40; museum designer, 172–73; in New York City, 27; in Puerto Rico, x, 70, 71–74, 81–83, 111–24; railroad freight transportation, 89–94; teaching, 181; for UNESCO, 143, 145–61; video producer, 210; in Virgin Islands, 75–80; war-related, 53, 58–59, 84–87; at WIPR-TV and Radio, 135, 142, 165–69. *See also* travel
Juan Bobo (Juan the Fool), 4

Kennedy, John, xi
Kiev, 4
King, Martin Luther, Jr., 168
Kormans (family friends), 15, 17

Laesley, Professor, 16
Land and Utility Project, Ponce, 72
Landman, Amos, 98
Lange, Dorothea, xix
Ledyard, Conn., 56
Lee, Russell, 31, 104, 109, 163–64, 183
Lindbergh, Jack, 12
Link, O. Winston, xvi–xvii
Llamado, El (Matos), 170
London, 157–59
Lorentz, Pare, 104
Louie (uncle), 5, 11
Lucío, Evy, 209
Lymans, Mr. and Mrs. Andrew, 46, 55

Magic Lantern, The (television show), 167
Mangialare, Silvia, 198
Maria, Doña, 175
Marichal, Poli, 178
Marvel, Lucilla, 162, 210
Marvel, Tom, 162
Matos, Luis Palés: *El Llamado*, 170; poetry of, 204, 205
Mauch Chunk (Jim Thorpe), Pa., 53
McCarter, Henry, 16, 17
Melcher, Daniel, 174
"Me voy a Ponce" (Delano, composition), 169
migrant farm laborers, 35–37
migrations: to Greenwich Village (New York City), 108; New York City to Puerto Rico, xii, 110; New York City to Washington, D.C., 30; Philadelphia to New York City, 26; Ukraine to Bristol, Pa., xii, 3–5. *See also* travel
military career: on First Aircraft Repair Unit (Floating), 97–100; Overseas Technical Unit, 104–7; secret mission to Peru, 101–3; still photographer, 97; training, 95–97. *See also* war
miners, bootleg, 23–25, 26
Moe, Henry Allen, 109–10
Monagas, Julio, 118
Moscow, 4
mother. *See* Ovcharov, Sonia (mother)
Muñoz Marín, Luis: death of, xi, 188–90; as first elected governor, 119, 167; influence of, x, xxi; introduction to, 113–14; wife of (Doña Inés), 113, 131, 168, 177, 206
music: "Amor America," 210; "Aves," 202; *La Bruja de Loíza*, 130; *Burundanga*, 204–5; "Cantarcillo Marinero," 169; "Los Catañecitos," 169; composing for ballet, 170–71, 199–200; "Cuatro Sones de la Tierra," 169; education in, 9–10; electronic, 124; for films, 121; "Me voy a Ponce," 169; *musique concrète*, 156; "¡A Navegar!" 169; *Ofrenda Musical a la Memoria de Luis Palés Matos*, 170; "La Oración de Jimena," 128; "Un Pétalo de Rosa," 209; for radio program, 126–27; "La Rosa y el Colibrí," 209–10; *Sinfonietta para Cuerdas*, 200; "Six Songs for Laura," 183, 193; Sonata for Viola and Piano, 127; "Three Preludes for Piano," 202; Trio for Violin, Cello, and Piano, 210; viola, 10; violin, 2, 4, 9

Index

name change, 21–22. *See also* Ovcharov, Jacob (Jasha)
National Negro Congress, 18
National Youth Administration (NYA), 15
Navaux, Pierre, 153
Neruda, Pablo: *Canto General*, 210
New Deal, xi, 18
Normandie (ship), 19–20

Office of War Information (OWI), 87, 108
Ofrenda Musical a la Memoria de Luis Palés Matos (Delano, composition), 170
Olga (Irene Esser's cousin), 17, 21
Olsen, Helen K.: *Stupid Peter and Other Tales*, 174
Onis, Federico de, 128, 130, 142
"Oración de Jimena, La" (Delano, composition), 128
Ovcharov, Jacob (Jasha), 1. *See also* name change
Ovcharov, Shlomo (uncle), 2
Ovcharov, Sol (brother), 3, 9, 10, 15, 200–202
Ovcharov, Sonia (mother), 1–2, 8, 163
Ovcharov, Vladimir (William) (father), 2, 8–9, 13, 154–55

Pablo Casals en Puerto Rico (film), 131, 134–35
Paris, 153–56, 159–61
Parks, Gordon, 90, 109
Passalacqua, Aida, 116
Peloteros, Los (film), xiv, xvii, 122–24, 153
Pennsylvania, University of, 15
Pennsylvania Academy of the Fine Arts, 15–16
"Pétalo de Rosa, Un" (Delano, composition), 209
Philadelphia residences: Cherry Street, 17; Franklin Street, 7, 8, 11; with Kormans, 15; Twenty-ninth Street, 12
Philadelphia Orchestra, 10
photographs: "The Bitter Years" exhibition, 163–64; Contrasts: 40 Years of Change and Continuity in Puerto Rico" exhibition, 184–88, 192, 195, 197–99, 211; developing, 49–50; importance, 214–15; at Library of Congress, 164–65; lighting for, 50–51; "Madres e Hijos" exhibition, 202; Santee–Cooper River Basin exhibition, 183; "vintage prints," 182–83; Virgin Islands exhibition, 196
Photo Mundo, 198
photo publications: *The Day the People Said Farewell to Muñoz Marín*, 189; in *New York Times Magazine*, 109; *Puerto Rico Mío*, 203; *De San Juan a Ponce en el Tren*, 115; *12 Million Black Voices: A Folk History of the Negro in the United States*, 40
picture frames, xiv, xv, 21
picture-within-the-picture imagery, xviii, xxii
Piñero, Jesús T., 112–13, 118
Ponce, P.R., 72, 211
Post, Marion, 29, 31, 109, 183
Pottsville, Pa., 24
Puerto Rico: Division of Community Education, 119–24; first trip to, 71–74, 81–83; Juncos muralists, xxii; Office of Information work in, 111–19; photographic book of, x, 109–10, 203; photographic exhibition of, 184–88, 192, 195; return to, x, 110
Puerto Rico Journalists Association, 168
Puerto Rico Mío (Delano, book), 203

Qué Pasa (magazine), 183

Raleigh News and Observer, 87
Raper, Arthur: Greene County, Ga., work, xv, 37–39; *Tenants of the Almighty*, 39, 40
Refregier, Anton, 26
Riga, Latvia, 4
Rivero, Ramón (Diplo), 122
Rockwell, Norman, 16
Roosevelt, Franklin Delano, xi, 52, 109
"Rosa y el Colibrí, La" (Delano, composition), 209–10
Rosskam, Edwin, xvii, xxii, 29, 31, 40, 109–10
Rothstein, Arthur, 109, 164, 183
Rotkin, Charles, 112

Sabios Arboles, Mágicos Arboles (Delano, book), 177–78
Sampson family, 55–56
San Juan, P.R., 71–73, 81–83
Saturday Evening Post, 16
segregation, 32–33. *See also* discrimination
self-portraits, xiii, xiv, 36
Settlement Music School (Philadelphia), 9
Shahn, Ben, 16, 51, 142
Sinfonietta para Cuerdas (Delano, composition), 200

"Six Songs for Laura" (Delano, composition), 183, 193
son. *See* Delano, Pablo (son)
Southampton, England, 4
Spain, 18
Standard Oil Company (N.J.), 108
Steichen, Edward, 128, 163
Stokowski, Leopold, 10
Strand, Paul, 25, 29, 56
Stryker, Roy, x, xix, xv, 29, 31, 32, 34, 163
Stupid Peter and Other Tales (Olsen), 174
Superfortress over Japan, 106

Tenants of the Almighty (Raper), xv, 39, 40
"Three Preludes for Piano" (Delano, composition), 202
Toli, Don, 186, 188
Tonner, Joe, 17
Tradition of Witchcraft in Puerto Rico, The (Vidal), 197
travel: on Cresson fellowship, xiii, 19–20; cross-country train, 91–94; Florida to Maine, 35–37; India, 147–50; Italy, 150–53; Japan, 145–47; London, 157–59; migrations with "Contrasts: 40 Years of Change and Continuity in Puerto Rico" exhibition, 195, 197–99; Paris, 153–56, 159–61; Pottsville, Pa., 24. *See also* jobs/assignments
Trio for Violin, Cello, and Piano (Delano, composition), 210
Tunbridge, Vt., 57
12 Million Black Voices: A Folk History of the Negro in the United States (Wright), 40

uncle. *See* Louie (uncle); Ovcharov, Shlomo (uncle)
United Nations Children's Fund (UNICEF), 127
United Nations Educational, Scientific, and Cultural Organization (UNESCO), 143, 162

Vachon, John, 31, 109, 163, 183
Vidal, Teodoro: *The Tradition of Witchcraft in Puerto Rico*, 197
Vigüe, Juan, Sr., 116
Vinnitza, Ukraine, 4
viola music, 10
violin music, 2, 4, 9
Virgin Islands, 70, 75–80, 196
Voroshilovka, Ukraine, 1

Wale, Fred, 119
war: in China, 18; FSA work during, 84–87; in Spain, 18; World War I, 1; World War II, 52–53, 75–77. *See also* military career
Weinberg, Jacob, 10
WIPR-TV and Radio, 130, 135, 159, 165–69, 171
Wise Trees, Magic Trees (film), 177–78
Workmen's Circle, 13
Works Progress Administration (WPA), 23
Wright, Richard: *12 Million Black Voices: A Folk History of the Negro in the United States*, 40
Writers Project (WPA), 23

Zeitlin, Emmanuel, 10
Zimbalist, Efrem, 10
Zuconni, Miss, 152